Campaigning for "Education for All"

Campaigning for "Education for All"

Histories, Strategies and Outcomes of
Transnational Advocacy Coalitions in Education

Antoni Verger and Mario Novelli (Coordinators)

with

Karen Mundy (guest contributor), Anja Eickelberg, Laura Grant, Selma Hilgersom, Joosje Hoop, Felice van der Plaat and Jonah Sarfaty

SENSE PUBLISHERS
ROTTERDAM/BOSTON/TAIPEI

ISBN: 978-94-6091-877-3 (paperback)
ISBN: 978-94-6091-878-0 (hardback)
ISBN: 978-94-6091-879-7 (e-book)

Published by: Sense Publishers,
P.O. Box 21858,
3001 AW Rotterdam,
The Netherlands
https://www.sensepublishers.com/

Printed on acid-free paper

CONTENTS

ACKNOWLEDGEMENTS

The idea for this research project began to take on a concrete form in May 2008, when we met with representatives of both the Global Campaign for Education (GCE) and Education International (EI) in the headquarters of the Dutch Ministry of Foreign Affairs and Cooperation (Minbuza). On that day the initial agreement was forged that this research would be independently carried out by the University of Amsterdam, but supported by both Education International and the Global Campaign for Education. It was also supported through resources provided under the umbrella of the IS-Academie: Education and Development – a four year research and capacity building initiative jointly funded by Minbuza- Education and Research Division and the University of Amsterdam – where both of the coordinators of this book were located. Institutionally, we would thus like to begin our acknowledgements by saying a big thank you to the GCE, EI, the University of Amsterdam and Minbuza – Education and Research Division. We would like to make extensive this acknowledgement to our contact persons from each of the participating institutions for their support and commitment to this project: Geoffrey Odaga and Jill Hart at the GCE, Monique Fouilhoux and Jefferson Pessi at EI, and Joris Van Bommel and Yvonne van Hess at Minbuza - Education and Research Division.

Secondly, we would like to thank all of those representatives of the national coalitions in each of the case study countries for facilitating this research, allowing our researchers access to the movements' history and to the voices of their members. They include Milton Luna and Cecilia Viteri in Ecuador; Raquel Castillo, Thea Soriano, Haydee Montoya, and Maribel A. Tanag in The Philippines; Daniel Cara, Iracema Nascimento and Maria Tereza Avance de Oliveira in Brazil; Leslie Tettey, Kofi Asare, and Awo Aidam Amenyah in Ghana; Miriam Chonya, George Hamusunga and Jennifer Chiwela in Zambia; Ramakant Rai and Sandeep Mishra in India; and Yanti Muchtar and Eny Setyaningsih in Indonesia. Similarly, we would like to thank all of the countless people who agreed to be interviewed of this research and/or participated in the consultation workshops.

Thirdly, we would like to acknowledge all of the authors of the individual case studies for their enormous amount of work and commitment to this project. Each national case study was carried out by postgraduate students as part of their Masters research – but their contribution and commitment extended well beyond the completion of their studies. Thus, our more sincere thanks to Anja Eickelberg, Felice van der Plaat, Jonah Sarfaty, Joosje Hoop, Laura Grant and Selma Hilgersom for their involvement and enthusiasm with the project. On a similar note we would like to thank Karen Mundy, an internationally renowned scholar and colleague for agreeing to contribute with a chapter on the history of the Global Campaign for Education which grounds the books research on national coalitions. We would also like to thank her for co-organizing with us the International Seminar 'Civil Society Advocacy and Education for All: Strategies, Outcomes and Future Challenges', celebrated in Amsterdam on February the 4th 2010, which contributed greatly to feed this project at both the theoretical and methodological levels.[1] Thanks also to all the participants (panellists, discussants and chairs) that made that seminar possible: Hanne Bondo Mawhinney, Marjorie Mayo, Robert O'Brien, Renato Emerson dos Santos, Jennifer Chan, Yusuf Sayed, Wouter van der Schaaf, Kees Biekart, Margriet Poppema, Inti Soeterik, Monique Fouilhoux, Olloriak Sawade, Martijn Marijnis, Geoffrey Odaga and Isa Baud.

Last but not least, we would like to extend our gratitude to Joosje Hoop, who apart from contributing an excellent chapter on the Philippines National Coalition, also went on to work with us on organizing the above-mentioned International Seminar and on the process of turning this book into a concrete reality. As a researcher and assistant you have been central to the success of this publication.

Mario Novelli and Antoni Verger
Amsterdam, September 2011

---

[1] The papers and presentations of this seminar can be downloaded from:
  http://educationanddevelopment.wordpress.com/past-events/civil-society-advocacy-and-efa/

ACRONYMS

ABI	Alternative Budget Initiative (The Philippines)
AIFTO	All India Federation of Teachers Organization
ANCEFA	Africa Network Campaign on Education for All
ASPBAE	Asia South Pacific Association of Basic and Adult Education
BESSIP	Basic Education Sub-Sector Plan (Zambia)
CAQi	Initial Student-Quality-Cost (Brazil)
CBDE	Brazilian Campaign for the Right to Education
CLADE	Latin American Campaign for the Right to Education
CMP	Common Minimum Programme (India)
CNE	National Council of Education (Ecuador and Brazil)
CNTE	National Confederation of Education Workers (Brazil)
CONEB	National Conference for Basic Education (Brazil)
CSE	Social Contract for Education
CSEF	Civil Society Education Fund
CSO	Civil Society Organization
EAC	Education Advocacy Coalitions
EDWATCH	Educational Watch research
EFA	Education For All
FCUBE	Free Compulsory Basic Education Program
FIFA	International Federation of Association Football
FNDP	Fifth National Development Plan (Zambia)
FUNDEF-FUNDEB	Fund for the Development of Basic Education and the Valuation of Teachers *(Brazil)*
GAW	Global Action Week
GCE	Global Campaign for Education
GDP	Gross Domestic Product
GER	Gross Enrolment Rate
GMR	Global Monitoring Report
GNECC	Ghana National Education Campaign Coalition
GPRS	Growth and Poverty Reduction Strategy paper
HDI	Human Development Index
IMF	International Monetary Fund
INGO	International NGO
MDGs	Millennium Development Goals
MoE	Ministry of Education (Zambia)
MoESS	Ministry of Education, Science and Sports (Ghana)
MST	Rural Landless Workers Movement (Brazil)
NCE	National Coalition for Education (India)
NER	Net Enrolment Rate
NGO	Non-Governmental Organization
NNED	Northern Network for Education (Ghana)

OECD	Organization for Economic Cooperation and Development
PEPE	Popular Education for People's Empowerment (The Philippines)
PGRI	Teachers' Association of the Republic of Indonesia
PNE	*National Education Plan (Brazil)*
PIECE	Partners In Education for Community Empowerment
POS	Political Opportunity Structures
PPPs	Public-Private Partnerships
PT	Worker's Party (Brazil)
RTE	Right to Education Act (India)
RWS	Real World Strategies
SMC	School Management Committee (India)
SWAP	Sector Wide Approach
TPE	All for Education (Brazil)
UNE	National Union of Educators (Ecuador)
UNDIME	National Union of Municipal Education Secretaries (Brazil)
UNESCO	United Nations Education, Science and Culture Organization
UNICEF	*United Nations Children's* Fund
UPA	United Progressive Alliance (India)
WEF	World Education Forum
ZANEC	Zambia National Education Campaign coalition

ANTONI VERGER AND MARIO NOVELLI

CHAPTER 1

Introduction to Civil Society Coalitions and Educational Advocacy:
Theoretical and Methodological Insights

INTRODUCTION

In the book *Poverty and Famines*, Amartya Sen presents the main findings of the outstanding research he did on the causes and effects of world famines. One of the starting points of his research was observing that similar types of food crisis (in similar climate conditions, with similar bad crops) that happened in India and China in the fifties had very different consequences in the two countries: Three million people starved to death in China, while many less died in India. So, the driving question of Sen's research was why did such big variations in the management of food crises in apparently two similar situations happen? (Sen 1983).

The main finding of his work was that, when famines happen, the important issue is not only the availability of food, but the distribution and the lack of purchasing power of the poor. However, and even more importantly for us, he also found that democratic institutions, free media and active civil society networks with the capacity to make their voices heard are determinant when it comes to avoiding the occurrence of famines. His study in India was contextualized at a time that the country had recently gained its Independence from the British Empire, and the country was trying to build a young democratic system sensitive to people's needs. In fact, the social movements that organised themselves to mitigate the effects of the food crisis were the same that contributed to Indian independence as well. Such institutional conditions were far from those occurring in China in the same period, but also in the colonized India of the forties. As Sen himself wrote:

> "Not surprisingly, while India continued to have famines under British rule right up to independence... they disappeared suddenly with the establishment of a multiparty democracy and a free press" (Sen 2001, p. 8)

On the basis of his results, Amartya Sen concluded that the state should be responsible for enacting laws that ensure food security for all, but that public action from below is equally important to put pressure on government bodies to guarantee that such laws are implemented and that, as a result, the right to food is enacted.

Sen's research on *Poverty and Famines* represents one of the first conclusive pieces of evidence on the social benefits of a well-articulated and independent civil

Antoni Verger and Mario Novelli (eds.), Campaigning for "Education for All", 1–15.

society. Even though this was not his main focus, Sen's work contributed to opening up a very important and fascinating area of inquiry on the role and impact of civil society in the warranty of the most basic of human rights. The book you have in your hands is similarly engaging with this still nascent area of inquiry and, specifically, with the role of civil society in the enactment of the right to education worldwide.

The lack of education and, specifically, the lack of relevant and quality education does not have the same dramatic and visual effects that famines produce. However, it too can also have dramatic consequences of a different nature. Lack of education deprives people from wellbeing and future opportunities, disempowers them in terms of civil and political participation and, more broadly speaking, limits their chances to enjoy a full, healthy and productive life. Fortunately, the international community is more and more aware of the important contribution of education to multiple dimensions of human and societal development. Since the nineties, and thanks to a great extent to the World Education Conferences that took place in Jomtien (1990) and Dakar (2000), governments, aid agencies and international organizations are formally committed to the right to quality Education for All (EFA) globally (World Education Forum 2000). In the context of the Dakar conference, they even signed and committed to a Global Action Framework on EFA that establishes six specific education targets that all countries in the world should achieve in the following decades (see Box 2.1 in Mundy's chapter, this volume). In parallel, civil society networks have organized themselves to make sure that these international commitments translate into concrete practice on the ground. Among these networks, the Global Campaign for Education (GCE) stands out as the biggest and most active civil society network advocating for EFA.

The GCE was set up in the late 1990s, in the run up to the Dakar Conference, with the objective of pushing for an ambitious EFA agenda. It brought together several International NGOs (Oxfam, Action Aid, Global March for Labour) and Education International (the global federation of teachers unions). With the passage of time, the GCE evolved into a multi-scalar organization by promoting and strengthening the role of civil society advocacy coalitions operating at the national and regional level. In the context of these coalitions, very different types of organizations work together to put pressure on national governments, donors and international organizations to honour financial and political agreements to deliver high quality education to all (World Education Forum 2000). To date, the GCE counts on the participation of 76 national coalitions and three big regional coalitions (see more details in Mundy in this volume)

ABOUT THIS BOOK

The main aim of this book is to understand *how and to what extent civil society coalitions are able to make the state responsible for expanding educational opportunities and improving the education experience of children in their countries*. This book is the main outcome of a three-year research project that has generated a range of empirically grounded case studies on the role and impact of civil society education advocacy coalitions (EACs) that are member of the GCE and that, as such, operate in a range of territories.[2]

The book is structured as follows. In this introductory chapter we detail the main conceptual, theoretical and methodological elements that have contributed to building the research framework upon which the book is based. The first chapter after this introductory one is written by one of the most knowledgeable scholars on global civil society and education governance, Karen Mundy. It traces the history, evolution and impact of the GCE at different scales, but with a focus at the supranational one (global and regional). In her chapter, Mundy reflects on the main achievements and challenges that derive from organizing a big social movement that operates at multiple political scales.

The following seven chapters analyse the evolution and the main outcomes of EACs operating in a sample of countries. The countries in question are Brazil, The Philippines, Zambia, India, Ghana, Ecuador and Indonesia. These case studies have been undertaken by junior researchers who participated in this project as part of their thesis dissertation in the International Development Studies MSc programme of the University of Amsterdam. The national EACs studies are very rich in empirical terms and are based on dozens of interviews and participatory workshops with activists and key informants and extensive document analysis in each country in question. The case studies contribute to recovering the history, the strategies, the challenges and successes, the main milestones and the internal learning processes that have occurred within the coalitions since their creation. They also highlight the main contributions that the different coalitions have made to the education field in their respective countries.

In the book's conclusion, the country case studies are analysed through a comparative strategy by the coordinators of this project. By doing so, we provide a synthesis of the core issues that have emerged out of the research, which include the varieties of education coalition's profile; the importance of agenda setting processes within the coalitions; the strategies and action repertoires that are more conducive to impact; and the factors explaining the different levels of internal cohesion of EACs, among others.

CIVIL SOCIETY ADVOCACY, AS A RESEARCH AREA

"Civil society" is a very broad and contested category. It includes a big variety of organizations such as international and local NGOs, trade unions, community based organizations, grassroots movements, independent research institutes, etc.[3] These organizations encompass very different numbers of members and manage very different amounts of human and economic resources; some of them are institutionalized and formalized, while others are more spontaneous and oriented

---

[2] See the Acknowledgements section for more details about the institutions supporting this research.

[3] If we take into account a more liberal conception of civil society, employers associations and corporate lobby groups could be also included.

towards collective political action; and so on. Given this diversity, the establishment of civil society *coalitions* usually implies the articulation of very different types of constituencies, interests and rationales in a single space, and this is not an easy task at all, as the book demonstrates.

Civil society organizations can decide to establish coalitions for different reasons, which include fundraising partnerships, providing innovative services or undertaking a research initiative. However, quite often, they do so to *advocate* something. Thus, coalitions are usually constituted with the explicit objective of influencing the agendas and decisions of governmental bodies in relation to a particular issue area or problem. This is clearly the case of the GCE coalitions that, as we said above, have emerged to put pressure on governments and the international community to fulfill their commitments with the EFA action framework.

Civil society advocacy coalitions have been understudied, especially in developing societies, and particularly in relation to educational politics and policies. The simple fact of their existence opens a range of areas of inquiry that are worthy of studying. Some of the main research issues around civil society advocacy coalitions, which to a great extent are addressed in this book, are the constitution and organization of coalitions – how and why did they form?; the internal cohesion of coalitions – how do different components of the coalitions interact?; the transnationalization of their operation and actions – How do they operate across geographical space?; and their main outcomes – What did they achieve?.

Constitution and organization

Research questions concerning this particular area of inquiry can be quite descriptive in nature, but they are necessary to get a first sense of the type of organization or movement we are talking about. They include: What are the main drivers for the constitution of civil society advocacy coalitions? Who are their promoters? Who are their members? Why do member organizations take part in such umbrella bodies, and with what level of involvement? Once coalitions have been created, how do they organize and fund themselves? Do the members institutionalize the coalition and, for instance, create a secretariat, or do they rather decide to work in a more informal and *de facto* way? Do coalitions plan to last in time or are they deigned to operate in a particular time juncture or in relation to a specific problem? What types of communication and information systems are built in the context of the coalition? How are decisions adopted? How is power distributed and representation ensured? Etc. etc.

Internal cohesion

Working in coalitions generates mutual learning processes and economies of scale, and can contribute to raising the profile of civil society groups in the public domain. However, coalition building is also a challenging process due to the fact that the parties involved might count on different political cultures and identities, and need to negotiate particular priorities, interests and objectives. In the process of building education coalitions, the relationship between teachers' unions with other sections of civil society is particularly relevant. Teachers' trade unions, as representatives of members largely within the public sector, have a tendency to be driven both to defend their members' interests, but also to some notion of 'public education'. In the current climate of neoliberal educational reform this is something that often forces them into conflict with the state and into alliances with other sectors of civil society (Robertson et al, 2007). However, this relationship is not without its problems. The balance between defending 'members interests' and the interests of 'public education' on behalf of unions, together with issues of different cultures of political organization, may provoke tensions within coalitions advocating for EFA.

Transnationalism

Civil society coalitions are re-scaling their activity and creating more links at the international level, in parallel to the increasing role of international organizations in the framing of national education policies (Bainton 2009, Gaventa and Mayo 2009). In a global governance scenario, advocacy coalitions feel an increasing pressure to build international networks and, more importantly, to become global themselves. These new types of organization opens up new political opportunities and advocacy strategies such as 'boomerang' effects (see Box 1.1), but also important challenges (Keck and Sikkink 1998; Mundy and Murphy 2001; Tarrow 2001). What is the potential and what are the challenges of organizing transnational advocacy networks? How are the activities coordinated between the local and the international parties of such networks, and what is the division of labor between the different scales of action? What is the comparative advantage for national coalitions to participate in supra-national networks? And, how is transnational advocacy translated into concrete political impact? From our point of view, these are some of the key questions that the globalization of politics introduces to research agendas on social movements and civil society.

Box 1.1: The boomerang effect

The *boomerang effect* is a civil society strategy whereby domestic groups whose demands are being blocked by the national state can try to utilise external pressure to make themselves heard internally – hence the boomerang imagery. It means that in order to overcome blockages and to open political opportunities at the domestic level they internationalize their demands through supra-national networks, key foreign states or international organizations and agreements that, they expect, will put further pressure on national governments to make them more attentive to their demands. To a great extent, the organization of the GCE as a pluri-scalar network, and the use of the EFA global action framework as a political tool, responds to this type of strategy.

Sources: Keck and Sikkink 1998, Tarrow, 2001

Outcomes

The *outcomes* or *impact* of civil society campaigns need to be understood in a multi-dimensional way. Different scholars consider that, at least, three dimensions of impact can be identified. They are: political impact, procedimental, and symbolic (Gomà et al., 2002, Burstein, 1999). *Political impact* refers to the specific effects of civil society action in observable policy outcomes (approval of a new law or changes in some aspects of the existing legislation; budget increases for education; governmental adoption of new education programmes, etc.). *Procedimental impact* refers to changes in the consultation and decision-making procedures that signify some sort of recognition of civil society organizations as legitimate interlocutors with the state. The *symbolic impact* refers to changes at the public opinion level, values or general beliefs concerning a certain theme. These three types of impacts are inter-related since, for instance, having more voice in consultative bodies might facilitate political impact over the short and medium term. Something similar could be said concerning symbolic impact, since changes in public opinion might force, at some point, a re-orientation of governmental educational policy.

THEORETICAL TOOLS

Social movements literature is rich in theories about the origins, the capacities and the impact of civil society actors in politics. According to the theory we are drawing on, different variables and other aspects of social movements' reality are highlighted and brought into focus. For the particular purpose of this research we have found two main theoretical approaches useful: on the one hand, frame analysis, which focuses on the role of ideas and discursive strategies in contentious politics and, on the other hand, the political opportunity structures approach, which focuses on the contextual factors that can enable or hinder the coalitions actions and claims.

Frame analysis

Mass mobilization and economic resources are important factors when it comes to understand social movements success. In social movements literature, materialist approaches, such as the 'resources mobilization' theory, are very well established. Such approaches assume that variables related to the organization and the management of resources (human, economic, etc.) are key elements when it comes to understanding the level of achievement of mobilization. However, more and more social movements scholars are also paying attention to the role of non-material and ideational factors such as persuasion strategies, the interpretation of social problems and the articulation of corresponding discourses by movements (Korzeniewicz and Smith, 2003). In fact, to a great extent, the strength and legitimacy of social movements depends on their principles and beliefs and, especially in the case of advocacy groups, on the scientific evidence they can draw on to support their claims.

Frame theory deals with the role of ideas and, particularly, with how ideas are constructed and disseminated in collective action settings. According to frame theorists, it is not only the content of the ideas that matters, it is also the process of how theses ideas are constructed (and framed) by the movements, and how they are linked to the social order (Benford and Snow, 2000). This approach necessitates looking at the coalitions as strategic producers of meaning and to ideas as dynamic resources in the movements' struggle. It focuses on the interactive processes by which frames are collectively constructed, sustained, contested and changed; the framing contests that occur between movement and non-movement actors such as the government, counter-movements or the media; the consequences of these processes for aspects of mobilization and political impact; and the hindering constraints and enabling factors on these processes (Snow and Benford, 2000).

Within the message of civil society groups, different dimensions of frames can be distinguished. They include *diagnostic* frames (problem identification and attribution of culpability), *prognostic* frames (possible solutions and alternatives to the problems) and *motivational* frames (telling people that action is viable and has a good chance of being effective). If one of these dimensions fails, is weak or is not coherently linked to the others within the discourse of civil society or advocacy groups, collective action has more chance of being unproductive.

Appropriate framing can contribute to a movements' success when the resulting message is clearly understandable by different sectors of society and/or when different social groups identify themselves with the problems that the movement points to (Goodwin and Jasper 2004). *Resonation* is a key concept in this respect. For a movement to make its message resonate in society, it needs to sound credible and salient. The *credibility* of a message is related to elements such us empirical commensurability (i.e. the apparent fit between the framings of the coalition and events in the world) or the status of the frame articulators (i.e. the greater the perceived expertise of the coalition representatives, the more resonant will be their claims). The *salience* of the message, on its part, corresponds to how important are the societal values and beliefs of the movement for its target population (whether it refers to decision-makers, some media groups, or to a broader public opinion), or to what extent the movement frames are resonant with the everyday experience of the population they want to convince or mobilize (Benford and Snow 2000).

Summing up, the greater the salience and the greater the credibility of the civil society groups' discourse the greater the resonance and the prospects of mobilization and political impact. In other words, an excessive distance between the discourse of the activists and the rest of society can reduce the effectiveness of mobilization (Dellaporta and Diani 2006). However, it should also be noticed that being too strategic in this respect could upset the more radical or principled-driven sectors of a coalition, which can perceive that they are becoming too adaptable to the *status quo* or feel that they have been co-opted (Maney et al 2009).

Political opportunities and other contextual elements

Putting excessive emphasis on frames and ideas when doing research on social movements could mean that we imply that politics can be reduced to a simple difference of opinion, or that reality can be changed by simply changing the opinion of key political agents (Olivier and Johnston 2000). Actually, when taking decisions, policymakers (or other actors usually targeted by advocacy coalitions such as the media) are not necessarily guided by the "truth" or by the most convincing arguments (Haas 2004). Electoral interests, ideological divergences, material interests, group loyalties and other political variables need to be contemplated as well to understand civil society influence. Here is where approaches such as the *Political Opportunity Structures* (POS) can contribute importantly to the analysis of the role and impact of civil society coalitions since they bring the 'political context' into the analytical framework.

Broadly speaking, POS refer to the political conditions that favour or make it difficult for movements to produce certain effects. Such conditions can refer to, on the one hand, systemic factors and, on the other hand, to factors of a more relational nature. *Systemic factors* include variables that refer to the main features of the political system in a certain territory. The main examples are the level of centralization (or decentralization) of the state, the level of openness (or closeness) of the political system to external actors, the independence of the different state powers (legislative, executive, judicial), and the level of repression existing in a certain country (Tarrow 1994). It should be also noticed that in some countries, the model of public administration is based on Roman Law, which is resistant to external contacts and influences, while in other countries, especially Anglo-Saxon ones, the administrative model opens more channels to lobbying and civil society participation (Dellaporta and Diani 2006).

The variation in these features of the political system affects the chances of social mobilization succeeding. However, it is not always clear in which direction these variables work. For instance, the level of decentralization of a country generates a sort of paradox for collective action. The more power is distributed to local governments the greater the chances movements have in accessing decision-making processes, since the nearer an administrative unit is to ordinary citizens the easier it is to gain access to it. However, decentralization also means that the field of struggle becomes more fragmented and that the demands of civil society groups are more difficult to penetrate at the national level (Dellaporta and Diani 2006). Something similar can be said about repression. Repression, while apparently discouraging mobilization, can in many cases lead to radicalization and the more effective organization of social movements.

Relational factors are less formal or permanent than systemic ones. They include the level of cohesiveness or the divide between political elites, the possibilities for the coalition to establish alliances with elites (or with other influential actors such as bureaucrats from certain public agencies), or the presence of antagonist or enemy coalitions in the political field (Tarrow, 1994, McAdam 1996). In relation to the latter, the coalition will be probably more successful if there are not powerful actors that prosecute opposing aims to the coalition ones in the same political field. In relational terms, the fact that left-wing political parties are in power often has the potential to affect the relationship between the movement and the state. The members of left-wing parties are normally involved in progressive social movements (they count on what is known as double militants). When these parties are in government, they are supposed to enhance the influence of protestors due to their personal links and the affinity between their ideas. However, the organic relationship between party and movements also has a price, since the government can try to co-opt the movement and/or try to manage and control the protest in a paternalistic way. When the left is in power, the claims of the movement might resonate deeper within governmental bodies, but, at the same time, mobilization becomes more difficult and the relationship between civil society and the state becomes more complex.

Another political factor to take into account is how strong the government in power is or feels (according, for instance, to whether it has been elected by a big majority of citizens or not). Governments that are strong and ideologically homogeneous tend to exclude opposing actors and 'external' ideas from their every-day action. In contrast, more heterogeneous governments are more open to the participation of external actors. A weak executive may ease access to the decision-making process, however it should also be acknowledged that it will have less capacity for implementing those policies that meet the social movements demands (Dellaporta and Diani 2006).

As we can observe, from the POS perspective it is very important to understand and pay attention to the state and its relationship with civil society actors, since "the state is simultaneously the target, sponsor, and antagonist for social movements as well as the organizer of the political system and the arbiter of victory" (Jenkins and Klandermans 1995: 3)

Beyond POSs, another contextual dimension to keep in mind when analyzing the evolution and outcomes of social movements refers to the *issue characteristics* of the theme that the movement in question deals with. In the same political context, there are not the same opportunities (or difficulties) to advocate over different issues. Climate change, peace, gender equality or 'education for all' are very distinct issues in nature that can count on very variable levels of centrality in political and media agendas and/or on very variable levels of support in society. In other words, the level of awareness, and the type of sentiments, beliefs or norms that prevail in society in relation to different policy issues, can vary substantially and this is something that frames importantly the opportunities and the strategies of different advocacy coalitions.

Today, many social and political agents agree on the importance of education in society, although they might do so for different reasons. Civil society groups usually do so because they see education as a human right, but other groups support investment in education for its strategic contribution to the economic competitiveness of countries, or for their positive externalities in health, family planning, or civic participation. Education advocacy is also looked upon favorably today because the issue of education is quite central in global agendas. In fact, education fulfills the three necessary conditions to be considered a so-called 'global political priority' (see Shiffman and Smith 2007). The first of these conditions is that international and national leaders have publicly expressed sustained concern and support for education; the best example of this can be found in the World Education Conferences celebrated in Jomtien and Dakar. Second, international organizations and governments have enacted policies to address the main education problems, such as the EFA global action framework or a range of Education Plans in many developing countries. And third, the international community has provided resources to solve these problems, both bilaterally and multilaterally, through mechanisms such as Fast Track Initiative (now known as the Global Partnership for Education).

However, being considered a global political priority alone is not sufficient to address education problems successfully. Education is a very complex and multi-dimensional policy issue. Many can agree in its importance for society broadly speaking, but disagree on the levels of funding that education should enjoy, on who should participate in the governance and funding of education, or on how it should be provided and regulated and by whom. In fact, today, the debate between what should be the role of the public and private sectors in different areas of educational policy is very central in the global arena (Robertson et al 2012). Everyone also agrees today on the fact that education access is not enough and that the education to be provided should be one of 'quality'. However, what quality education means is also the object of passionate discussions in both the academic and political fields. In these types of variables and details, and not necessarily on the importance of education in abstract terms, is where the struggle of the EACs actually focuses.

To sum up, what the POSs and the 'issue characteristic' approaches tell us is that the context in which advocacy coalitions operate is 'selective'. As we develop below, in different periods and places, the context favours certain strategies, actors and discourses over others. Therefore, not all the outcomes are possible for every coalition, for every strategy and in every moment (Hay, 2002).

Through a more integrated framework

As we noted earlier, placing too much importance on frames and ideas can make researchers have an understanding of the political field that is too intentionalist and ideationalist. As the Political Opportunity Structures approach warns, the power of actors advocating a cause is sensitive to the power of the political context to inhibit or enhance political support, as well as to the power of their allies and enemies (Shiffman and Smith 2007). However, at the same time, we also should bear in mind that an excessive emphasis on POSs could neglect the importance of activists' agency and their ideational and non-ideational strategies (Meyer and Minkoff 2004).

Therefore, to try to solve this 'structure-agency' or 'context-ideas' dilemma, it is necessary to understand that while coalitions are strategic actors with the potential to transform their context, they are also operating in strategic and discursively selective contexts. The context imposes 'discursive selectivity', selecting *for* and selecting *against* particular ideas, narratives and claims (Hay

2002). However, at the same time, as Tarrow (1994) noted, political opportunities, even when they are consistent, are not necessarily formal or permanent and, even more interestingly, they can be altered by social movements agency.

Thus, in social movements research frameworks, structure and agency, context and ideas need to be understood as mutually constituted. 'Ideas' and 'context' are not independent or totally differentiable elements. Ideas play a crucial mediatory role in the relationship between the context and the strategy of the coalitions. For instance, the analysis of the environment carried out by advocacy coalitions – whether this is done in a more explicit or implicit way – plays a crucial role in the formation of the coalition actions, claims and messages and, consequently, affects the political change process they try to promote. In this sense, what matters are not only the objective opportunities or difficulties that political opportunities provide, but also the perception of these opportunities and difficulties by activists. In other words, ideas and, particularly, *reflexivity* are important concepts to link structure and agency since they provide the point of mediation between actors' strategies and their context.

Box 1.2. Reflexivity and social movements: Are activists too optimistic?

Reflexivity requires agency (and giving importance to agency in analytical terms), and refers to the capacity of actors to reflect on the environment, its previous actions and its consequences. We should keep in mind that there is always some relationship between the context and the ideas actors hold about that context, but not a perfect correlation. In other words, reality is something different from the perception of actors over their own reality. Strategic actors need to make assumptions over the context and build hypotheses over the future consequences of their (and other agents') actions over the context.

Some scholars perceive activists as people that are optimistic by default about opportunities and, to some extent, as 'naïve agents' that do not necessarily calculate with any rigor the prospects for successful mobilization or generating policy reform: "they just keep trying". However, this is not necessarily negative. There are cases in which movement activists have interpreted POs in ways that emphasize opportunities rather than constraints and, by doing so, they stimulate actions that change opportunity, making their opportunity frame a sort of self-fulfilling prophecy.

Sources: Hay, 2002, Meyer and Minkoff, 2004

In the following figure (Figure 1.1) we detail how we have sought to integrate reflexivity and the other theoretical concepts developed in this section in a single but dynamic analytical framework. The figure, is based on the political analysis framework suggested by Hay (2002), and shows how critical reflexivity over both the context and the previous actions of coalitions over the context is a key element when it comes to framing the new strategies pursued by the coalition. These new strategies will partially transform the context, but will also allow internal learning processes within the coalition and, as a consequence, contribute to the following round of strategic actions as shown in the figure.

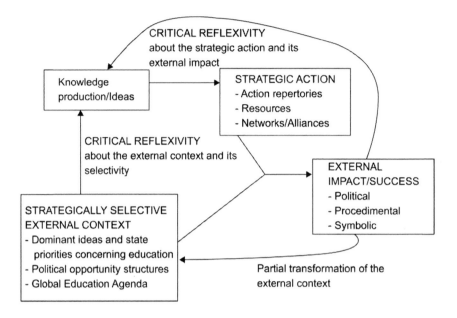

Figure 1.1. Context, ideas and coalition strategies

To sum up, looking at the structural or political opportunities without considering the cognitive processes that intervene between structure and action could be misleading. Because of this reason, this research tries to integrate ideas within both agential and structural factors when it comes to understand the role and impact of civil society coalitions in educational politics. This theoretical point has important methodological implications because it means that it is important to retrieve data about the activists' understandings and interpretations of the available opportunities for them, and document what are the lenses through which they view potential opportunities for their movements. In the following section we advance some of the methodological strategies that we have developed in order to address this challenge.

METHODOLOGY

Analyzing the role and impact of advocacy coalitions is not an easy task. There are so many variables in the political influence game, that identifying regularities and causal factors through research is very challenging. There are three main methodological problems that scholars that analyze civil society influence face at some point in their research.

The *first* problem consists on the attribution of causality, i.e., how to ascertain that the social movement or coalition action is the explanatory variable of a certain political outcome. For instance, let's take the case of coalition A that organizes a campaign that advocates an education budget increase in country X. Some months after the campaign starts, the government of X makes public that they will increase the education budget for the next year. A superficial observer would be tempted to deduce that the government took this decision because of coalition A's pressure. However, the government may have done it because another coalition or lobby that is also acting in the country (coalition B) had a similar demand, or because the government already planned to do it before coalition A's campaign started. Finally, we should also consider the possibility that the coalition campaign had political effects and outcomes, but that these effects were not related to their explicit claims and demands (unintended effects) (Giugni 1998).

A *second* problem is how to analyze the political impact of advocacy coalitions in a context where politics have been deterritorialized and where the state authority has been distributed beyond the national scale, both to local and to supra-national scales. Quite often, social movements research has a methodologically nationalist bias, i.e. it assumes that the nation-state is the main unit of analysis and that decision-making dynamics are not affected by agents and processes that are based 'outside' the borders of the nation. However, civil society organizations are intervening today in a context in which international organizations, on the one hand, and local (sub-national) governments, on the other, are more and more involved in political processes affecting education. Thus, in the global era, a new set of political actors and political scales introduce complexity to the analysis of the political influence of non-state actors

A *third* problem is how to get the appropriate and the necessary data to empirically demonstrate the political impact of advocacy coalitions. On the one hand, what are the sources, the time periods and the empirical evidence we need to consider to rigorously attribute to coalitions action the responsibility of a certain political change? And, on the other hand, are the stakeholders' sources reliable? We raise the latter question because it is well-known that activists usually have a triumphalist and, consequently, biased discourse about the impact of their action. At the same time, a government representative could also tell the interviewer that they have met the demands of the civil society groups, because they know how to articulate a politically correct discourse on the importance of civil society participation, democracy, and so on and so forth. Again, the superficial analyst would take the activist or the policy-maker's words as the truth and, consequently, would reach easy conclusions that might not correspond with the complexity of influence dynamics.

These are, indeed, very different methodological problems in nature. To a great extent, they need to be resolved by resorting to theoretical tools as, for instance, those specified in the section above. However, in parallel, we can also apply a range of methodological strategies that contribute to the validity and reliability of our results. Specifically, in the context of this research project we have applied the following:

a) *Process tracing and thick description.* Quite often, the best way of explaining a phenomenon is by describing it in-depth. Process tracing requires the detailed historical reconstruction of different advocacy campaigns, its key events and its relation to broader policy processes. It also requires the systematization of the chain of actions and interactions hosted by different actors in such policy processes (Bestill and Corell, 2001). Process tracing will allow us to examine how political opportunities work and how the responses that social movements provoke alter the grounds on which they can mobilize and influence (McAdam 2001).

b) *Multi-stakeholder analysis.* To overcome the bias that particular stakeholders might have when assessing the role and impact of civil society campaigns, a range of actors and key informants that are both internal and external to the coalitions and that operate at a range of scales should be interviewed (including activists, researchers, policy-makers, local governments, international NGOs, donor agencies, journalists, etc.)

c) *Document equivalence.* Another way of contrasting empirically the effects of civil society groups' actions is to compare the advocacy documents they produce with the documents (laws, agreements, etc.) finally approved by decision-makers.

d) *Counterfactual analysis.* Counterfactual analysis means understanding 'what something is' in relation to 'what it is not'. This type of analysis assumes that we can only discern the necessary, constitutive properties of a phenomenon by relating these properties to what is not constitutive (but rather an accidental circumstance). According to counterfactual analysis, after having done the empirical work, we should be able to answer the counter-factual question: "Would the outcome of the policy process be different if coalition X had not intervened?" (Korzeniewicz and Smith, 2003, Guzzini, 2005).

e) *Comparison.* Research on the influence of coalitions can finally benefit from explicit comparisons across different contexts. Comparative research is especially adequate to analyze the political impact of civil society actors, due to the fact that it allows us to explore the conditions and circumstances of the realization (or non-realization) of the impact (Giugni et al., 1999). A comparative strategy will allow us to answer the question why do similar coalitions obtain different political outcomes, or, alternatively, why do coalitions operating in similar contexts obtain different results.

Finally we would like to note that we selected the country sample for this research on the basis of two main criteria. The first criterion was choosing coalitions that are highly active in their countries.[4] This would allow us to compare organizations that are similarly active, but that operate in different political, cultural and socio-economic contexts. The second criterion was geographical representation. As a result we have case studies from Asia (India, Indonesia and the Philippines), Africa (Ghana and Zambia) and Latin America (Brazil and Ecuador).

---

[4] Because of methodological reasons, we have selected seven coalitions that are very active and relatively successful in the territories where they operate. Thus, this book does not necessarily reflect the reality of the GCE member-coalitions globally.

CLOSING WORDS

On the basis of the theoretical and methodological elements described above, this book analyses the strategies and outcomes of civil society coalitions in advocating for the right to education. While the book focuses on a specific organization, the Global Campaign for Education, we hope our work contributes more broadly to a critical reflection on the emerging role of civil society actors in global governance structures and to a better understanding of the potential, but also the challenges, of organizing transnational coalitions that can act at a range of scales, from the local to the global.

Furthermore, for research purposes, we hope this book contributes to further reflection and debate on methodological strategies and instruments to better understand the outcomes of civil society at different levels (agenda setting, recognition, political outcomes, etc.) as well as on the levels of cohesiveness of coalitions in a far more rigorous way.

Centrally, we hope that this book will help practitioners and activists that are part of civil society groups to better identify those strategies and practices that can strengthen the quality of the advocacy processes they are involved in, and in that way to make a modest contribution to progressive political change in the education field.

Finally, we wish to conclude this chapter by returning to Amartya Sen's findings mentioned in the beginning on the importance of civil society. As the reader will note as they read through the chapters of this book, while civil society advocacy in education is composed of a varied and diverse set of practices and activities, in all of the cases here presented it has succeeded in contributing to the better provision of public education in their respective countries. While there is a great deal that remains to be done, children in the countries studied are receiving better education today because of the commitment and activities of these coalitions. For education to be guaranteed as a human right, the state should remain the key actor in the funding, delivery and coordination of education. However, education is far too important a task to be left to the state alone. An active and organized civil society – linked together transnationally - advocating for the right to education, and lobbying national and international organizations to ensure that they deliver on their commitments, is one of the best ways to ensure that one day all children in the world will enjoy relevant and quality education.

KAREN MUNDY

CHAPTER 2

The Global Campaign for Education and the Realization of
"Education For All"

INTRODUCTION

Formed in 1999, the Global Campaign for Education (GCE) has emerged over the past decade as the globally recognized voice for civil society actors on the issue of "Education for All" (EFA). From its early founding by a small cluster of international nongovernmental organizations, the GCE has grown enormously. Today it has affiliated members in over 100 countries, including the participation of major international and regional non-governmental organizations, Education International (the international federation of teachers' unions); three regional umbrella bodies (ANCEFA in Africa, CLADE in Latin America and the Caribbean, and ASPBAE in South-East Asia),[5] and a growing number of nationally-based coalitions (76 at most recent count, up from 37 in 2002).

The scope of its aspirations, geographic membership, and funding, places the GCE among the largest of the transnational advocacy organizations active on issues of human rights and world poverty. This chapter explores its origins, evolution, key achievements and challenges. It describes in some detail the way that the GCE has sought to support national educational coalitions, whose work is the focus of this volume. The chapter will conclude with an assessment of the GCE's efforts to frame a global right to education and achieve political and policy changes to affect its achievement.

ORIGINS AND EARLY EVOLUTION OF THE GCE: 1999-2007

The Global Campaign for Education was born in 1999 at a meeting hosted by ActionAid, Oxfam International, Education International (the international federation of teachers' unions), and the Global March against Child Labour (a grassroots movement formed in 1998 that links education with eradicating child labour). It was initially conceived of as a short-term campaign focused on ensuring that *"the World Education Forum in Dakar, April 2000, would result in concrete*

---

[5] ANCEFA: Africa Network Campaign on Education for All; CLADE: Campaña Latinoamericana por el Derecho a la Educación; ASPBAE: Asia South Pacific Association for Basic and Adult Education.

Antoni Verger and Mario Novelli (eds.), Campaigning for "Education for All", 17–30.

commitments and viable policies to implement the Education for All (EFA) goals, including gender equity by 2005, universal enrolment in and completion of free primary education by 2015, and a 50% reduction in adult literacy by 2015" (GCE Constitution 2001).[6]

The early GCE was influenced by the different approaches to advocacy and campaigning taken by its founding members. Oxfam, an International Non-Governmental Organization (INGO) not previously active in education, had decided in 1998 to use the theme of "education for all" as a venue for advancing its broader advocacy for debt relief and better development cooperation. Its "Education Now" campaign was launched with an empirical study of global trends in educational access and funding, and included new EFA targets and demands for the revitalization of international funding for EFA. Oxfam efforts were linked to the highly visible Jubilee 2000 campaign for debt relief, and included direct advocacy to senior officials in the World Bank and Unicef about its proposed plan of action. This led to a spot for Oxfam on the inter-agency EFA Steering Committee in the summer of 1999. From the Oxfam campaign, the GCE inherited a strong focus on education finance and a tradition of working for direct change in international networks.

Box 2.1: Education for All Goals

1. Expand and improve comprehensive early childhood care and education, especially for the most vulnerable and disadvantaged children.
2. Ensure that by 2015 all children, particularly girls, those in difficult circumstances, and those belonging to ethnic minorities, have access to and complete, free, and compulsory primary education of good quality.
3. Ensure that the learning needs of all young people and adults are met through equitable access to appropriate learning and life-skills programs.
4. Achieve a 50 % improvement in adult literacy by 2015, especially for women, and equitable access to basic and continuing education for all adults.
5. Eliminate gender disparities in primary and secondary education by 2005, and achieve gender equality in education by 2015, with a focus on ensuring girls' full and equal access to and achievement in basic education of good quality.
6. Improve all aspects of the quality of education and ensure the excellence of all so that recognized and measurable learning outcomes are achieved by all, especially in literacy, numeracy and essential life skills.

Several other organizations also launched education for all campaigns in 1999, including ActionAid and Education International. ActionAid's Elimu campaign

---

[6] In addition to these four institutional members, key Southern education networks (members of ActionAid's Elimu campaign on education) were present at the meeting. A Steering Committee was elected, consisting of six Southern representatives and the four founding members.

focused on the development of national level NGO networks capable of engaging in local educational policy debates – a focus that would be picked up by the GCE. Education International's campaign concentrated on re-invigorating the advocacy role played by teachers unions and teachers associations at the national and international levels. From EI, the GCE would inherit a strong interest in issues of teachers work, as well as an absolute insistence on publicly provided and finance education while from Actionaid and important focus on building the capacity of local citizens in the majority world to demand a basic right to good quality equitable education. A final founding member, Global March Against Child Labour, joined the GCE as a founding member in recognition of the important link between campaigns against child labour and educational opportunity.

In the months that followed its establishment, the GCE network expanded and began to focus on ensuring a place for civil society at the World Education Forum (Dakar 2000). The Campaign grew rapidly, to include over 30 national coalitions, 8 regional members, and 8 INGOs and international networks. At the World Education Forum in Dakar, the GCE emerged as the leading voice for civil society, playing an important role in ensuring that the financing of EFA remained at the centre of conference discussions. The GCE also influenced the World Bank's presentation of its first version of the Education for All Fast-track plan, for which the GCE announced its support (World Education Forum, 2000). It was nominated to speak on behalf of civil society in the final drafting committee, where it succeeded in keeping such issues as international financing targets and the idea of education as a basic right on the forum's agenda (Mundy and Murphy 2001; Murphy and Mundy 2002). It helped to ensure that the Dakar declaration referred to "free" (rather than affordable") education for all; included all six of the EFA goals set at Jomtien; and included language that recognized civil society as policy partners and not only providers of services (see Table 2.1, below). These were all significant achievements. Subsequent to Dakar, universal primary education was named as one of the Millennium Development Goals.

Table 2.1. Influence of Campaigners on the Dakar Framework for Action

Early Draft of Dakar Framework for Action	Final Text
1. "Affordable" not free education	Free and compulsory education by 2015
2. NGOs as service providers	CSOs as partners in policy dialogue, planning, and monitoring
3. EFA structures did not provide for participation or representation of Southern governments or civil society in the South	EFA structures to be democratized and streamlined. Focus is on building from National EFA Forums upwards, with civil society engagement specified as essential at all levels
4. No clear/time-bound national level follow up	National EFA plans by 2002 developed by government through

		transparent and democratic processes with civil society
5.	Emphasis on UPE	National plans to address all six Dakar goals
6.	No provision made for monitoring implementation of Dakar framework	Emphasis on high level annual review "to hold global community to account for commitments made in Dakar"
7.	No concrete targets for increased aid to education	Donors "to ensure viable national education plans will not be thwarted for lack of resources"
8.	HIV-AIDS mentioned	Separate strategic objective on HIV-AIDS
9.	Quality gap not linked to equity gap	Language "equity in quality" adopted
10.	No commitment to change in donor practices	Donor support to be "consistent, coordinated and coherent"
11.	No concrete targets for increased domestic spending	National plans to include appropriate budget priorities

Source: Elimu (2000) World Education Forum – Dakar, Senegal: Outcomes and Next Steps. http:/www.elimu.org/newstest1.htm, (as cited in Murphy and Mundy 2002).

Success at Dakar led the members of the initial GCE coalition to establish a more permanent organizational structure. At its first World Assembly (Delhi 2001), the GCE adopted a constitution and set up its key governing structures (a General Assembly, a 13-member Board and a small Secretariat). A key decision was made to give Southern voices a greater percentage of the Board's voting power (Gaventa and Mayo 2009), and to encourage the expansion of national coalitions and regional networks. Mass mobilization led by its regional and national members around an annual EFA Global Action Week quickly became a hallmark of the campaign, with millions of participants in dozens of countries by 2004 (Culey, Martin and Lewer 2007: 16).

From this starting point, the GCE continued to grow, according to one evaluator: "incrementally and organically...rather than consistently towards a long-term strategic goal" (Culey, Martin and Lewer 2007: 12). At the GCE's second World Assembly (Johannesburg, 2004) members revisited the tensions between the GCE's commitment to highlighting the full EFA agenda, and the tendency of its secretariat to focus more on the Millennium Development Goals related to primary schooling (Culey et. al 2007). There were renewed calls for building and strengthening national coalitions and ensuring that Southern voices and Southern citizenship activism remained a core focus for the organization. Fundamental differences in the views and approaches to education for all taken by NGOs and teachers unions emerged – a theme which surfaces in some of the case studies in this volume. The campaigning objectives of the organization – which focused on quantifiable financial targets for aid and for improved global policies -- tended to chosen in a top down manner and thus were sometimes in tension with the organization's other identities as looser, social movement network, and as a capacity building forum for national and regional civil society advocacy.

Post Johannesburg, efforts followed to strengthen GCE's organizational capacity so that it might meet all three of these objectives. A permanent Secretariat based in Johannesburg was established, and a decision was taken to pool existing financial contributions from founding members into a common budget for the organization. Fund-raising led to the GCE's first grant, from the Hewlett Foundation, which subsequently provided the organization with a substantial part of its core operating costs (more than US $5 million) between 2004 and 2010. Funding was also received from the Dutch government for the Real World Strategies program to support member coalition capacity in the South (25 countries under phase 1; 43 under phase 2), as highlighted in chapters of this volume (see also Moriarty 2010). A second window of funding emerged when GCE UK members convinced the British Government to establish the Commonwealth Education Fund, to provide direct support to Southern national coalitions in 16 commonwealth countries, as well as the GCE itself (Tomlinson and Macpherson 2007a; 2007b).

Throughout this period the GCE's membership grew rapidly, rising to 25 international members and 46 national coalitions by 2007 (up from 15 in 2000). At the global level, it maintained a strong presence at international meetings and gained permanent representation on the Fast Track Initiative Board, the UNESCO High Level EFA Working Group, the board of UNGEI, and the board of the UNESCO EFA Global Monitoring Report. Despite some criticism from its members, it proved itself adapt at playing an insider/outside role in these venues – for example, by sponsoring critical reviews of the FTI while also participating in the FTI Board (Rose 2003).

Yet tensions within the coalition continued. At the end of 2007, an external evaluation of the GCE was carried out, in preparation for the Third World Assembly in Sao-Paulo in January 2008 (Culey, Martin and Lewer 2007). This evaluation pointed out the enormous improvements in organizational and partnership capacity that had been made between 2004 and 2007. But it also identified several crucial challenges for the GCE. Among these, it pointed out that while the GCE was now at the global policy table for EFA, its ability to shape policy change was less clear. The GCE was felt to be underplaying its capacity to call for change in the global aid architecture and only weakly monitoring the quality of aid to education. The GCE's use of media and its communications with members were weak. The evaluation also pointed out that the GCE faced very difficult political opportunity structures going forward: education had become a 2nd tier issue in global development, while global commitments for basic education were stalling. What, the evaluators asked, should GCE do to respond to the fact the 6 EFA goals were unlikely to be met? Thus the report highlighted the "need for a single, coherent, long-term strategy." (Culey et. al, p. 59).

But the largest challenge facing the GCE was clearly at the national level – where the opportunities created by the popularity of the Global Action Week were by and large not being translated into effective policy analysis and policy advocacy by strong national advocacy groups in the poorest and most educationally marginalized countries. A renewed call in Sao Paulo – familiar from goals adopted at the 2001 and 2004 General Assemblies, was for "more focus on the national level" and better efforts to "realize the potential of the regions" (p. 59).

THE EVOLUTION OF THE GCE, 2008-2011

The past four years have been momentous ones for the GCE. For the first time the organization could boast a reasonably clear and targeted strategic framework; a stable secretariat; and new sources of funding to expand both its reach and the activities of its members.

At the GCE's Third World Assembly (Sao Paulo, January 2008), the organization adopted its first three-year strategic plan. This plan suggested three goals around which GCE activities would be oriented for the period 2008-2011. The strategy established three key goals and three cross-cutting themes for the GCE, as described in the figure below.[7]

Table 2.2. Goals and Themes of GCE's 3-year Strategic Plan, 2008

Goals	Strategic Themes
1. To demand that state bodies make measurable progress towards the achievement of education for all at the national level in poorer countries. 2. To demand that richer countries and international institutions deliver good quality aid to reach the "fair share" investment and conducive policies to realize a global compact on EFA. 3. To Have Grown the Scale and Strength of the GCE, GCE members and the Education for All Movement.	1. Focus on Impact and Results 2. More focus on Poorer Countries, Quality and the Full EFA agenda 3. Bolder messaging and actions all year round

The Strategic Plan also laid out the key actions that the GCE believed need to be taken to advance each of its three Strategic Goals. Under *Goal 1* (progress in poorer countries) the GCE's planned actions focused on enabling national

---

[7] The GCE members also put forward 26 motions on EFA, ranking them in importance, which gave the GCE clarity on where members thought its emphasis should be (top 5: quality education; enforcing the right to education; adult literacy; financing quality education; abolishing fees. The GCE has no document in which it addresses how the Strategic Plan was modified to reflect the members' priorities.

coalitions to become better policy influencers (with attention to policy advocacy and mass mobilization). Actions listed under *Goal 2* (progress among donors) had two dimensions: GCE-led efforts to influence donor governments and international donor organizations; and capacity support for Northern coalitions. *Goal 3* is a cross-cutting goal, mainly focused on mass mobilization, but also with some attention to expansion of the GCE membership and improving organizational capacity.

From this summary of goals and actions, one gets a clearer picture of the GCE's central theory of change. Most prominently, the GCE believes that widespread public pressure by citizens based on the realization of their human rights is necessary to encourage Southern governments and Northern donor institutions to meet EFA goals. In the GCE's analysis:

> "the main barriers to achieving the goals are political. The technical and financial barriers to achieving universal education can be overcome – if, but only if, there is sustained and substantial public pressure on leaders to take the steps necessary....the GCE and the wider education movement need to achieve our own breakthrough in the level of civil society campaigning and influence on education, so we can secure new political spaces and build a mass movement backed by millions, in order to amplify our demands so loudly that they cannot be ignored." (GCE Three Year Strategic Plan, 2008: 3)

Mass mobilization and campaigning techniques are proposed as the *central* way to create public pressure and the necessary political will. This is to occur both in the North (targeting support for increased aid) and in the South (targeting increased government commitment to EFA). At the same time, GCE also planned to balance mass mobilization with insider and outsider forms of policy advocacy, relying on research, policy analysis, and direct engagement with policy makers to achieve policy change. Insider techniques involve direct collaboration with policy makers – for example, GCE sits on the FTI board and has established a group of Government Champions through its Class of 2015 initiative. Outsider techniques are more confrontational, as for example, the GCE's critical publications on the World Bank and the IMF efforts to impose wage ceilings that limit spending on teachers; or its efforts to single out "failed donors" in its annual School Report Card publication. Finally the GCE aimed to support national coalitions to use both traditional advocacy and mass mobilization techniques to directly influence national governments. In turn, the GCE planned to aggregate and coordinate popular demand for EFA at the international level.

To support this agenda the GCE has had remarkable success in fundraising. The GCE's core secretariat budget stood at a little over $2 million/annum in the 2009/2010, based on funding from the Hewlett Foundation, its founding members (ActionAid, Oxfam, Education International) and membership fees. But it is in funding for special projects that the GCE saw its greatest successes. In addition to the Real World Strategies programs funded by the Dutch government, the GCE was successful in attracting short term funding for its 1Goal campaign from Britain, FIFA and other OECD donors; it also received a grant from the Education for All Fast Track Initiative of $17.6 million over four years to support national civil society coalitions and the establishment of Civil Society Education Funds (FTI 2011: 48-56). Combining it secretariat budget with special project funds, one estimate put its total budget at $12.2 million in 2009 (Mundy and Haggerty, 2010).[8] This amount of overall funding places the GCE comfortably within the category of well-resourced transnational advocacy campaigns on issues of world poverty.[9]

This funding has enabled the GCE to achieve a great deal in symbolic, procedural and political terms at the global scale. The GCE has not only been "at the table" in global discussions – it has increasingly been able invite others to its own table, for example by creating a group of high level champions drawn from governments and the private sector, through its Class of 2015 initiative; as part of its 1Goal campaign with the World Soccer Federation; in its support for the creation of a Global Fund for Education and the reform of the Fast Track Initiative; and in its more recent high-level panel on EFA, which is led by Gordon Brown. Though intermittent, its work in tracking international funding for EFA – mainly through its publication of national "School Report Cards" – created and framed the debate on "fair share" in global discussions on international financing for education, adding this to notion to the lexicon of global education policy makers. The GCE has also expanded its efforts to track multilateral funding and policies and their impact on education – with key analytic works on the IMF and the World Bank. In its global work the central frame has been on greater financing for EFA – a theme that is reflected in the activities of the coalitions represented in this book. As discussed below, the GCE's challenge since 2008 has been to find a way of advancing this financing frame in the context of a global economic crisis and donor fatigue. More pointedly, GCE's focus on financing is not aligned with the strategy of its key funder, the Hewlett Foundation, which wants attention to shift from inputs to learning outcomes.

---

[8] The GCE prefers to count only the portion of project funds that are used by the Secretariat as part of its overall budget. However, since the GCE is the formal recipient and manager of these funds, including them as part of GCE's overall budget seems equally accurate.

[9] Comparison was drawn to the Millennium Development Campaign (recent annual budget just over US$6 million) and the GCAP campaign (3-year global-level budget of US$2.4 million between 2006 and 2008). In contrast, the GCE Secretariat is far less well-resourced than the ONE campaign against extreme poverty, which received a little under US$28 million from the Gates Foundation in 2009 for its advocacy work over the next 4 years (http://www.gatesfoundation.org/Grants-2009/Pages/The-One-Campaign-OPPGD1050.aspx).

Table 2.3. Number of countries and people participating in Global Action Week, 2002-2009

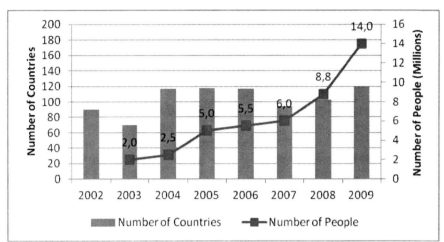

Source: Mundy and Haggerty, 2010, p. 43 (based on data from Culey, Martin and Lewer, 2007; GCE Big Books 2004-2009).

Table 2.4. Membership Growth of the Global Campaign for Education, 2002-20010

	2002	2005	2007	2008, Jan.	2010 Jan.	*Breakdown of Members, Jan. 2010*
National Coalitions *(paid members)*	37	42	46	56	64	23 African; 12 Latin American; 11 Asian 17 Northern; 6 Middle Eastern
International and Regional Members	16	19	n/a	31	35	10 regional members; 23 INGOs; 1 Education International; 1 Global March

Source: Mundy and Haggerty 2010.

At the national level, GCE achievements have also been substantial. Its Global Action Week has continued to grow in size and strength (see figure above), and in a recent survey was described as a very highly valued part of the GCE's overall work with its members (Mundy and Haggerty 2010). Research conducted in Nigeria and India by Gaventa and Mayo (2009) suggests that one reason the GAW has such high legitimacy among members is that it has allowed for significant input from members coalitions, whose voice and achievements are also recorded and collected as part of the larger gains for the whole coalition, in the annual publication of the GCE "Big Book". While there are still concerns about the relevance of the GAW among some members (see Philippine case study in this volume), overall the GCE's Global Action Week seems have moved to new levels of efficacy. It now not only provides a common moment for the GCE's global membership and rising numbers of supporters to feel connected to a global movement, but also links more frequently than ever before to year-round strategies for policy influencing.

Furthermore, through the Real World Strategies Initiative and the Civil Society Education Fund program, the GCE can be credited with supporting the development or strengthening of national education coalitions in more than four-dozen countries. The overall number of formally registered national coalitions belonging to the GCE has virtually doubled (see table above). Several recent studies, as well as chapters in this book, provide examples of increased capacity to influence policy within Southern coalitions, including reports of impact on external policy outcomes, and of intermediate outcomes, such as routine inclusion of civil society in education decision-making at the national level, and examples of good quality policy analyses (Mundy and Haggerty 2010; Moriarty 2010).

Box 2.2. The GCE's Main Programs to Support Southern Coalitions

---

1. Real World Strategies II Program
Fund: 5 million Euros from 2006-2010 from the Dutch Government (The pilot RWS-I from 2002-2005 addressed 26 coalitions).
RWS-II is a program managed by GCE, ASPBAE, ANCEFA and CLADE to support capacity development in 51 national coalitions. Each region developed a slightly different focus: in Africa most workshops appeared to be skills-based (communications, budget tracking, and campaigning); in Asia workshops were focused on creating national analysis of progress on EFA ("Education Watch reports") and supporting campaigns; in Latin America the focus was on justiciability, advocating for free education and quality education. The RWS initiative has also supported regional partners to coordinate advocacy targeted at regional policy bodies, and to create opportunities for cross-organizational learning.

2. Civil Society Education Fund Program
Fund: $17.6 million over three years (2009/10-2011/12), provided by the Fast Track Initiative. (Additional funds raised from Spain to support CSEF in Latin America from 2010).

Funding to provide core support to coalitions in up to 65 FTI approved countries. The project aims to provide support to the core work of national education coalitions so that they can fully engage in the development of education sector programmes with government and donors, and track the progress of national governments and local donor groups in working towards the EFA goals. As part of this program each coalition is to establish a National Civil Society Education Fund and raise funds to support advocacy initiatives in their country. Only the core funding for the coalitions is provided under this grant, at typically between $75,000-250,000 per coalition per annum. Capacity support is primarily delivered by ANCEFA, ASBPAE, and CLADE, each of which hosts a CSEF Secretariat, while financial oversight is provided by Oxfam, EI and ActionAid, and funding decisions are made by a regional funding committees comprised of representatives from a range of INGO and other CSOs

---

However, an expansion of funding and activities on this scale – particularly funding that comes in the form of project funding, can be a double-edged sword for an organization that is trying to manage relations among a large and diverse membership.

For example, ensuring that the growth in national educational coalitions is matched by strong advocacy capacity within these coalitions has been a vexing problem for the GCE (Mundy et al, 2006). Both philosophically, and because of the small size of its secretariat, the GCE early on made a decision to push its funding for national coalition capacity development out to its regional coalition members: ASPBAE, ANCEFA and CLADE. The different capacities and approaches to advocacy taken by the three regional bodies has led in turn to highly uneven results among member coalitions, contributing (for a variety of reasons[10]), to particular weaknesses in the advocacy capacity of coalitions in some of the poorest countries in the world. The decision to keep the secretariat small and push capacity development out to the regions has also undermined the ability of the GCE to act as a relay of information across scales (from national coalitions to global policy discussions) and across coalitions themselves. As studies in this volume suggest, the result has been a certain unevenness in members' sense of "belonging" to the campaign, and their engagement with global campaign initiatives. Thus a recent study of the Real World Strategies initiative comments:

> "It seems reasonable to conclude that so little focus was given at the global level that it had a detrimental effect on the project's potential outcomes. The global centre could have served an important function in terms of centralised mechanism for sharing materials, facilitating cross- project learning and actions, and making more explicit links between national and international advocacy....GCE did not fully implement its vision of change through RWS II. It was not able to adequately connect the local level concerns to the international policy objectives of GCE. And it failed to create meaningful links between coalitions from different parts of the world. (Moriarty et al, p. 44 & 50).

The GCE's 2008 Goals included a commitment to support coalitions' ability to do research and monitoring of national policies; and to support for them to do research and policy advocacy in such common areas of concern: transparency, national EFA plans, quality education models, justiciability; goals re-articulated in the GCE's new plan (GCE 2011). While case studies in this volume (and other recent reports) suggest some progress in all of these areas, the sustainability of such efforts and GCE's ability to contribute to them is arguably more precarious today than ever, since the Netherlands has pulled out of the Real World Strategies Program, and the Fast Track Initiative funding window that financed the Civil Society Education

---

[10] As Moriarty (2010) shows, each of the regional bodies has taken a different approach to capacity development – ANCEFA has focused on building the number of coalitions in its region, and supports more than two times the number as compared to the other regional networks; ASPBAE has focused on coaching a small number of coalitions to produce high quality policy analysis and advocacy strategies; CLADE has played a stronger role in building a regional agenda for advocacy (p. 28).

Fund (CSEF) initiative has been closed (Mundy and Haggerty 2010; Moriarty 2010; Fast Track Initiative 2011).

The GCE's success in funding-raising for its global advocacy work has also brought mixed blessings to the organization. In particular the agreement to accept large scale, one year funding for the 1Goal campaign with FIFA, without wide consultation among the GCE membership, undermined confidence in the Secretariat among some key members. Some critics (including core funders of the GCE) questioned the 1Goal campaign for its reliance on online "sign up" campaigning. This type of campaigning – popularized by the UK based Make Poverty History Campaign and ONE, is quite different from the GCE's customary focus on sustained grassroots organizing, and its concentration on finance and access goals (Martin, Culey and Evans 2005; Chapman and Mancini 2009). Others believe it cemented a UK centric focus in the GCE's global campaigning approach, leaving it poorly positioned to switch its advocacy efforts in ways appropriate to the global power shift occurring between the West and emerging economies, and the tailwinds of an ongoing economic crisis (Mundy and Haggerty 2010, p. 29-35).

Box 2.3. The 1Goal Campaign

In June 2009 the GCE signed an agreement with DFID and FIFA to host a large, mass mobilization campaign leading up to a media of world leaders at the 2010 World Cup in South Africa. A significant feature of the campaign was an online sign-up, which yielded more than 12 million signatures. The British government committed £1 million for the campaign.

Whatever the validity of these criticisms, the sheer shifts in staffing within the secretariat required to implement two multi-million dollar projects (CSEF and 1Goal) in 2009 and 2010 left many of the organizations' core functions understaffed. Basic competencies that might be expected of any civil society organization – transparency and communication about the sources of its funding, publicly available reports on its projects and their outcomes, updated information about policies and governance structures; and the development of clear, democratic, and effective structures for communication and engagement of members on key strategic decisions (many of which are taken between World Assemblies) were neglected.11 At a time of rapidly growing membership in both southern and donor countries, the GCE's ability to coordinate and build synergies across national, regional and global scales did not keep pace with the growth of its membership. Efforts to expand the organization's ambitions based on short term and unpredictable finance had the

---

11 For a brief on basic principles of transparency and accountability see CIVICUS. (2007). Understanding LTA [Legitimacy, Transparency and Accountability]. Retrieved April 10, 2010 from http://www.civicus.org/lta/1237

ironic side effect of leaving the organization particularly vulnerable when these sources of external funding began to shrink in 2011.

WAYS FORWARD FOR THE GCE

Although the Global Campaign emerged initially as a short term, issue oriented coalition in the lead up to the Dakar World Education Forum, over time it has expanded into what Sidney Tarrow has described as a "campaign coalition," distinguishable from both event coalitions and longer term, formal federations by its combination of longer term sustained collaboration among a rather horizontally organized platform of members (see also Gaventa and Mayo 2010). It has been remarkably successful in expanding the resource base for both its global and its national advocacy efforts in recent years, and it has made significant achievements at both of these scales, using a variety of advocacy strategies and tactics. At its recent World Assembly the GCE promised to continue these efforts – by continuing to advocate for national and global policies to ensure expanded and more equal educational opportunities, by building the capacity of its members, and by focusing more specifically on discrimination in education as a common mobilizing theme for its membership (GCE 2011a).

The GCE's procedural gains – those that build space, voice and recognition for citizen claims making at national and international scales – have arguably been its most substantial. Gaventa and Moyo, in their comparative study of global social justice movements, describe the GCE as particularly successful in developing a common framework for advocacy across diverse national contexts, in ways that both scale up to citizen voice on a global scale, and deepen citizen engagement at the national level. The GCE has managed to sustain a diverse membership of organizations committed to working together to achieve a common set of goals in more than 100 countries, and it has supported a global movement to ensure that civil society actors sit both at the national and international policy tables for education.

Symbolically, the GCE and its membership have done much to keep basic education in the public eye. It has been innovative and taken risks to keep education on the public policy agenda, experimenting with new forms of mass campaigning via 1Goal, and rapidly expanding its efforts to support southern advocacy capacity. Unfortunately, these efforts – based on short term project funding -- may have had negative consequences for the organization, in terms of internal trust and core organizational capacities, highlighting some of the longer term tensions between vertical and more centrally driven forms of campaigning; and more diffuse, horizontally organized forms of social movement organizing.

The GCE's political impact on the decisions of governments and the international community have been less even, but still important. Despite the rapid expansion of both its global advocacy and national coalition building efforts since 2005, there has not been a substantial increase in aid for basic education or public expenditures. Perhaps this is too much to expect, especially in the more recent context of global economic restructuring. Still the coalition can lay claim to having contributed to sustained aid commitments from the UK government and recent announcements of expanded funding from the World Bank ($750 million) and Australia ($5 bn) in 2010. It has played a profound role in publicizing the need to reform the Fast Track Initiative (recently rebranded the Global Partnership for Education). At the national level, much evidence in this volume and elsewhere suggests that at least some among the GCE's national coalitions have had success in advocating locally for policy changes and budget share. The GCE's new strategy recognizes the need to build on these successes, and commits the organization to a renewed focus building national advocacy capacity.

Going forward, the GCE faces a series of challenges. It needs to re-think its approaches to advocacy in light of softening global support for education aid, and the expected near-term contraction of fiscal space for education in the national budgets of least-developed countries. It is yet to find a sustainable funding base for its activities and is extremely vulnerable to cuts in its core funding from private donors. It will need to undergo a major process of organizational reform and reflection on its theory of change if it wishes to maintain its core identity as membership driven "campaign coalition" capable of bringing together both domestic and international monitoring of states' commitments to the right to education.

Yet there is no other body in the EFA policy arena with as large and wide a reach as the GCE, nor with as strong and committed a membership in the societies of the majority world. It has proven how valuable a civil society counterbalance can be in global efforts to frame "education for all" as a dimension of global social policy.

JOOSJE HOOP

CHAPTER 3

People Power for Education: Civil society participation in the
Philippine educational politics

INTRODUCTION

The focus of this chapter is the role and impact of the *Philippines' civil society network of education reforms*, also known as Education Network Philippines or E-Net, in the field of education in the Philippines. E-Net was born out of the perceived lack of civil society participation in the first Philippine Education for All (EFA) decade (1990-2000). The network now counts 156 members, varying from individuals, INGOs, to academics and teachers' unions, all united to ensure all Filipinos have access to multi-cultural, gender-fair, liberating, life-long education as a basic human right. They specifically aim at reforming the Philippines' education system and developing alternative learning systems with a particular concern for marginalized, excluded and vulnerable sectors.

Currently, the Philippines' education system is facing a range of challenges such as low average student participation, poor performance of students in local and international standardised tests, persistent inequalities in basic learning resources, corruption, and alarming drop out rates.

The Philippines is often mentioned in literature on democratic transitions and democratic governance. The 'People Power' revolution of 1986 is an example of a non-violent, popularly based, overthrow of authoritarianism. In this revolution, massive democratic opposition was mobilized to put a stop to President Marcos and his corrupt regime. Civil society gained national importance in the latter part of the martial law regime, fulfilling functions the government did not.

In addition, the Philippines is seen as a country that successfully re-established democratic institutions under the leadership of Corazon Aquino. However, things are not as democratic as it seems. Philippine politics are still facing problems like corruption, favouritism and election fraud. The inability of the Philippine democracy to produce sound governance is often blamed on the weak party system that is elite-led (Rogers 2004:114). Furthermore, the lack of equal justice is considered a barrier to further democratic progress. While civil society is a rooted concept in the Philippines, it is questionable how much space they have in the political spectrum. Over the years, the role of civil society has changed from service delivery to policy advocacy, to hold governments accountable for their responsibilities to their citizens. This chapter looks into the impact of E-Net and explores the factors that contribute to or hinder this impact.

Antoni Verger and Mario Novelli (eds.), Campaigning for "Education for All", 31–50.

The case study is based on data gathered during fieldwork from March until June 2009. Primary data consists of twenty in-depth semi structured interviews with members, board members, academics, teacher union representatives, government officials, and journalists, exploring their stories and opinions. In order to avoid a research only in the capital, Manila, the interviews were conducted country wide, both in urban and rural areas. Furthermore, a collaborative workshop, held in Manila in June 2009, was used for data gathering as well, which brought together various members of the nationwide coalition. This primary data was supplanted through analysis of secondary data including reviews of network and government documents, as well as literature on social movements' impact and politics in the Philippines.

The chapter is divided into five sections. In the first section the political opportunity structures in the Philippines will be discussed, focussing on the relationship between the state and civil society and the educational climate in the Philippines. The second section will explore the origin, structure, scale and strategies of the network. The focus of the third section will be the strategic development of E-Net, and how they've adapted their strategies over the years. In section four E-Net's success will be discussed while looking at both internal and external impact. In the last section I conclude by answering the question that has guided this research: how does E-Net matter in education in the Philippines and which factors limit or contribute to the success of the movement?

POLITICS AND EDUCATION IN THE PHILIPPINES

When analysing a civil society movement in any given context, the political contextual factors should be addressed carefully as they influence the possibilities of interaction with the government. Furthermore, as E-Net is advocating for Education for All, the educational context should be analysed as well. In the next section, the political and educational context in which E-Net is operating is discussed.

Political climate - opportunities for E-Net

The democratic republic of the Philippines has a turbulent past. It has been occupied by the Spanish, Americans, has been invaded by the Japanese, and endured a dictatorship from 1972 until 1986 when President Ferdinand Marcos declared Martial Law. After the People Power revolution in 1986, the return of the democracy and government reforms were faced with issues such as national debt, government corruption, and coup attempts (Carino 1999).

The Philippines is a democratic republic, where the president is head of the state and head of government within a multi-party system. Before the Second World War, for most of the American colonial regime the development of political parties was noted for its extremely elitist orientation. In response, mass-based radical parties were formed to challenge the dominant elite parties.

The non-violent overthrow of the authoritarian regime of Marcos became known as the 'People Power revolution'. This revolution marked the powerful, but short-lived coalition of various organised groups, dissatisfied military forces, as well as many unorganised individuals, who joined to oust Marcos. However, due to the extreme variance of political interests which have their base in centuries-old inequity, the fragile political coalition soon dissolved. One of the most important consequences of the People Power revolution was the passage from a 'parochial and subject' political orientation to a 'participant orientation'. This involved an awareness of decisional political processes and outputs, and a belief that citizens have the right to participate (Canieso-Doronila 1997:101). Although no major electoral reforms have been legislated to change the composition of the elite-led Congress, the issues and demands raised by various groups have been included in the 1987 Constitution and legislation (ibid. 101). Furthermore, several laws and policies derived from the 1987 Constitutional mandates for nation building, have been created. These include: agrarian land reform law, Local Government Code, Philippine education reform, language policy, human rights education, and others. These examples can be seen as attempts by the government to accommodate the social demands articulated by the social movements. Nonetheless, as the mandates are clear, according to the social movement the elite-led government didn't consider all the demands, and they have failed to address the historical roots of the problems (ibid. 103). Furthermore, for the majority of the population, the lack of information and knowledge about the Constitution and laws, insufficient knowledge of the legal language (which is English) and the general lack of participation in national decision-making processes, results in remaining outside the mainstream of public opinion making. Therefore, as no broad social consensus has been reached on the issues proposed in the legislation, civil society continues their struggle for reform and change (ibid. 103).

The successor of Marcos, President Corazon Aquino, is remembered for the 'restoration of democracy' and the realisation of a new constitution, which limited the powers of the presidency. Her administration put strong emphasis on civil liberties and human rights. In many sections of the new Constitution of 1987, the importance of people's participation was recognised. The constitutional emphasis was on the role of NGOs as *guardians of the public interest* (Carino 1999:84). Several laws provided for civil society organisation representation in Congress and in local special bodies. Although it seemed the state provided an enabling and facilitating environment for civil society organisations to exist, the question remains how powerful these organisations could be in influencing government and policies. Even though the mechanisms for consulting civil society were in place throughout government, real civil society participation was not necessarily taking place (Diokno 1997). Advocating for issues of social justice and equity within the newly installed democracy seemed a difficult task.

Former President Gloria Macapagal-Arroyo came to power in 2001, initially with support from grassroots movements. However, accusations of fraud in the 2004 elections reduced her popularity. During the administration of Gloria Macapagal-Arroyo, E-Net came into existence and civil society participation became increasingly more important on the international agenda. It was during this administration that the fieldwork was carried out. Gloria Macapagal-Arroyo claims to have increased civil society participation, but critics question whether this is more rhetoric than reality. After almost nine years in office, many civil society organisations criticize the former president for the lack of pro-poor policies, and only serving the interests of the middle and upper classes (Interview Outsider, ExecutiveCommittee, 2009).

Education in the Philippines

According to Guzman (2003), the impact of the three colonizers is still reflected in the current education system's thinking and practices. The Spaniards were successful in propagating Christianity, and making the Philippines the only Asian country practicing the Catholic religion. The Americans laid down the foundation of a democratic system of educationa focus on English language and literature. The American influence made the Philippines the third largest English speaking nation in the world. Furthermore, the exposure to the Japanese made the Filipinos aware of their position as an Asian country with great possibilities to develop (Guzman 2003:40).

After Marcos was overthrown, a new Constitution was drafted. The Constitution of 1987, which is still in effect today, contains the fundamental aims of education in the Philippines. One of these aims is the right of all citizens to quality education. As not all Filipino's could exercise this right, there was an urgent need for government to provide for at least basic education. The period 1990-2000 was declared the decade of Education for All (EFA), and a National Committee was created to prepare a National Plan of Action and to manage the EFA structure. However, the committee proved to be short-lived as after 1993, it was never again convened (Raya and Mabunga 2003:14). Along with EFA, the Philippines also committed itself to the Millennium Development Goals (MDGs). The MDGs and EFA goals remain the leading frameworks for education policy and reform (Bauzon 2007:19).

When by the end of the first EFA decade many problems with access and/or quality of education had not been solved, a second EFA decade was launched. A new EFA plan was drafted and it was not until 2006 that this new National Action Plan for Education for All 2015 (EFA 2015) was signed. The new action plan aims at creating functionally literate Filipino's, and emphasizes the need to provide basic education for all, with additional focus on youths and adults. E-Net was involved in the creation of the Plan of Action, and as a member of the National EFA committee keeps track of the progress made towards the EFA goals.

What's wrong with the system?

When looking at the state of Philippine education, questions are raised. While the Philippines used to be high on the Asian education list, it seems countries like Indonesia and Myanmar are now outperforming them (GMR 2009). The quality of education has decreased over the years and the Philippines is experiencing a setback in its progress towards the EFA goals (Caoli-Rodriguez 2008:93). Currently, the education system is facing challenges such as: low average student participation poor performance of students in local and international standardized tests; persistent inequalities in basic learning resources; and susceptibility to being adversely impacted by political and economical developments unfolding within and outside the country (Lapus 2008:2). Furthermore, high drop out rates, illiteracy, and corruption in the Department are other factors that hinder the Philippines from reaching the goal of Education for All.

There is an overall consensus among all education stakeholders that action needs to be taken to address the problems. The country has put in place major reforms and programs throughout the years to create a policy environment supportive of the EFA goals. Yet, limited progress in basic education outcomes has been achieved. Frequent changes in education leadership and lack of political consensus, among others, are likely to undermine progress in fiscal and public sector reforms (Interview Outsider, 2009). Since the formation of E-Net, there have been six secretaries of education, each with new policies, new views and new networks. The high turnover has influenced the way E-Net works as they had to adjust to the new people and ways of working in the department.

A possible (part) explanation for the low performance and deteriorating quality of Philippine education is the huge and increasing resource gap. While enrolment in basic education has been growing at an average of 2.5% per year, the education budget on the other hand has grown at a slower rate of 2% annually. This has resulted in a decline in per pupil expenditure (Raya 2007:26). The Philippines is among the lowest spenders on education in Asia, and the world. Although the government claims the biggest part of the budget is spent on education, the current level of expenditure is too low and falls short of the requirement for quality education and reaching the EFA goals. Debt service actually gets the biggest share of the budget, which effectively shifts much needed resources away from priority basic services (ibid 27). The education budget should be increased, as high population growth and a limiting fiscal situation contribute to poor education outcomes (Caoli-Rodrigues 2008:399).

Table 3.1. Progress towards EFA goals in the Philippines

EFA 2015Goals	Indicators	
	Baseline	Latest
1. Expanding and Improving early childhood care and education (ECCE)	2001* GER in ECCE: 17.86% Percentage of Grade 1 with ECCE experience: 55.81%	2008** GER in ECCE: 49% Percentage of Grade 1 with ECCE experience: 70%

2. Universal Primary Education	SY 2000-2001 (%)*			SY 2007-2008 (%)**		
	Indicators	Prim.	Sec.	Indicators	Prim.	Sec.
	GER	109.85	81.53	GER	110	82
	NER	96.77	57.55	NER	92	
3. Learning needs of all young people and adults	2000* (Basic Literacy Program-LSC only#) No. of learners: 58,360 No. of completers: 6,791 1999** Out of school children 1,139,000 # Literacy Service Contracting Scheme			2005 (BLP-LSC only) No. of learners: 38,563 No. completers: 32,754 2008** Out of School Children 961,000 Out of School Adolescents 372,000		
4. Improving levels of adult literacy	1994 FLEMMS Simple Literacy: 93.9% Functional Literacy: 83.8% Male: 81.7% Female: 84.9%			2008 FLEMMS Simple Literacy: 95.6% Functional Literacy: 86.4% Male: 84.0% Female: 88.9%		
5. Eliminating gender disparities in primary and secondary education	2000* Gender Parity Index			2008** Gender Parity Index		

Indicators	Prim.	Sec.	Indicators	Prim.	Sec.
NER	1.01	1.11	NER	1.02	
GER	0.99	1.08	GER	0.98	1.09

Indicators	GPI	Indicators	GPI
ECCE GER	1.06 (2002)	ECCE GER	1.02
Simple Literacy	1.00 (1994)	Simple Literacy	1.02 (2003)
Functional Literacy	1.05 (1994)	Functional Literacy	1.05 (2003)

6. Improving quality of education	2000 National Achievement Test (Mean Percentage Score) Primary: 51.73% Secondary: 53.39%	2008 National Achievement Test (Mean Percentage Score) Primary: 64.81% Secondary: 49,26% 2007 Drop outs: 27%

Sources:
* Caoli-Rodriquez (2008), p 397
** UNESCO Global Monitoring Report 2011
Functional Literacy, Education and Mass Media Survey (FLEMMS) National Statistics Office, RP (1994, 2003, 2008)
Basic Education Information System (BEIS), DepEd
Bureau of Alternative Learning System (BALS) DepEd

EDUCATION NETWORK – E-NET

After the 1990 Jomtien World Declaration on Education for All and the World Education Conference in Dakar in 2000, the importance of including civil society in the efforts of reaching the EFA goals was widely accepted. While the DepEd had several initiatives to improve the education situation in the Philippines, the improvements were moving slowly. The government sought the support of particular organisations in certain areas, but at no point did civil society organisations have access to the EFA process. It was through the help of Oxfam Great Britain that meetings between DepEd and CSOs were facilitated. Through these engagements with the government, CSOs became aware of the need for a broad network to rally around the education issues. In 2000, the perceived lack of civil society participation in the first Philippine Education for All (EFA) decade (1991-2000) led to the creation of the Civil Society Network for Education Reforms, also known as E-Net Philippines. Most founding members were education oriented, but not all. What they had in common was a background in activism and fighting injustice, which still influences E-Net today. Among the founding members were: Oxfam Great Britain, Action for Economic Reforms, Education for Life Foundation, Popular Education for People's Empowerment (PEPE), Alliance of Concerned Teachers, Philippine Rural Reconstruction Movement, and the Asian South Pacific Association for Basic and Adult Education (ASPBAE) (Raya and Mabunga 2003:24).

The newly created network E-Net received institutional funding from Oxfam GB. Although Oxfam GB has been a great influence in the creation of E-Net, they didn't force their agenda on the network and let the many CSOs -that had been working on education improvements for many years- create their own agenda. Several members of E-Net carried out research to clarify issues around education financing and alternative learning systems, and island wide consultations took place in 2001-2002 to identify issues for education reform and to bring out local stakeholders' view and recommendations on the education situation. At that time, there were no other civil society networks that had a focus on advocacy for education. This influenced the power relations with the government, as there was no 'competition'. As civil society participation gained international importance, E-Net was the civil society party the government could intervene with regarding education. E-Net agreed to push for public education system overhaul, instead of revolutionary transformations. As mentioned by some members, the call for mass-oriented, nationalist education was left to political groups, while E-Net decided to push for reforms within the public education system (Interview Executive Committee, 2009). The aim was to build partnerships with the Department of Education and other allies as E-Net believes that in order to obtain the best education for all, many different EFA constituencies and advocates are needed on many different levels (Interviews Secretariat, Board Member, Executive Committee 2009).

VISION - MISSION

During the founding meeting in 2000, the vision and mission of E-Net were drafted. As stated in the Education Reform Agenda, 'E-Net Philippines envisions a Filipino society where quality education is a basic human right, and everyone has access to multi-cultural, gender-fair, liberating, life-long education' (E-Net website). In order to achieve this vision, the following mission was formulated: 'E-Net Philippines commits to expand and strengthen civil society participation in reforming the Philippine education system and in developing alternative learning systems with special concern for marginalized, excluded and vulnerable sectors' (E-Net website).

E-Net's vision on education is much broader than most of the international education agreements, which tend to focus on only primary or formal basic education. E-Net has a more holistic view on education, including early childhood education, life-long-learning, gender and alternative learning systems. As mentioned by an E-Net member:

Our work is not confined to schools; we also serve those who are out of school (Interview Secretariat, 2009)

The focus on excluded and marginalised groups has always been the framework as some of the founding members of E-Net are working on life-long-learning and alternative learning systems, such as Education for Life Foundation and Popular Education for People's Empowerment (PEPE), all derived from the Marcos era, when civil society was more focused on service delivery rather than on advocacy purposes.

PIECE

Additionally, E-Net is collaborating with the implementers of the Partners In Education for Community Empowerment (PIECE) program in Southern Mindanao. This program, which started in 2007 under the Aid to Uprooted People program of the European Commission, focuses on strengthening schools and community structures as focal points for community reconstruction. The main implementer of this program is Oxfam GB (Cotabato City office) and E-Net serves as a project partner. E-Net has set up an office in Mindanao with three E-Net staff members working on the project. Through the PIECE project, E-Net can advocate for the whole EFA agenda both at the local level, reaching the conflict affected area of Mindanao, and at the national level.

This PIECE project is a comprehensive assistant for rural communities, covering many areas of assistance. We believe education is the best medium, an instrument in transforming the situation of peace and development in time, but maybe in a long period of time. And we do also believe that school is the best institution, best structure, for transforming this kind of education (Interview Secretariat, 2009).

The fact that there is an E-Net office there has had a positive impact in terms of carrying out activities and advocacies in the province (Interview Secretariat, 2009). This shows the importance of physical presence in an area, and it could be a strategy for E-Net to expand their office to other localities as well.

Composition, scale and scope

E-Net now has 156 members, varying from (International)NGOs to individuals, from Teacher Unions to grassroots organisations, from academics to media contacts. Their members are committed to expanding and strengthening civil society participation in reforming the Philippine education system and in developing alternative learning systems with special concern for the marginalised, excluded, and vulnerable sectors. The focus on these sectors is influenced by the inclusive political background of the founding members, who have been working on non-formal education and creating a counterforce to the elite-dominated government. The network is coordinated by the Board of Trustees of ten representatives of all regions, a National Executive Committee, as well as regional coordinating bodies. Furthermore, the Manila based national secretariat is responsible for the daily work and management of E-Net. The biannual General Assembly is the highest decision making body.

Guided by a rights-based approach, E-Net uses the international Education for All framework for mobilising and carrying out their advocacy:

...EFA was a good frame by which... (to) hold government accountable and rally a broad sector of society (as well as) the international community into advocacy (interview E-Net Member, 2009).

Impelled by the international agreements the government also uses this framework to address education policies. This frame alignment could contribute to the success opportunities of E-Net.

E-Net identified four main goals:

• Establish, build and strengthen E-Net to sustain its initiatives in education reform,
• ensure and institutionalise civil society's active participation in the entire education process and in the pursuit of education reform,
• pursue reforms that will improve the content and system of Philippine education,
• strengthen international solidarity in order to redress existing disparities that prevent us from achieving the goals of Education for All (Raya and Mabunga 2003:26).

With these initial focus points in mind, E-Net makes use of different strategies to pursue their mission, including building legitimacy, social mobilisation, networking and communication, political pressure, evidence based advocacy, research and knowledge production, engaging the government and targeting education politicians and officials.

As the network is based on a principle of 'inclusiveness' and consists out of various members each having their own skill and interest, working groups were created to focus on specific themes. There are five working groups: Early Childhood Care and Development, Education Financing, Quality Formal Education, Gender-fair Education and Alternative Learning Systems, and Non-Formal Education. The division of these groups allows the network to work on the complete EFA agenda, and allows the members to work according to their strengths.

From Local to Global, and Back

While E-Net is a national network advocating for education reforms in the Philippines, the national level is not the only level on which they are active. E-Net is recognised as the Philippine national coalition affiliated with the Global Campaign for Education (GCE), and they are also a member of the regional organisation: Asian South Pacific Association for Basic and Adult Education (ASPBAE). These international relations benefit E-Net in several ways. The fact that E-Net is related to an internationally renowned global campaign adds to their credibility, which enables them to benefit from the reputation of the GCE. While the GCE continues to pressure international institutions and donors to meet the EFA commitment, it is also constituted by national coalitions to pressure national and local governments to reach EFA. E-Net can use their relation with the GCE to learn about the international education discourse and debates, and through its links with the international GCE, E-Net remains up to date on the international campaigns. The current president of E-Net is also a board member of the GCE international Board. This connects E-Net more directly and organically to the GCE and, at the same time, allows the GCE to learn from the Philippine experience for their international advocacy work.

Furthermore, the internationally organised Global Action Week (GAW) receives a lot of attention which E-Net can use for their advocacy at the national level. The international magnitude adds to the status of the event and this helps to attract high profile people. However, the GAW dates and topics are decided globally and do not always coincide with the Philippine education debates and priorities, but, more importantly, the GAW is held when schools are closed for summer vacation. E-Net has creatively reacted to this by creating a Global Action *Month*, which coincides with the end of the school year so that school children and parents can more actively participate in the activities.

From a regional perspective, E-Net has active ties with ASPBAE. The value of the linkage between ASPBAE and E-Net is a stronger coordinated voice from the South, especially South East Asia and South Pacific. According one ASPBAE representative put it in a workshop:

In many conferences abroad, South East Asian delegates seldom talk. They are so soft spoken, they are so polite and they don't push their agenda as much as the other sub-regions do. For example, as much as South Asians or Africans do. We hope we could have this stronger voice from Philippines, Indonesia, Cambodia and all other countries (Workshop Transcription 2009:22).

Therefore, the linkage between E-Net and ASPBAE is important as it helps to develop a message together. Another benefit of the partnership of E-Net and ASPBAE is getting to know and engaging with other sub-/regional platforms such as UNESCO-Asian and the Pacific, South East Asian Ministers of Education (SAMEO), Association of South East Asian Nations (ASEAN), the Asia Pacific Parliamentarian's Forum (APPF), and even the Asian Development Bank (ADB). For E-Net, it is important to keep track of and participate in these (and other) platforms, as this is where the secretary of education, congressmen, senators, donors and funders are also engaged in.

Moreover, through the membership of GCE and also ASPBAE, E-Net members can participate in international and/or regional conferences and events. These are perceived as good networking opportunities to engage and establish links with other education stakeholders. When national coalitions participate in regional conferences where government officials are also present, the experience is that these officials become more open to negotiations with the coalition when back in their country. An example of this is given by one of the interviewees:

When E-Net gate-crashed at the UNESCO Bangkok EFA Coordinators' Meeting, we met DepEd people. Before that meeting, we have been knocking at DepEd's door, but they would not let us in. After the meeting [in Bangkok], they began to entertain us (Interview Secretariat, 2009).

For ASPBAE it is important to obtain information from the national levels to use for their regional advocacies. In the Philippines, this is provided through E-Net. This way the organisations strengthen each other.

Furthermore, the Real World Strategy (RWS) funds are channelled through ASPBAE. This fund aims to contribute to achieving specific policy changes at the global, regional and national level to escalate EFA progress. One of the initiatives derived through the fund is the Education Watch initiative. Education Watch is an independent, citizen based assessment of the status of basic education at regional, national and local level, designed to monitor the progress towards EFA, carried out by ten Southeast Asian coalitions including E-Net. The initiative was successfully implemented by the coalitions, who developed ownership of the project, became stakeholders amidst what they described as 'a kind of belonging, a feeling of solidarity' between the different Southeast Asian 'colleagues' (Razon 2008:25). RWS initiatives like Education Watch, help E-Net to engage both governments and donors on their policy reviews and plans for EFA, compelling attention to the neglected goals and neglected groups for concrete and systematic action. The RWS is an important financial resource for E-Net that allows them to work together with ASPBAE on (sub-)regional and national education initiatives.

The close ties of E-Net and ASPBAE might be partly related to the fact that the previous national coordinator of E-Net now has a leading position with ASPBAE. Although E-Net would have been part of ASPBAE even without this link, it shows that personal linkages can sometimes be beneficial for the coalition.

ASPBAE works as an effective platform for E-Net to engage with other national coalitions in the region. The coalitions can share experiences and learn from each other. In fact, E-Net is considered as an example for other Asian countries (Interview ASPBAE rep, 2009).

Although not all members, especially the ones working on a more local basis, are directly aware of the work done on the regional or international level, other members recognise the importance of having those international linkages:

> So this is the thing without GCE, without ASPBAE, E-Net has maybe only one wing, but because GCE and ASPBAE, E-Net has more or less two wings (Interview Secretariat, 2009).

On the national level, E-Net doesn't only engage with the government and its members, but on many occasions, they also communicate with other education groups like Philippine Business for Education (PBEd), Synergeia, and Education Nation which aimed to put education high on the agenda of the presidential candidates for the 2010 elections. Even though these other education coalitions might have slightly different aims and approaches, possibilities of collaboration are explored when there is a common ground that fits E-Net's reform agenda. E-Net is the only civil society coalition that takes the whole EFA agenda into consideration, but as they recognise that education is a multi-stakeholder business, they use their networks to strategically work together to push for their Education Reform Agenda and the realisation of EFA.

STRATEGIC DEVELOPMENT - REFLECTING AND ADAPTING

Ever since the formation of E-Net, they have been strategically selecting their moves and adapting their strategies to the various situations. As mentioned earlier, the first strategic decision during the formation of E-Net was to advocate a system overhaul, not a drastic revolution and be clear on the willingness to work together with the government. As some civil society groups were considered more militant, this clear statement of willingness to cooperate had positive influence on the relation with the government.

Another enabling factor can be found on a more personal base. After the People Power revolution, several presidents have appointed civil society leaders to government positions. Because of this, the President of E-Net, Edicio dela Torre served as director of Technical Education and Schools Development Authority (TESDA) for three years under the administration of Estrada. The fact that E-Net has a president who is familiar with the ways of working both from civil society and inside the government, made them more reliable/trustworthy for the government.

During the first EFA decade the Philippine government created the EFA plan 2015, placing early childhood, formal basic education, education financing, and non-formal education on the agenda. Realising this, E-Net created its own agenda. During the formation in 2000, E-Net chose to create several working groups, which correspond with the working groups within the Department of Education. From its members, they identified experts on all topics. The working groups created for their core advocacies are:

- *Early Childhood Care and Development*: This task force develops advocacies and coordinated initiatives in Early Childhood Care and Development. It also undertakes engagements with Government in the implementation of key legislations in this area.
- *Education Financing*: This task force updates studies and popularize issues on key reforms in education financing. It is also mandated to build capabilities of E-Net for advocacy on education financing at the local and national levels, and among donor countries and agencies.
- *Formal Education*: Examines and monitors issues in formal education, such as quality and equity issues, and continuously inputs into the reform agenda.
- *Non-Formal Education & Alternative Learning Systems*: This working group aims to further develop alternative learning systems and contribute to the creation of standards that will build a respected constituency in the topic at par with its formal counterparts. Working with the Bureau of Alternative Learning System, Literacy Coordinating Council, Bureau of Non Formal Education and agencies like the National Council on Indigenous People and the National Commission on Culture and Arts, to put together a 'core Indigenous People curriculum.' Furthermore they do research and case studies on culture-based education.

Linking their own agenda to the topics used by the government is a strategic move. Some years later, a working group on Gender was created as this was a missing topic in both the government and E-Net agenda. In the process of maturing, E-Net adjusted their strategies. While in the beginning there was a strong focus on being recognised by the government and increasing civil society influence in the EFA process, now that E-Net has gained an institutionalised position alongside the government, they altered their strategies. Through strategic reflection they realised being 'in' is not enough, and that there is a need for advocating both from within and without.

Box 3.1. Campaigning Inside and Outside - The Out of School Youth

One of E-Net's core advocacies is developing alternative learning systems with special concern for the vulnerable, excluded and marginalised sectors. This includes the Out-of-School Youth (OSY). While the government has not yet published official data on the number of OSY in the country, E-Net estimated that 11,6 million youth aged 6-24 were out of school. Most of these youth come from poor families, which are most effected by inequality in education.

As many of these OSYs cannot (instantly) return to the formal education system, the government's Bureau for Alternative Learning Strategies is the department that should reach out to them. Unfortunately, while the alarming number of OSY reaches the number of youth who are in school, the Bureau of Alternative Learning receives a meagre budget from the Department of Education. E-Net has been advocating for bigger allocations to the BALS budget.

One of their strategies to strengthen their advocacies is to let the OSYs speak for themselves. E-Net organised a two-day workshop for OSYs, to teach them about lobbying, policy advocacy and public speaking. This way, they could demand education programs for the Out-of-School children and youth.

The workshop was concluded with a rally at the Department of Education on the day of school opening. As outside of the Department several OSYs were demonstrating and generating media attention with their chanting and slogan covered signs, some OSYs were invited into the Department to be heard by government officials. This was a very literal example of campaigning inside and outside.

Over the years, E-Net has also realised the importance of the "localization" of its EFA advocacies. This coincided with the new politics, decentralisation and political measures, such as the Local Government Code, DepEd's School First Initiative and other decentralisation policies.

That is part of the general governance strategy in the Philippines, even while we hope for and struggle for improvements at the central government level, there is more hope and in some ways more effort electing local officials, and influencing local officials, more transparent, more participatory government. That's smaller scale, so maybe we can influence better. But this is maybe the development of the last 5 or 7 years. Before that we thought advocacy work was at national level (Interview BoardMember, 2009).

Through their members E-Net is increasingly working together with Local Government Units, Parent-Teacher-Community-Associations, and other local stakeholders of education. The current education debate includes questions on how to set up local EFA committees that will keep track of the local progress towards the Education for All goals.

Through advocacy workshops, EFA orientations, education financing workshops, alternative learning systems trainings, and a course on early childhood education, E-Net has developed the capacities/competences of their members. The network strategically uses the expertise of the members. For example, the working group on education financing carried out research on the finance of education and effectively used their findings for financing workshops for members all over the Philippines. As the budget deficit is one of the biggest problems of Philippines' education, this core advocacy is important to all members. The working group shared their knowledge on education financing and creatively opened new possibilities to access funding through assigned education budgets of the Local

Government Units. This way, members learn from each other, which is an example of the added value of collective action.

The collective identity of E-Net and the internal relations are also constantly reflected upon. Strategic learning takes place at various occasions, such as coalition meetings, after specific campaigns, and during the General Assembly, where the members evaluate the previous experiences and set the agenda for the new term. But besides these occasions, E-Net carried out a self-evaluation of civil society participation through ASPBAE in 2003, and had an external evaluation by Oxfam GB in 2006. Both occasions were good moments to reflect on the work done so far and on the strengths and weaknesses of the network.

The recommendation of the 2003 research was to 'unify and clarify' its position on education. Furthermore, it was recommended that civil society should focus their advocacy initiatives on key issues to achieve maximum impact and involve more networks and members in the EFA campaign' (Raya and Mabunga 2003:28). Since then, E-Net has taken up this strategy, and has brought out issue based policy statements, specific campaigns, and has included even more members in their campaigns.

The research done by Oxfam GB in 2006 showed that with the passage of time E-Net's work, the impact of the network should not be underestimated as many members are improving the quality of their work and undertaking more effective advocacy (Oxfam 06). Unfortunately, the currently increased workload of the secretariat prevents them from being able to thoroughly reflect on their numerous advocacy activities in a more systematic way. While some reflection spaces are open, usually ad hoc, the limited capacity urges the members of the secretariat to move on and to focus on the next project, meeting, or activity.

In 2009 the funds that were given by Oxfam GB for institutional strengthening finished, and there was a need to redefine the network for all members, including board, and secretariat. The new reality of diminished institutional funds necessitated new responsibilities for the members:

> Because previously we had money, and the secretariat could work on its own. But now that we don't have money, it's up to the network to sustain its advocacy (Interview Executive Committee, 2009).

Over the years E-Net got more global Asia oriented. Through the collaboration with the Asian South Pacific Bureau for Basic and Adult Education (ASPBAE), and their participation in the Real World Strategies, sub-regional (Southeast Asian) collaboration gained more importance. This led to sharing of learning experiences, strategies, and working together to strengthen civil society and create a stronger voice from the South. By strategically reflecting on the context and their own actions and impact, E-Net was able to adjust, develop and improve their activities in order to have a bigger impact.

E-NET'S CONTRIBUTION TO EFA

When looking at the success or impact of E-Net, this could be divided into internal (network cohesion, structure, resources and collective identity) and external (political, procedural and symbolic) impact.

Internal impact

One of the main internal successes is the broad constituency E-Net has built over the years. For the first time, over 150 civil society organisations that are working on education and reforms have come together to form a common agenda and advocacy strategy. They are working together according to their particular strengths, and despite their political differences. The growing number of members illustrates the success of this collaboration. E-Net is the biggest civil society coalition working on EFA and education reforms in the Philippines. This status gives them a stronger position, which might influence the recognition of the government. The members are spread nation-wide, which is beneficial for retrieving local information. Furthermore, the members have different backgrounds, varying from local service deliverers, alternative learning systems trainers to large (I)NGOs, researchers and teacher organisations. This wide variety of members is useful for the different advocacies and strategies as they all bring various expertise to the network.

Furthermore, the members seem to agree and respect the structure and purpose of the network. The collaboration of the different organisations causes no major power struggles amongst the members. If there are issues that will not fit E-Net's agenda, these will be carried out separate of the network. Although some tensions may occur, so far there have been no major break-ups or problems that damaged the network (Interview E-Sec, 2009). Because of the collaboration there is also stronger alignment of individual programs and better access to information. As information is distributed among the members through E-groups, workshops, meetings and through the secretariat, they can learn from each other and share best practices. Moreover, the collaboration with actors from other areas in education contributes to the understanding of the complete EFA agenda. Furthermore, E-Net has always been focused on building the capacity of their members. Through workshops and information sharing, they aim to strengthen the position of their members in order to advocate their educational rights. The sharing of expertise, knowledge, experiences, and making use of networking and scalar interaction strengthens the network and the members. For example, during a seminar-workshop on education governance in Southern Mindanao, where civil society and local government representatives were invited to share their best practices, the participants learned from each other and from the experiences at the national level presented by the organisers. In turn, the best practices shared during the workshop could be used as information to feed the national advocacies.

Something that is important for the Philippine case is the strong relationship between Teacher Unions and NGOs. In civil society literature, tensions between

NGOs and unions in the education field are common (Archer 2007). The fact that the Philippines has no central teachers' union, but several fragmented ones based on various ideological backgrounds, prevents the teachers' organisations from becoming too big and influential, which could cause tension. One could also argue that the repressive environment within which teachers' unions operate in the Philippines also generates solidarity from other stakeholders and amongst the several teachers' organisations. Teacher unions in E-Net are mainly working with the working group on formal education. Although the various organisations do not always agree on certain issues, they seem to be collaborating for the common agenda. Issues on which they do not agree are discussed outside the E-Net arena (Interview E-NetMember, 2009).

EXTERNAL IMPACT

Looking at the external impact, the division of Burnstein (1999) is used, focusing on political, procedural and symbolic impact. *Political impact*, according to Burnstein (1999) refers to the specific impact of the movement in observable policy outcomes. When looking at political impact, it is difficult to attribute changes in policies solely to the work done by E-Net. Other actors and external factors might have contributed to the change in policies as well. Despite this difficulty, there are some examples of policy outcomes where E-Net has certainly played a role.

Probably one of the best examples of the political impact of E-Net is the Alternative Budget Initiative (ABI). Since its formation in 2001, E-Net has been involved in budget monitoring and advocacy. The working group on "Education Financing" conducts research, identifies critical gaps in education performance and outcome and proposes policy measures and specific budgetary allocations to address such gaps. In collaboration with other civil society groups like Social Watch Philippines and the Freedom for Debt Coalition, E-Net is pursuing its budget advocacy initiatives (E-Net ABI 2008).

In 2006, the budget advocacy campaign made a significant breakthrough. Civil society groups, for the first time, were able to effectively lobby for reforms in the national budget hearings in both the Upper and the Lower Houses. NGOs collaborated with legislators and formulated an alternative budget aimed at realising the Millennium Development Goals and Education for All-goals. The campaign coalition was initiated and coordinated by Social Watch Philippines, and E-Net was responsible for the education cluster of the campaign.

In 2007, the campaign had another breakthrough. For the first time in history, the Committee on Appropriations of the Lower House had allowed the participation of CSOs in budget hearings and has vowed to make such practice permanent. The members of the Alternative Budget Initiative, including E-Net, presented their views, comments and recommendations on the General Appropriations Bill. They recommended an alternative budget that puts social services at top priority and eliminates unreasonable, big, and vague budgetary allotments (E-Net ABI 2008).

Because of the constructive interventions by the members of the Alternative Budget Initiative in the national budget process, education and health services were given better allocations. This effort has been recognised by the National Economic Development Authority, who highlighted in the 2007 MDG Report that the Alternative Budget advocacy in 2007 resulted in an increase of 22.7 billion Philippine pesos (PhP) in additional proposals for MDG-related activities, and an approval of the PhP 5.5 billion in the 2007 national budget for social services. Furthermore, the ABI campaign for the 2008 budget resulted in PhP 6.3 billion increases for social services, meaning more allocations for health, environment, agriculture, and education.

While the ABI campaign is a multi-sectoral campaign, the education sector has been the biggest gainer, as it covered half of the increase in the budget. However, in the process of budget amendments, particularly in the education budget, the lower house version of amendments did not match those of the Senate's. During the bicameral conference committee meetings, there were discussions to reconcile the figures, making the education budget once again the bone of contention. Fortunately, it resulted in PhP 3.2 billion additional funds for the Department of Education (E-Net ABI 2008). This advocacy experience has opened new opportunities in ensuring greater and more direct participation of stakeholders in the budget process.

Furthermore, E-Net has supported the passing of several bills regarding education reforms. For example, E-Net has been supporting the amendment of the Magna Carta Act for Public School Teachers, which aimed at additional benefits to teachers. Another bill E-Net has supported is the bill for Multi-lingual education.

Local budget advocacies of E-Net members have also been successful in some advocacy initiatives, for example ESKAN was able to mobilise financial support for education for child labourers, PEPE was able to access financial support from the Mayor's office in Atok in support of the mentoring for indigenous children, and PILCD was able to access a resource centre in Buguias (E-Net Project Report 2009).

Furthermore, DepEd Order 94 series 2009 on Guidelines in Creating Regional EFA Committees is based on draft guidelines presented by E-Net in a meeting of the National EFA Committee (E-Net Project Report 2009). These are all examples of how E-Net has influenced both national and local policies regarding education.

Somewhat easier to distinguish is the procedural impact, which refers to implicit changes in the decision making procedures of policy makers that recognize the civil society movement as a legitimate actor. E-Net has achieved being formally recognized by the government as being co-chair on the national EFA committee. This official status is, of course, a big procedural accomplishment. The fact that civil society participation has been institutionalised is a big difference from the Philippines some decades ago. This is the result of the CSOs' push for civil society influence in policy making over the years. Partly it might also be addressed to the international framework/climate of the growing importance of civil society advocacy.

However, while it is considered a great achievement, the question remains how real this co-chair status is. Does being co-chair also mean having co-responsibility? And does being co-chair mean equal positions? One could say although E-Net is recognised as a NEC co-chair, it is not recognised as a full partner in policy formulation and decision-making. As one of the interviewees pointed out, the relations between the chair and co-chair are not equal:

> He said "you're co-chair! If DepEd doesn't call a meeting, call a meeting!" But do you really think any government ministry will come to a meeting called by civil society? Probably not! (Interview Executive Committee, 2009).

The position of co-chair is also considered a big achievement by the members of E-Net and they are proud of this realisation. On a local level, they can also use this in order to gain more respect and win over local government unit representatives. In this sense, it also has a symbolic value:

> In local politics sometimes the dynamics might be difficult, that some local member of E-Net is not so acceptable to the major or governor. But when, and that's what we were trying to do, if you get the papers from the national and we say look E-Net is co-chair, we are not an anti-government organisation, we are willing to operate, it helps a little (Interview E-Net Member, 2009).

Linked to their position in the National EFA Committee, E-Net also has civil society representatives in the Technical Working Groups of the committee. Therefore their influence reaches further than only the National Committee itself. In this way, E-Net members link up with the government agencies and officials working on specific topics, which provides them with an opportunity to link up with possible 'champions' inside the bureaucracy.

Another example of procedural impact is that E-Net is invited to official meetings, such as bill hearings in the Senate, public hearings of the Senate Committee on Education, Arts, and Culture (Interview Secretariat, 2009). The fact that civil society is officially invited to these meetings shows how their status has improved over the years.

Symbolic impact refers to changes at the public opinion level and to transformations in belief systems and ideologies. Although symbolic impact is probably the hardest level of external impact to measure, there are some matters that can be considered as such. Over the years, E-Net has been successful in raising awareness on Education for All. Before E-Net started its advocacy, not many people were aware of the concept of Education for All and the associated goals. While many people have been working on education, whether formal or non-formal, not everyone knew of the existence of the Education for All goals. E-Net has been introducing and promoting 'EFA' to a bigger audience, and even introduced the concept to some people within the Department of Education who were not aware of it (Interview Executive Committee, 2009).

Through research and advocacy E-Net has created more awareness on the state of education in the Philippines. The Education Watch initiative 'Mapping Out Disadvantage Groups in Education' is an example of knowledge production based on local members' participation. The findings of the initiative were integrated in official government reports such as the Mid-Decade EFA Assessment (E-Net Project Report 2009) which illustrated the real education situation and problems on the local and national level.

Another example of symbolic impact can be seen in the capacity building of local communities. Though workshops, E-Net is making local communities aware of their education rights. In this way, they influence the public opinion at the local level. A group of education budget advocates, EFA campaigners, organisers and advocates, organised and developed capabilities through EFA orientations, education financing workshops, alternative learning trainings/orientations, advocacy workshops, and a course on Early Child Care and Development (E-Net Project Report 2009). However, while their media strategies could be strengthened, E-Net has had symbolic impact through knowledge sharing, capacity building, and raising awareness on EFA.

CONCLUSIONS

There is still a long way to go before all Filipino's have access to multi-cultural, gender-fair, liberating life-long education, as the education situation is alarming. But the recent democratisation of the country and the increasing institutionalisation of civil society participation has created new possibilities for the education situation to improve. In the ten years of existence, E-Net has matured from a group of justice activists who were brought together by an international NGO to address the alarming education situation in the Philippines, to an independent network of over 150 members, spread nationwide, who officially co-chair of the National EFA Commission, and who advocate for education reforms and increased importance of education Filipino political debate.

Although members have different ideological backgrounds, the network is valued very important, and members take their convictions beyond the network. The added value of belonging to the coalition can be found in various means of capacity building, information and knowledge sharing, and a sense of camaraderie. The all-inclusive character of the network on the one hand leads to an overfull agenda with positions on many things, but on the other hand covers expertise on the whole EFA agenda. Members are working according to their strengths and can learn from each other.

Going back to the question of whether civil society 'matters', in light of the research presented, an answer in the affirmative is most certainly warranted. The question of *how* civil society advocacy coalitions matter largely depends on the national political context in which they are embedded. Especially in countries where the government rhetoric differs greatly from reality and is mainly serving the elite, a strong civil society that can counter balance the power of elites is needed. In this study, the impact, strategies, and challenges for civil society were shown. Although there is great room for improvement, E-Net has proved to be an important actor in the education sector in the Philippines.

JONAH SARFATY

CHAPTER 4

*Civil Society and Education Advocacy in Ecuador: Building a Social
Contract for Education*

INTRODUCTION

'Only Education Can Change Ecuador'. This is the slogan used by the *Contrato
Social por la Educación* (the Social Contract for Education in Ecuador, CSE), a
participatory civil social movement in Ecuador. The CSE was founded with the
intention of defending and exercising the human rights of the Ecuadorian
population, and in particular their right to a good quality education (CSE 2002: 1).
The CSE, in its 8 years of existence, has forced itself into a strong position in the
national education field. They have been able to create broad awareness on a range
of social issues related to the development of the country. The rising interest and
commitment of the population at this moment to the goal of a good quality
education, the members say, has been partly attributed to the work of the CSE
(Participatory Workshop CSE, August 2009).

This chapter analyses whether and to what level the CSE has contributed to
improve education access and quality in Ecuador. The arguments are based on
research carried out by the author between March and May 2009. During that
period I interviewed members of the coalition and other key informants,
participated in the movement's events and activities and analysed their core
documents. Specifically, I interviewed around 20 coalition members, three policy-
makers, four journalists and other independent actors, all in order to make the
research more comprehensive. These interviews were backed up by participant
observation in the CSE headquarters and at their organized events and meetings. I
also did various informal interviews with the coalition members, as well as with
other actors in society. I spread my interviews over different regions in the country,
visiting people in Ecuador's three biggest cities, Quito, Guayaquil and Cuenca, as
well as making fieldwork trips to the countryside. At the end of my research I
sought to test my initial findings by organizing a participatory workshop for some
of the members of the coalition. Around thirty members attended the workshop and
through the focus groups organized in the context of the event I was able to build
in feedback loops and check the validity of my assumptions with core informants.
Through these different methods I sought to get an insight into the complex ways
that the movement operates in order to get a sense of its own institutional memory.

In this chapter I seek to offer a broad insight into my findings of the goals,
strategies, effects and successes of the CSE, as well as the lessons the movement

Antoni Verger and Mario Novelli (eds.), Campaigning for "Education for All", 51–64.

has learned in the years since its creation. In order to address these issues and to increase the understanding of this movement, it is first important to analyse the context in which this coalition was constructed and has evolved. The chapter is divided into six sections. The first section seeks to analyse the existing socio-economic and political situation of Ecuador in terms of the political opportunities for the development of a civil society movement committed to improve education in Ecuador. In the second section I will explain how the movement has developed over the years. Specifically, I will focus in on their goals and strategies, their membership and the power relations between the members. In the subsequent section I will then explore the external relations of the movement with the state, the media, and other sections of the Ecuadorian society. Finally I will explore the impact that the movement has had on the educational scene in Ecuador in terms of political, procedural and symbolic effects. The chapter will then end with a discussion and conclusion. Throughout the chapter I will emphasize the lessons the movement has learned over the years to enhance its strategic interventions in Ecuador.

The Ecuadorian Context

David Meyer's article 'Protest and Political Opportunities' emphasizes the central role that societal context plays in the success of social movements. Meyer argues that social movements can 'make history' in a country. However, movements that try to make history do so not in situations of their own choosing, but rather in social and political circumstances peculiar to their given society. The national context determines the activities, mobilizing strategies, and the final effects of any social movement (Meyer 2004).

The educational context in Ecuador, as in many other Latin American countries, is marked by a strong inequality between the white-mestizos and 'black'-Indigenous groups. The discrepancies can be traced back to historical times in which education was used by the colonial power to subjugate the Indigenous inhabitants to their Hispanic and Christian values. In 1830, when Ecuador became independent from Spain, educational policies were adjusted in the constitution and aimed at using schools to promote homogenization and assimilation, in order to construct a proper nation state. Then, as of the 1960s, international actors came into play constructing new educational programs more focused on participation and experimentation (Oviedo and Wildemeersch 2008).

In the 1990s, neoliberal reforms in educational policies had the effect of increasing inequality in the country. Inequality rose as a consequence of the Structural Adjustment Programs initiated by the World Bank and the International Monetary Fund (IMF) whereby the amount of public spending on education decreased. A further reason for rising inequality in Latin America has been a tendency of upper and middle classes to self-select out of public education and opt for private education as a reaction to the educational inclusion of groups previously excluded from the educational system. Consequently, as Bonal (2004) argues, 'rather than being a strategy for fighting poverty, education seems to be a sphere in which the ravages of poverty are laid bare and made visible' (p. 658).

In the last twenty years most educational indicators have improved in Ecuador, although at a very irregular path and not by benefiting all social groups at the same level. The gender-gap, highly present in Ecuador in former decades, decreased substantially and the enrolment rate for boys and girls is almost completely equal nowadays, as Table 4.1 below demonstrates. Another indicator that has evolved in Ecuador is the total years of schooling, which has increased in the last decades. In 2006 the average number of schooling years for Ecuadorians was 8.1 (see Table 4.2).

In recent years however, the rate and pace of change in these improvements has slowed in comparison to previous years. Whereas the enrolment rate between the 1970s and the 1980s increased by 20 percentage points, in the 1990s it only went up one percentage point. Most indicators have thus shown some improvement, whether small or large. While improvements have slowed, one indicator has markedly deteriorated: education inequality. As can be observed in Table 4.2, children living in rural areas have almost 50% fewer years in schooling than their urban counterparts. Aside from urban and rural, there is also a notable division along ethnic lines between indigenous, black, white, and *mestizo* children.

Table 4.1. Enrolment Rate in Ecuador by Gender in 1990 and 2001

	Primary		Secondary	
	1990	**2001**	**1990**	**2001**
Male	88,6	89,9	42,0	43,9
Female	89,2	90,4	44,1	45,4

Source: Ponce Jarrín 2008: 10

Table 4.2. Number of Years of Education in Ecuador in 2006

Total in Ecuador (2006): 8,1			
Male	Female	Urban	Rural
8,3	7,9	9,5	5,3
White	Mestizo	Afro	Indigenous
8,7	8,4	7,0	4,3

Source: Ponce Jarrín 2008: 3

Politically speaking, Ecuador has gone through some turbulent times over the past ten years. Despite the average presidential term being constitutionally defined as a four year period, Ecuador has had eight different governments during the last decade. The country has also been increasingly influenced by external actors, particularly in education. Actors from the World Bank through to the United Nations have had a strong impact on the national education agendas and policies.

In 2007 Rafael Correa was elected as president. His appointment followed along similar lines to many other Latin American countries where there has been an increase in left-wing parties being elected to power. Following Correa's appointment the government has taken a more active role in education, and many view him as a change agent capable of redressing Ecuador's legacy of inequality and poverty.

Under Correa, The Ministry of Education has brought a broad education agenda to the table, and the state has sought new ways to increase the quality and equality of education. This new strategy was implemented on the 16th of June 2006 when the *Consejo Nacional de Educación* (National Council of Education, CNE) came together to construct guidelines for a ten year plan to improve the educational situation in Ecuador, which they called the *Plan Decenal*. Even though the plan was put in place before Correa's appointment, the new president adopted the strategy and reinforced it. The CNE met at the request of the Ministry of Education and consisted of 'representatives from the National Educators Union, the Confederation of Catholic Education Schools, the Confederation of Private Education Schools, the National Council of Higher Education and the National Secretariat for Planning and Development'. The then Minister of Education, Raul Vallejo Corral, was also president of the CNE.

The CNE thus comprised many actors in the education field. Other important groups of civil society were however excluded, such as the teachers union UNE (*Unión Nacional de Educadores*), indigenous movements and social movements such as the *Contrato Social por la Educación* (Meeting CSE Ample Committee, March 2009). This omission of the CSE in the CNE is an example of the sometimes difficult relationship between the state and civil society in Ecuador. I will go into these relationships more thoroughly in the next section.

AN INSIGHT INTO THE CSE

Its origins and membership

The *Contrato Social por la Educación* was founded in 2002, a national election year. As said before, in the years leading up to these elections Ecuador was a very unstable country with drastic political changes happening at a governmental level, almost on a yearly basis. This instability peaked in 1999 when there was a social, political and economic crisis in Ecuador. This had a big impact on the country as a whole, mostly because society lost hope in a better future (Interview Secretariat 01).

> 'The Ecuadorian reality was characterized by a deep social instability. That is to say, in ten years almost ten Presidents or Ministers of Education were in office. We would work ten months to enable Ministers and then they would leave again. They did thus not manage to install political means for the improvement of education in the country before they would leave again, and

this political instability was seriously affecting the right to education' (Member of UNICEF Ecuador, 4-20-2009).

UNICEF decided that a critical voice against the state was needed, a role however that they, as a social movement, were unable to play. During this time a group of twenty Ecuadorian personalities came together to try bring about the earlier experience of unity and hope the country had initially experienced. Under the influence of UNICEF they decided that children were the way to improve the country's situation. Their focus came to rest on education, using the topic in a political way to give hope to the country for the future. The group wanted to construct a national agreement, something that would speak to everybody in society (Interview Secretariat 01).

These twenty individuals were from different sectors of society, ranging from the corporate sector, to academia, the media, the political sphere, social movements, and the church. All were highly educated and with high social positions. Furthermore, the group consisted of people from different geographic regions and of different political opinions, so that no single political current was overrepresented (Interview Secretariat 04).

The 20 members established the 'Contrato Social por la Educatión' (CSE), the Social Contract for Education. The organization was thus literally meant as a contract to raise awareness and serve as a sort of national constitution for all actors working in the education field, from teachers in small rural schools to the president himself.

CSE's first action was to create an Agenda composed of three main goals, containing seven strategies to reach them. The first and most important goal was to ensure that all Ecuadorians up to ten years of age would be able to have access to a good quality basic education. The CSE argued that the country would never be able to develop with the huge inequalities present in the Ecuadorian society and its education in particular. The second goal was to adopt standards of quality in education taking into account the entire ethnic and cultural diversity of the country. The final goal was to locate Ecuador on the map as one of the countries within the Latin American region with a better index in basic education (CSE 2002: 1). The group of personalities asked a very diverse range of actors to sign the contract, by which they made a promise to commit themselves to the cause of the Contrato Social por la Educación to improve the national education level.

The new movement's first public action used the slogan 'If your candidate doesn't know how to change education, change your candidate' during the time of the national presidential elections. Members of the CSE say that this slogan was very successful in achieving their goals, because while at the start of the presidential campaigns there were only two candidates that addressed educational issues, by the end of the campaign all twelve candidates used educational points in their campaigning (Interview Secretariat 04). In this way, CSE was able to not only raise awareness from the start, but also to ensure education having a higher place on the political agenda.

The structure of the CSE can roughly be divided into three substantial organs. The first one, the Promoter Committee, is an executive governing council constituted by the twenty personalities that established the movement. These persons are all well-known in Ecuadorian society, have a busy life and are, one could say, elites. Once a year this Committee meets to discuss the year's results and the future focus of the movement (Interview Promoter Committee 03). Because of the public functions of these personalities they do not have the time to run the movement. This group thus serves more as a backbone and gives the movement an advantage in being seen as a legitimate partner in the policy-making processes in the education field (Interview Secretariat 04). A second group was formed in 2004 to be in charge of the day-to-day campaigns, events, strategies and challenges of the social movement. This group, the Technical Team, is composed of five full-time employees.

Over the years the movement started growing by more and more people signing the Agenda and joining their cause. The CSE soon became the biggest actor in the field of education with the exception of the national government and the teachers union (Interview Secretariat 04). In order to give all the actors that signed the Agenda a place, the Technical Team constructed the third body of the coalition: an Ample Committee. This group consists of almost 200 individuals who are invited to the events the CSE organizes, and who are actively involved in constructing and redefining the Agenda of the movement. The Technical Team organizes meetings according to external events. For instance in times of elections the Ample Committee meets more frequently to discuss the CSE's tactics on influencing the candidates and the election at large. In this division of the three committees the idea within the CSE is that the Ample Committee is eventually responsible for the final decisions of the entire movement.

The decisions within the CSE are made at two levels. The Technical Team decides on proposals that they want to focus on over the coming years, after which the Ample Committee is asked to broaden those proposals and make them more concrete. The members of the Technical Team can thus be seen as facilitators in the decision making process within the movement. Since all members have an equal say in the process there is very little sense of hierarchy in the decision making process (Interview NGO 02).

In 2006 a new Agenda was created. This constitution was a bigger and more concrete mandate than the original Agenda of 2002. Whereas the CSE started off in 2002 with just a small group of people, by the time they constructed the second Agenda in 2006 the movement had grown substantially. This growth has been very influential in the adjustment of the Agenda. The first Agenda, which the 20 personalities constructed, was more of a broad set of goals designed to have mass appeal so as to attract more signatures. The goals were therefore comprised of rather all-encompassing phrases on education policies that could attract broad based support. By 2006 the CSE was more constructed of NGOs and other social movements; actors that worked directly with the people teaching or running schools. When constructing a new agenda, these agents gave ideas for more concrete programs and had more ideas and expertise in terms of how to go about realizing them. It is not surprising then that the Agenda of 2006 became bigger and made a shift from being abstract and idealistic to being concrete and particular.

While the CSE may appear to be very democratic, there are problems of manifested inequality when it comes to the participation of the members within the movement. One of the critiques often heard was that the focus of the actions of the CSE is too much directed to politics, and thus centred around Ecuador's capital, Quito. As a result, many experiences of small provinces have been excluded and almost seem to be of lesser interest to the Technical Team. Moreover, by organizing most of the events and meetings with the Ample Committee in Quito, Guayaquil and Cuenca, Ecuador's three largest cities, the CSE excludes certain members of society. For many people in the outskirts of the country, usually the poorer rural communities, it is financially not possible to come to all the meetings, resulting in their voices not being heard.

This bias can be understood in the sense that the three main cities of the country house the biggest percentage of the national population (Interview NGO 01). However, since CSE is fighting against inequalities in the country as a whole, a bigger focus on all parts of the country would represent a more coherent territorial strategy.

The way activities are organised does not only affect actors from outside of the city however. Some argued that the CSE also made it difficult for them to participate by organizing day filling events. For instance, a member of a big NGO argued that they have a busy schedule and important events to attend and/or organize and cannot afford the "luxury" of dropping their work for an entire day to discuss the new strategies for the CSE. She concluded that this system of setting up events, both in the city as well as for a whole day, results in the Technical Team having more to contribute to the discussion than other people within the movement (Interview NGO 01), the result being that the Ample Committee is not as effective as it could be.

Its regional relationships

When the *Contrato Social por la Educación* started of in 2002, its focus was on constructing a *national* civil social movement in Ecuador. Whereas their focus is still mostly on the national Ecuadorian experience, the movement is now slowly trying to expand its borders and share its experiences with other countries. Around the year 2006 the CSE started forming alliances with international actors in the education field such as the *Campaña Latinoamericana por el Derecho a la Educación* (CLADE) (Interview Secretariat 04). CLADE regularly organizes meetings and seminars in different countries in Latin America.[12] If possible a member of the Technical Team of the CSE joins these events to bring the Ecuadorian perspective to the table and share ideas and strategies with their regional colleagues. The CSE is planning on increasing these international contacts over the coming years. Among other initiatives, they are thinking of organizing annual meetings to share experiences between the civil movements in the different Latin American countries (Interview Secretariat 01).

---

[12] http://www.campanaderechoeducacion.org/. Visited on November 13th 2009.

On the global level, the CSE is, also since 2006, part of the international organization the Global Campaign for Education (GCE). The most visible result of this relationship is the organization of a one-week annual event, which is organized in all the member countries of the Campaign, called the Action Week. In 2009 the Action Week was called 'The Big Read'. The GCE states that in 2009 '774 million adults cannot read this, and 75 million children who are not in school will be denied the chance to learn to read and write' (GCE 2009). In order to change this immense amount of illiteracy the GCE wanted to spread awareness in many countries around the world by funding the national coalitions to organize events on this topic. The relationship between the CSE and the GCE is at this moment however still small. As one member of the Technical Team explained:

'[The GCE] only helps with sponsoring the world-wide action week with about 2000 or 3000 dollars per year, which is very little. But what I believe is that the support they're giving is not economic, but more political. One feels backed up and that their proposals extend or go beyond the national border. So I say it is more a way of providing us with legitimization than to feel part of a world-wide movement, part of a world-wide opinion' (Interview Secretariat 04).

In 2009 the Technical Team organized three debates during the Action Week concerning education. The other members of the CSE, those in the Promoter Committee and in the Ample Committee, were however not aware of the connection between these activities and the GCE.

In general when asking about the relationship between the CSE and international actors, such as the GCE, the most heard answer was that they were unaware of the details on the relationship (Interview Promoter Committee 02 & 04; Interview NGO 04). The only contact there is between the global actors and the CSE thus lies with the Technical Team, showing the extent of the relationship.

There is certainly scope to improve and strengthen both regional and global alliances. A stronger relationship with CLADE and the GCE could increase successes for the movement because alliances lead to increased interaction and broader participation as well an added political legitimacy and extended access to financial resources. The Technical Team acknowledges these positive effects of alliances with international actors and is thus planning on strengthening them in the future.

Its relationship with the State

At the moment of the research the CSE was more focused on the relationship with the national government. With the election of Rafael Correa as president some windows of political opportunity opened for the CSE. However, at the same time, the level of openness to the political system was altered and to some extent some opportunities diminished for civil society coalitions such as the CSE.

Originally the Technical Team was very positive with the election of a socially oriented president. They thought that they now did not have to stress the importance of Education for All (EFA) in the country, but that the state itself would take action. The situation was however not as rosy as they expected. Because of his popularity in the presidential elections Correa felt that he had the whole population behind him. When social movements criticized him he therefore did not give them much notice, the CSE felt. In the past, with neoliberal presidents, the CSE were able to stress the importance of equality in the country and promote the cause of the most vulnerable parts of society. With a socialist government in power, this position was less powerful; they felt like preaching to the converted.

The national context in Ecuador in 2009 is that of a presidential and relatively centralized government. The country came from an era of dictatorship and has now recently elected a socialist president. All these factors are shown by Della Porta and Diani (2006) to be limiting to social movements. This can also be seen for the CSE; the movement is very much dependent on their relationship with the state, seeing their focus is on the national policy making processes. The movement has to be very creative therefore to not lose their role as a critical actor, but at the same time trying to influence and correcting the state, while keeping an amicable relationship.

With the new Ecuadorian government in power, there were in 2008 plans of the state of constructing a new national constitution, one more fitting the new stage the country was in. The CSE saw their chance and introduced a number of points they thought should be present in this new national constitution. Many of their suggestions were later used in the parts of the constitution on education. The Technical Team concluded that as much as 80% of the new constitution constituted of their proposed points (CSE 2008: 2). After this claimed success of having an influence in the political educational sphere of the country, the focus of the CSE came to lie on the new laws that the country wanted to construct according to the revised constitution. The CSE, just as the Ministry of Education, the teachers union UNE and the indigenous movement CONAIE, have been active with writing proposals for national laws.

The fact that the CSE is one of four actors that are involved in this process of constructing the national laws in Ecuador, shows that they, even though some aspects of the political opportunities in the country do not favour the CSE, are able to have some recognition or even impact on the political decision making processes within Ecuador.

INTERNAL COHESION

Besides the state, the CSE also has other national relationships to maintain. Seeing the focus of the *Contrato Social por la Educación* is centred around the Ecuadorian state at the level of state governance, the CSE's strongest and most often used coalitions are with other national actors in the political education field, such as UNICEF, PLAN and *Fe y Alegría*. In their strategies the movement is very focused on establishing coalitions on the national level, of which they have many; already more than 200 other social movements and NGOs are part of the CSE in its Ample Committee.

In this open space of participation one of the biggest actors in the educational debate is missing however: the teachers union, the *Unión Nacional de Educadores* (UNE). When the CSE started in 2002 this teachers union was part of the movement. This soon changed however. The CSE was taking stances that the UNE did not agree upon and they therefore quit the Promoter Committee (Interview Secretariat 06). One of the biggest reasons the CSE names for this 'break-up' is the fact that before the establishment of the CSE, the UNE had some sort of a monopoly on influencing the government on their educational policies. At the time there were only two substantial actors in the educational debates: the state and the teachers union. When the CSE was created the UNE however had to share their position as trustee of the state with another actor. When it became clear that the CSE had different ideas about how education should be arranged in the country, the UNE did not want to be involved with the movement (Interview Secretariat 04).

The relationship between two of the biggest actors in the Ecuadorian educational field is very tense. One of the ongoing struggles is the question of teacher evaluation. Milton Luna, the national coordinator of the Technical Team of the CSE, wrote in his biweekly column in *El Comercio*, one of the biggest newspapers in Ecuador, that, 'Without a doubt one of the central strategies for true educative change is the social and economic re-evaluation of the educative profession. For this we have to shape the evaluation of teachers...' (El Comercio 5-16-2009).

The UNE feels that, with teacher evaluation policies, their teachers are being blamed for problems they did not create. UNE fears that when teachers would now be evaluated many might not meet the standard assumed by the state. This would mean that many of its affiliates, maybe even thousands, would lose their jobs. And this, they argue, would be detrimental for the national economic situation in the country (Interview UNE 01). The UNE also thinks it is unfair to blame a bad educational system solely on the teachers. The teachers, they argue, are educated by the state and use the books provided by the state. Often teachers have to work in rural, hard to reach schools, and because of the roads they are unable to come on time or more than a few days a week. They are also often forced to work for little or even no money, seeing there are not enough funds provided by the government. The fact that the government does not provide good education for the teachers, nor good infrastructure or appropriate salaries should not be put on the teacher's shoulders, and it should most definitely not be solved purely by evaluating the teachers on their abilities, the UNE says (Interview UNE 01). The effect of this argument is that the three biggest actors in Ecuador concerned with the national education level: the Ministry of Education, the CSE and the UNE are not working together to improve education in the country. The Technical Team of the CSE does not see this weak relationship with the UNE as a bad thing however.

'[this difficult relationship] is only limiting in terms of a bigger voice, but not in terms of our principles. I would want you to go to any person in the street and ask what he or she thinks of the UNE, this is not just our vision, more we have tried to be the spokesmen of the opinions of the whole society. Of course if we would construct an alliance with UNE it would be very nice and it would definitely increase our presence, seeing it has 200 thousand affiliates. But when we begin to criticize the teachers UNE will not agree and we will have a rupture in the movement. (...) we are not going to let our principles go just to have a bigger presence (Interview Secretariat 06).

It could be considered that these relational difficulties between the CSE and the UNE are limiting the impact of civil society in education. One of the biggest civil movements and the vast majority of teachers in the educational field are not part of the CSE. This clearly has an effect on the amount of people the movement will be able to reach. The UNE moreover is a union that counts on many resources. All their members pay a small contribution and seeing that there are around 120.000 teachers in Ecuador of which approximately 110.000 are members of the UNE, the union has quite some leeway financially speaking (Meeting CSE Technical Team, August 2009). To have such a movement as an ally instead of an enemy would in my eyes be very beneficial to the sustenance and influence of the CSE on the national politics. The different views on education reform and other political aspects make reconciliation between the CSE and the UNE unlikely however.

THE IMPACT OF THE CSE

One of the Technical Team pointed out that part of the CSE's success is evident in the fact that it has been active for over eight years, which is a testament to the relevance of its initial goals and strategies (Interview Secretariat 03). To a large extent, the success of the CSE can be to a big extent traceable to their strong focus and relationship with the politics of the Ecuadorian state, which since 2002 has become increasingly more centralized in Quito (Participatory Workshop CSE, August 2009).

The main goal of the movement is to universalize education in Ecuador. They try to reach this, on the one hand, by pressing the importance of this issue to the state and, on the other, to provide a space for civil society to discuss educational issues. They have been able to reach new advantages for the Ecuadorian society, such as the universalization of the first year of basic education and the abolishment of the voluntary fee of 25$, but they have not changed the educative access and quality drastically.

In their struggle the CSE has been able to clear the road; according to CSE members, the state had hitherto been a closed entity, but through CSE's struggle they have been able to pave the way, which has resulted in the state becoming more comfortable with the influence of civil society actors in the political arena. Prior to CSE, the only actors involved in the education sphere were the *Ministerio de Educación* and UNE, the teachers union. Without the CSE, many members argue, the situation of a centralised and closed state with few influential political actors would not have changed (Participatory Workshop CSE, August 2009). The CSE however was not represented in the *Plan Decenal* of the ME. This shows that true acceptance by the state through influence in the decision making process is yet to be realised.

The aspect of visibility of the movement can be seen as a success. Other actors in educational and political fields know the movement well, and especially the alliance with the media is very strong. The national coordinator of the Technical Team has a biweekly column, the goals or activities of CSE are named, but they are also asked for their opinion on certain topics. The media coverage of the CSE is thus quite big. This derives in them being seen as a legitimate actor in educational debates in the country (Interview Media 04).

Outside of the political sphere the movement is not widely known however. The Technical Team therefore started organizing dialogues with rural schools. At this moment they have had dialogues in more than 900 schools. The impact of these dialogues is not only that the movement is able to raise awareness on the importance of good quality education, through these meetings the CSE has at times also been able to change the situation for the individual schools, for instance by redirecting the funding of local governments to issues more important for that particular school. The dialogues are also fruitful for the CSE itself. Due to its strongly established ties of communication with the general population, the CSE is able to see and understand the educational situation in the country by being directly in touch with public discourse of educational issues. This strengthens the construction of their policy proposals to the Ecuadorian state (Dialogue with Rural Schools, March 2009).

DISCUSSION

The CSE in a changing context

The relationship with the Ecuadorian government, and the political opportunities the CSE therefore receives, is one of the most important factors for their success as a movement. The CSE therefore constantly has to adjust their tactics to adapt to its changing external context. This flexibility can already be seen in the start of the CSE; the movement was set up out of the necessity to deal with external challenges. UNICEF found that the work they were trying to achieve was getting increasingly difficult with the ever changing government; every time UNICEF were able to construct a fruitful relationship with the ruling national state, the ministries would change once again. The movement thus argued that constructing a political civil movement, in charge of this political aspect of social change, was the right way to have an impact in the national policy making processes, as it created continuity. This is a big reason for many NGOs to be part of the CSE. Through their membership they are able to channel their critical demands, without affecting their direct relation with the state.

A sign of reflexivity can also be seen in the fact that the CSE feels the need to revise their Agenda regularly to adjust their ideas to new circumstances. Around five or six times a year a meeting is organized for the Ample Committee and in these meetings the priorities of the CSE are discussed. People share their stories or their worries on the upcoming elections or criticize the direction the CSE is taking. With the results of these meetings the CSE adjusts their focus and their strategies.

Self-criticism is crucial in the process of growing as a movement, Milton Luna, the national coordinator of the CSE, argues. Having meetings with the Ample Committee enables the movement to see itself in a mirror and can thus be very interesting and, more importantly, beneficial (Participatory Workshop, August 2009).

The effect of the new political context in the country was that the focus of the CSE changed; when constructed in 2002 they had basic education for all children as a priority, but in 2009, with Correa in charge, the movement shifted to participation issues and recognition of civil society in the political decision making processes.

The movement is now also revising the structure and membership base of the coalition. The CSE, as explained earlier, is made up of three main parts: the Promoter Committee, the Technical Team, and the Ample Committee. Of these three groups the Promoter Committee serves as a legitimizing backbone, showing that 20 high standing, well known figures in the Ecuadorian public life support the movement. This concept served very well in the times before Correa was elected. Most, if not all of the members of the Promoter Committee are part of the elite level of society and most of their members are situated ideologically to the right of the current government. The political situation in the country is at the moment one in which the president portrays himself as being a president of the people, a person opposing the ruling class system in the country. To thus have a very visible group of people serving as spokespeople for the movement from elitist, right winged background, can be detrimental to the movement in their relationship with the state. The CSE now seems to the state to be a movement supporting old-fashioned neoliberal policies and ideas. The Technical Team is looking for ways to change this perception and is thinking about replacing some people in the Promoter Committee for famous public figures from the left, such as some famous artists. This strategy comes with the hope that the CSE gets more respected by the socialist state and does not lose their position as one of the actors in the education political decision making field (Meeting Technical Team, August 2009).

The difference between the Promoter Committee and the state are not the only limitations. The discrepancies between the Promoter Committee and the Ample Committee are growing. Both groups have different ways of working and differ in thoughts on educational policy. The diversity of opinion and array of focus areas has narrowed the possibility for consensus, and decreased the possibility for agreement except for on broadly principled policy statements, such as the necessity of education for all. Diversity has always been one of the CSE's greatest strengths. As the movement has grown, diversity has also become an impediment. As a result the CSE has become hamstrung by focussing on internal challenges, which has limited its role of influencing the state. In this respect, many of the institutional blockages manifest in its organisational setup first need to be addressed in order to increase the CSE's efficacy going forward.

CONCLUSIONS

From the outset, *Contrato Social por la Educación* was founded on a will to influence the political aspects of the educational field. This emphasis has mostly been seen as positive seeing the educational policies are constructed at the state level. CSE's civil society movement is at this moment the third biggest actor in the education field, besides the Ministry of Education and the teachers union UNE, which is not a bad result at all after being active for only eight years. The relationship of the movement with the state will however always be a balancing act. The members of the CSE need a good and fruitful relationship with the state in order to have political influence, although they are also aware of how important is not to lose its independence and its criticizing role.

While political influence is one of their core competencies, CSE's primary focus on the political sphere in education subjects their movement to the vicissitudes of political change. The composition of the members of the movement, especially in the Promoter Committee, is now seen as a liability for the CSE. In order to stay a successful movement the CSE has to think about how Correa's government receives them, and whether their committee has the legitimacy to remain influential regardless of the government in power. They would benefit from ensuring that the message of high-quality education for all Ecuadorians maintains a bi-partisan appeal regardless of the ruling party.

Many new members of the CSE regard the emphasis on state politics as a major limiting factor, and consider that they should focus further on more localised problems and in rural areas. Government officials will leave every four years, they argue, but teachers will stay in their position a lot longer, and the CSE should therefore work more out of the classroom. The difficult relationship between the UNE and the CSE stands in the way of this thought however. Although the teachers unions are one of the most important groups in education, they do not participate in the activities of the CSE, which has lead to the two groups frequently talking at cross purposes.

The emphasis on national politics limits the regional and global relationships of the CSE as well. Even though the CSE is part of international coalitions such as CLADE and the Global Campaign for Education, the amount of contact is very sporadic. The influence of the CSE in society could increase when these alliances improve, as can their financial means and their knowledge.

In Ecuador there is still much inequality between different sectors in society regarding the access and quality in education. The goal of a social movement such as the *Contrato Social por la Educación* to universalize education within the country can therefore make a big difference. Hopefully, over time, the CSE can contribute to change Ecuadorian society by ensuring equal opportunities in life by promoting a high quality education for all.

FELICE VAN DER PLAAT

CHAPTER 5

Striving for Education for All in Ghana: the role and impact of the Ghana National Education Campaign Coalition

INTRODUCTION

This chapter analyses the history, development, context, strategies, actions and impact of the Ghana National Education Campaign Coalition (GNECC). GNECC functions as a civil society coalition, institutionalized in 1999 to advocate for the achievement of universal quality and enjoyable basic education for all in Ghana. It is one of the first national coalitions of the Global Campaign for Education (GCE) and it has played an active role in conferences and workshops from the GCE and the African Network Coalition for Education for All (ANCEFA). Because Ghana's democracy has only been fully in action for the last two decades, it is a fascinating country to conduct research in on the impact of civil society actors. The constitution that was reborn on January 7, 1993 opened the way for human rights improvements, media freedom and for a more liberal economic environment in Ghana. Since 2001 there has been a significant improvement in the quality of governance in Ghana, especially concerning transparency within governmental affairs, voice and accountability. Furthermore, there is more space for an independent civil society and the government has become more responsive to their voices (Gyimah-Boadi, 2004). The establishment of GNECC thus fits within a democratic Ghana where the voices of civil society are valued by the national government. Furthermore, it fits in an era where civil society is asking for poverty reduction and accountability from its government and where it tries to improve these conditions in cooperation with other actors.

This chapter looks into the history of education and of state/civil society relationships in Ghana, with a focus on the role of GNECC, the internal structure of the coalition, strategies and mission. Subsequently, the impacts of the coalition are analysed by looking at a specific campaign carried out between 2005 and 2009. Finally, the coalition's impact at procedural, political and symbolic levels is reviewed.

The fieldwork for this research took place from February to May 2009, followed by a workshop in July 2009, which was organized with the coalition to reflect upon the findings of the research and to obtain new insights. The majority of the fieldwork took place in Accra, but several interviews were also held in Ghana's different regions with regional and district members. Data was obtained through semi-structured interviews with coalition members, media outlets, government

Antoni Verger and Mario Novelli (eds.), Campaigning for "Education for All", 65–82.

officials, GNECC's partners and the donor community. These were complemented by participatory observation of the day to day activities of GNECC and a critical review of policy and academic literature which was undertaken during the period of research.

COUNTRY CONTEXT

Prior to Ghana's independence in 1957, the education system was managed through colonial missionaries (Kadingdi, 2007). After independence, the education sector was handed over to the newly formed post-colonial government led by Ghana's first President, Kwame Nkrumah. In 1960, fee-free compulsory primary and middle school education were introduced. Nkrumah's vision on the use of education was unmistakable: to reduce poverty through increased economic productivity stemming from the development of education in Ghana (Akyeampong, 2007). In this period, Ghana's education system was considered to be one of the most developed and effective in West Africa (Foster, 1965) but by the 1980s it was in near collapse and unable to reach the many goals of the country (Peil, 1995).

The 1990's came with some promising changes. With the new constitution of 1993, education once again became very prominent on the government's agenda (Rolleston, 2007). Achieving universal primary education and gender parity became a legal requirement from that date onwards. To deliver on these promises, the Government of Ghana launched the Free Compulsory Basic Education Program (FCUBE) in 1996, which promised free universal basic education for all by the year 2005. FCUBE intended to abolish school fees with the purpose of increasing the school enrolment levels country wide (Thompson and Casely-Hayford, 2008). Although FCUBE was accompanied by great donor support for primary education projects in Ghana and major improvements primarily in terms of access to education were made, free basic education is yet to be realized.

The government continued working towards its overall goal by developing new policies and signing international agreements such as the Education for All (EFA) goals and the Millennium Development Goals (MDGs). In 2003 the Ministry of Education, Science and Sports (MoESS) launched the first Education Strategic Plan (ESP) 2003-2015 to facilitate realization of the goals that are spelled out in the EFA goals and in MDG 2 (Government of Ghana, 2003). The ESP functioned as a long-term plan to provide a strategic framework to ensure the development of the education sector until 2015 (Government of Ghana, 2003). It formed the basis for a Sector Wide Approach (SWAP) for education sector development arranging partnership and joint responsibility between the MoESS and all development partners. In 2007 a revised version of the ESP was launched. The Government furthermore developed the Growth and Poverty Reduction Strategy paper (GPRS) I and II that are intended for realizing the MDGs and to accelerate the growth of the economy of Ghana in order to become a middle-income economy. (Government of Ghana, 2005) The right to basic education is prominently presented in the GPRS papers. In GPRS I, the government aimed to equalize access by providing six-years of mandatory education, for all children up to the age of 12 years (Government of Ghana, 2003b). In GPRS II, it is stated that EFA should be obligatory for children between the ages of 4 until 15. Hence the government almost doubled the years that children are required to go to school. This was reinforced by the Education Act of 2007 (Government of Ghana, 2007). Furthermore, while in GPRS I the government primarily focus on providing access for children to go to school, GPRS II focuses on improving the quality of the curriculum, school buildings and facilities, teachers and the standards of literacy and numeracy.

STRUCTURE OF EDUCATION SECTOR AND IDENTIFIED PROBLEMS

Access to quality education is not only viewed as a global human right, but also as an important tool to facilitate long-term national development, poverty reduction and a necessary process to improve the quality of life for individual citizens (MoESS, 2003). Despite these aspirations, there are a number of prevalent problems, which can broadly be characterized as such: access to and quality of education. Meaningful access to education requires more than enrolment; it entails high attendance rates, progression with little or no repetition, and learning outcomes that prove that the pupils master the necessary skills. When looking at access it is thus also important to look at what type of service pupils have access to as well as their educational outcomes (CREATE, 2008). The most common tools used to express access to education are the Gross Enrolment Rates (GER) and the Net Enrolment Rates (NER).[13] According to the EFA goals and the educational policies of the MoESS, in 2015 all school-aged children should be enrolled. As is shown in Table 5.1, the GER of Ghana in 2007 for primary education was 95.2%; for Junior Secondary School it was 78.8%; 93.8% respectively in Ghana as a whole; and 65.3% in the deprived districts. The NER was 83.4% for primary education and 53% for JSS in Ghana as a whole, and for the deprived districts it was 77.9% and 43.8%. In 2007 Ghana had almost a million children of school-age out of school, while over 4.1 million children were enrolled in primary and JSS education (Ampiah and Adu-Yeboah, 2009). The lack of access to education can be attributed to several factors. Firstly, poverty continues to be a hindrance to children of school going age, especially since the indirect costs of education are not eliminated. Secondly, traditions concerning gender result in less girl-child enrollment rates. Other factors that contribute to lack of access of education for children include: distance to schools, teacher absenteeism, and insufficient schooling opportunities for disabled children. Furthermore, the fact that child labour continues to be an issue in Ghana is an extra tragic impediment.

---

[13] The primary NER is the share of children of primary school age that are enrolled in primary school. The GER is a related indicator. The primary Gross Enrolment Rates indicates how many children, regardless of their age, are enrolled in primary school, relative to the population of primary school age.

Table 5.1. Education sector statistics 2007 (source: MOESS, 2008)

	National	Deprived Districts
Adult literacy rate	61,7	
Gender parity at primary level	0,96	
Gender parity at Junior High School (JHS)	0,92	
% of trained teachers at primary level	42,9	37,2
% of trained teachers at JHS	76,4	62,9
Gross Enrolment Rates (GER) primary level	95,2	93,8
GER JHS	78,8	65,3
Net Enrolment Rates (NER) Primary Level	83,4	77,9
NER JHS	53	43,8
Primary Pupil Teacher Ratio	34,1: 1	38:1
Secondary Pupil Teacher Ratio	17,4:1	18.9:1
Pass rate BECE	63	49% (2006)
Completion Rate Primary	88	81,4
Completion Rate JHS	67,7	54

Despite this great number of out of school children, access has increased since the mid 1990s. Unfortunately, the quality of education did not improve simultaneously (Interview Key-observer03, 2009). The majority of public schools lack sufficient and adequate classrooms, sanitary facilities, teaching materials and electricity. Furthermore, the professionalism and availability of teachers is a huge problem. As a result, students are unable to obtain a satisfactory level in basic literacy, numeracy and social studies. This results in students being insufficiently equipped to move to Senior High School levels of learning (MoESS, 2003).

Another problem is the UNEQUAL opportunities between public and private schools. Facilities are generally less developed in public schools, unlike private schools, where children enjoy more hours of schooling and private school pupils start with schooling in English from the moment they enter the education system (Interview Member05, 2009). As a result, pupils from private schools perform much better at the Basic Education Certificate Exam than children from public schools (see Table 5.1).

STATE/ CIVIL SOCIETY RELATIONSHIP

Since the Constitution of 1993 the relationship between civil society and the state in Ghana has improved remarkably. Their interaction has evolved from limited contact until the beginning of the 1990s to enhanced inclusion and participation. This improved interaction is most notable in increasing representation of civil society in public bodies, in government meetings and decision-making processes; as well as improved information sharing between the state and civil society and vice versa. The government also proves that it recognizes the importance of civil society by attending events organized by CSOs, publishing civil society press statements on its website, and by recruiting officers that work primarily with civil society. In an attempt to exhibit's its commitment, the Ministry of Education recruited an officer whose main responsibility is to collaborate with GNECC.

Improvements have taken place at district, regional and national levels of governance (Darkwa et al, 2006). A Professor and the former Director General for Education in Ghana agreed that Ghana has moved towards becoming more responsive towards civil society inclusion during the past decade:

> 'Ghana is now more democratic than it used to be. A space for dialogue has opened for civil society. They pushed the perspective that government should consult civil society organizations and that they have a role to play. In the education sector the GNECC is the most effective (coalition) among the non-union based civil society organizations' (Interview Key-observer01, 2009).

There are several factors that can be linked to the improved participation and recognition of the role of civil society in Ghana. Firstly, the 1993 Constitution of the Republic of Ghana provides space for CSO engagement in advocacy in the media, lobbying with governmental bodies and participation in stakeholder meetings. Secondly, initiatives such as the GPRS I and II and the ESP give way for participation and inclusion of CSOs in the policy-making processes. They promote responsiveness from the government towards civil society advocacy to bring about public change (Ahadzie, 2007). Thirdly, donors are progressively requesting to include civil society in decision-making processes (Interview Key-observer03, 2009). A fourth contributing factor is that over the past decade, civil society in Ghana has moved its focus from primarily implementing activities, to the foundation of a number of strong research and advocacy-based organizations and coalitions. The outputs and activities of these organizations have been relevant to the public policy processes in Ghana, including considerable participation in national policy-making (Ahadzie, 2007). For civil society to be successful in Ghana it seems to be important to be complementary to the government, to base their campaigns on evidence from the ground and to advocate with the government (Interview Policy-maker01, 2009).

Although civil society participation has been steadily growing, it is important to highlight some factors that hinder the opportunities for civil society participation in Ghana, namely: poverty, the lack of information and technology infrastructure, economic and social crises, and pervasive adult literacy are all notable limitations to a functioning Ghanaian civil society (Darkwa et al, 2006). Furthermore, civil society engagement in politics is not equally spread and efficient, active engagement is limited to the top-end urban based civil society groups (Ahadzie, 2007).

HISTORY AND STRATEGIC DEVELOPMENT OF GNECC

Ghana's major civil society voice in education is the Ghana National Education Campaign Coalition. GNECC was established in 1999, shortly before the World Education Forum in Dakar (2000) and was also one of the first organizations to join the Global Campaign for Education. The rationale behind its constitution was to obtain a stronger unified voice on education in Ghana by building strategic partnerships between the different civil society actors, social movements, nongovernmental organizations and teacher unions. Before GNECC came into being the different CSOs on education had a piecemeal and individualistic approach to education development. By uniting as a coalition they sought to strengthen their voice and work towards achieving a common agenda.

When GNECC first started, the coalition neither had a defined structure nor a constitution. In the first years, the coalition was hosted in the office of a member organization, and there was no secretariat in place that dealt with the daily business of the coalition. During this period the bulk of the coalition's time was spent fostering governmental commitment toward achieve the EFA goals, and the campaigning of GNECC was rather small scale. 2005 however, was a milestone in the history of the coalition. In this year, an organizational assessment took place to review its functioning and to provide suggestions for improvement. Its chief outcome was that the coalition became a legally registered body, with a constitution, a General Assembly, an Executive Council, regional bodies, and a functioning national secretariat that dealt with the coalition's day-to-day business. Subsequently, GNECC designed a three-year Strategic Plan for 2006-2009 and, based on this Plan, annual programs and quarterly reports could be designed. Additionally, from 2005 annual audits took place to improve the accountability and transparency of the coalition. The restructuring of GNECC bore fruit, because it not only grew its membership significantly, but it was also able to attract more funding. Then it became clear that the GNECC improved its institutions and organization structures. This led to enhanced partnership between the coalition and donors such as the Commonwealth Education Fund, Oxfam Great Britain, Oxfam Novib and Action-aid. Additionally, since its reformation the membership base of the GNECC has been steadily growing (GNECC, workshop, July 2009).

At the time of the research, the GNECC, together with its counterpart from the three Northern regions of Ghana, the Northern Network for Education (NNED), is comprised of over 200 members spread throughout Ghana's 10 regions. The members are interested and engaged in the promotion of the right to quality basic education for all (EFA), and is comprised of a diverse array of individuals, registered civil society organizations, NGOs, faith-based organizations, research institutes and grassroots organizations. The members form the General Assembly, which is the highest decision making body of the coalition. The General Assembly meets annually, each time in a different region to evaluate and review the activities, projects and actions of the GNECC of the previous year.

The Executive Council is the main executing and governing body of the coalition. It consists of fifteen members: ten members are regional chairpersons from the ten regions and the other five elected members are the chairperson, the vice chairperson, the treasurer, the national coordinator as an Ex-Officio member, and one representative of the Disability Network. The fifteen elected members should be representative of the coalition in terms of background, gender, expertise and experience. The Executive Council is responsible to the General Assembly and its main task is to initiate the policies, project, programs, rules and regulations of the GNECC; to endorse work plans and prepare the budgets and accounts of the coalition; to recruit and monitor the secretariat staff; to ensure that collaboration is maintained with relevant government departments and with strategic alliances and other suitable networks. Finally the Executive Council has general responsibility over the coalition's finances, documents and correspondences.

The National Secretariat deals with the daily business and management of the GNECC and is headed by the national coordinator. It is accountable to the EC, and is also responsible for raising funds for the GNECC. Furthermore, the secretariat implements, co-ordinates and monitors programs and activities of the GNECC. Therefore the secretariat is also busy with collaborating, networking creating and maintaining close contacts with strategic allies such as: government offices, local governments, international networks and donors.

Crucial components of the GNECC are its regional secretariats and District Education for All Teams. These regional committees are in charge of the day-to-day business of the regions. The regions all have their own regional coordinator, chairperson, vice-chairperson, accountant and regional members, which reach out to the different districts. Decentralization is crucial for the functioning of GNECC. As the regional chairperson for the Greater Accra Region states:

'Decentralization is a key aspect for the coalition and local research could not exist without the regional teams. When research is to be done on the local level, I would call on members from my districts to go to the communities. These local researchers speak the language, are familiar with the people and they have contacts to conduct the research successfully. (Interview Member05, 2009)'

The establishment of regional committees handed the GNECC an opportunity to obtain specific local knowledge and to design programs that fit local conditions. The regions and districts are in charge of budget tracking and they share their research findings with the national office and with regional governmental bodies (Interview Secretariat02, 2009). The national secretariat then uses their input for their evidence-based reports and campaigns. Using evidence from the field increases the voice of the coalition significantly during policy dialogue, because they can actually document what the local situations in the education sector are.

STRATEGIC DIRECTION AND PARTNERSHIPS

The philosophy of the GNECC is that education is a fundamental human right and key to breaking the cycle of poverty. In order to fulfil the right of each Ghanaian to access high quality education, free education, the coalition works toward changing attitudes and practices in Ghanaian policy elites. The coalition uses several strategies to achieve this goal. Its main strategy is analysing policies, identifying gaps in the policies and demonstrating these shortcomings by conducting research in the different regions and pointing out which errors in the education system exist. The results are then put into reports, which are issued to the government through press releases, evidence-based campaigning, through engaging in policy meetings, and through direct dialogue with the relevant governance figures. Budget tracking and monitoring the implementation of policies is another key strategy of the coalition. A further tactic of GNECC is networking with relevant partners, such as research institutes and donors and engaging in relevant campaigns of other stakeholders. An important campaign in which the coalition engaged is the Violence Against Girls campaign, initiated by ActionAid in 2008. By aligning to this nation-wide campaign, GNECC was able to receive resources, to engage in policy dialogue and to strengthen its relationship with ActionAid, which is one of its key donors. Networking and collaborating with like-minded organizations are key strategies to increase civil society voice and advocacy.

Collaborating with the press is another vital strategy of the coalition. Throughout the years GNECC has established an excellent working relationship with the media in Ghana and they have been requested to speak on education issues as the voice of civil society in the press. At the start of a campaign, the coalition released a press release that was depicted on the national TV, radio and in the newspapers. Furthermore, every three months the GNECC publishes a tabloid called the *Education Agenda* within the newspaper called the Public Agenda. The Public Agenda is a key partner of the GNECC, and approximately every two weeks it publishes a section about the coalition and its work (Interview Secretariat04, 2009). Common media attention is especially strong in the period shortly before and during the Global Action Week and during governmental elections.

Partnering is one of the main strategies of GNECC. Through collaborating with local and global partners GNECC can rely on a global support base to help them meet their goals. Partnering with the GCE and other allies can also cause a 'boomerang effect' (when national civil society actors liaise with transnational actors to achieve goals in their own country) for the GNECC (Keck and Sikkink 1998).

The coalition's main international partners are:

- The Global Campaign for education (GCE): The GCE works as a space that acts as a catalyst for frame alignment between the different national coalitions, which is something that increases the voice of the movement as a whole. Through the GNECC's partnership and membership with the GCE they have been able to increase their status and fame internationally, through participating in international meetings and advocating their work globally.
- The Africa Network Coalition for Education for All (ANCEFA): ANCEFA is the regional branch of the GCE. The coalition participates actively in their workshops and activities. Also, the annual event of the Global Action Week ensures that GNECC hits the news.
- World University Services Canada (WUSC): the GNECC has a working relationship with this Canadian university, which provides the coalition with students to intern with them and to help the coalition to build its capacity.

INTERNAL COHESION

It could be expected that a coalition with a membership base of 200 members would experience some internal tensions. It is not always easy to agree on shared goals and strategies when there are so many different members with different interests. Currently, the majority of the members of GNECC are teachers, largely due to the involvement of the different Teacher Unions of Ghana in GNECC and to teachers' strategic role in public education systems. The Unions have a strong voice within the coalition and teachers' specific perceptions on education influence the vision of the coalition (Secretariat02, Accra, March 2009). The secretariat is responsible for ensuring that, in their programming, no one group of members dominates, but that the EFA goals remain central (Interview Key-observer07, 2009).

Start-up issues

In the period between 1999 and 2005, when the GNECC was not formally structured and hosted within one of the member organizations, power was very much centralized within a few organizations. Without a formal written constitution people could hijack the coalition and pursue their own agenda. There was also a lack of accountability and transparency at stake. The formal institution of the GNECC and its legal constitution in 2005 improved the internal cohesion significantly. The constitution provided a space for every organization to function and to be involved. One commonly heard complaint however is that the constitution is nowadays out-dated. The power division between the different levels of the coalition (local, regional and national) and between the different bodies of the coalition (the Executive Council, the National Secretariat and the General Assembly) as defined by the constitution has led to new power struggles that take place both between the local level and the national level, and even more obviously between the EC and the national secretariat.

The national versus the regional level

Within the GNECC constitution, there are guarantees that every region in Ghana has a say in the coalition. Every region is represented at the Executive Council, and the regions and district teams tend to be fully involved in advocacy, campaigning and in engaging with the media and the Ghana Education Service. There are however differences in levels of activity between the different regions, some are highly involved while others are less involved. This is not only to be blamed on the commitment of the members, but also of the lack of resources available for the region's activities. The regions are dependent on the national secretariat for funding. The fact that money flows from the national to the local level makes their relationship one that is top- down (Interview Member05, 2009). Some of the constraints include a delay in the transfers of funds for projects or regional meetings, and the simple fact that the national secretariat can decide not to fund a certain project. As a consequence, regions may feel that the national level is not responsive to their needs and that they are centralizing all the money for national concerns (Interview Member03, 2009).

Relations between the secretariat and the Executive Council

Another issue is the power division between the Executive Council (specifically the chairperson) and the national secretariat. It is important that both parties join forces in the interest of the coalition and do not hinder the other parties work. However, the secretariat sometimes experiences that the Executive Council does not carry out its responsibilities timely. For example, money can only be signed off when both the chairperson and the treasury provided signatures. When one of them is out of the country this hinders the execution of campaigns for example. Furthermore, a complaint from the secretariat is that the division of tasks between the Executive Council and the national secretariat is not well defined (Interview Secretariat01, 2009). For some activities it is unclear if the secretariat should be responsible, or if the chairperson, vice chairperson or treasurer should do it. This is for example the case with attending government and donor meetings. As stated by an official of the Ministry of Education, the representative of the GNECC needs to be highly knowledgeable, confident and he needs to possess great lobbying and negotiation skills to be a supportive part of the meetings. An employee of IBIS believes that the position of the chairperson is too much a position of power (Interview Donor03, 2009). The constitution gives him a powerful position, while he is not involved in the day to day functioning of the GNECC. This sentiment is well encapsulated by one comment of the national program officer of the GNECC:

'The position of the chairman is more or less a position of a monarch. So if we have a chairman who is not level-headed, who does not understand development and the developmental needs of the coalition and reduces its power to parochial petty interests, this can be dangerous. A revision of the constitution and the role of the chairman should be discussed at the Annual Assembly. The national coordinator should have more power. (Interview Secretariat02, 2009)'

A suggestion prompted by most working groups during the workshop (GNECC, Workshop, July 2009) was to revise the constitution and to make a clearer division between the roles of the secretariat and the Executive Council and chairperson in general. By doing this, the members hope to improve the working relationship of the EC and the secretariat and to improve the unified voice of the coalition when campaigning for policy change.

CAMPAIGNING FOR EFA: THE CAPITATION GRANT

Since 1999, GNECC has been involved in several campaigns striving for the achievement of the different EFA goals in Ghana. In this section the 'Capitation Grant' campaign is highlighted, which aimed to achieve truly fee-free basic education for all in Ghana. The coalition started campaigning for the establishment of the Capitation Grant in 2005, and their efforts were quickly followed by the enactment of the Capitation Grant in Ghana, which allows the government to allocate funds to schools per student. The idea behind this is to make education more affordable for families by limiting or diminishing the costs that parents contribute to their children's education. GNECC advocated heavily for the establishment of this grant and, when the grant was put into being in 2005, the coalition started to monitor the implementation as well as advocating for a further increase of the amount given per child.

Problem identification

The Government of Ghana dedicated itself in 1996 to achieving Free Compulsory Universal Basic Education by 2005. The hard reality, ten years after the launch of the FCUBE programme, was that this goal of universal coverage and free basic education remained unachieved. According to a report of the Core Welfare Indicators Questionnaire for 2003, 25% of children between ages 6-17 dropped out of school because of the cost of education (GNECC, 2005). According to GNECC, lacking access to education is a principal challenge in Ghana affecting the wellbeing of its population as well as the country as a whole, which should be tackled accordingly. Without any changes, GNECC envisioned that the government would not only fail to achieve Free Compulsory Universal Basic Education, but it would also keep lagging behind on achieving the MDGs as well as the EFA goals. One way of making education more accessible to students is by diminishing the costs of schooling. Before the Capitation Grant was put into being in 2005, the government worked with an alternative cost-sharing scheme to cover non-tuition fees that was included in the FCUBE program in 1996. This first initiative did not work as well as the government planned. The main reason why a persistent amount of children remained out of school was because parents could not afford the levies charged by certain schools. Levies are used by schools to get finances for school repairs and activities. Poor families in particular were unable to send their children, particularly girls, to school. According to GNECC, this situation could be improved by providing a sufficient amount of money per pupil to schools, so as to ensure that education was truly free for students by limiting the amount of indirect costs that families need to pay. The government introduced the Capitation Grant in 2005, allowing each school to receive 3 Ghana Cedi (2 US$) per child. However according to the coalition, a further increase of the grant would be needed to ensure all indirect costs of schooling would be covered by the government.

Problem attribution

The coalition believes that the prime stakeholder responsible for getting children into school and completing quality education is the government. Therefore, GNECC holds the government responsible for ensuring that parents do not have to cover any costs for basic education. GNECC asked the government for the Capitation Grant to be put into public schools so as to ensure equal opportunities and access to education for children across the country. Furthermore, after the government introduced its first version of the Capitation Grant in 2005, which promised that schools would receive 3 Ghana Cedi per child per school year, the coalition kept tracking whether this amount of 2 US$ per pupil would actually lead to fee free education. As stated by GNECC in a press release in 2005:

It is in this context that we pat the back of Government for deciding to pay capitation grants to cover fees for public basic schools. The purpose, it must be understood, is to remove user-fees, which have become a barrier to many poor families and communities. (GNECC, 2005)

Once education is truly free of costs for families and children are still out of school, the coalition sought other issues to be tackled. GNECC identified a wide range of economic, social, physical and cultural aspects that hinder children from attending education. Examples of these are: distance to school, teen pregnancies, sanitary facilities at school, child labour, and the quality of education (Interview Member05, 2009). GNECC is concerned with all these issues, but their first concern is to make education truly fee-free, so that the other broader issues can be dealt with.

Motivational framing

The coalition believes that when school fees are abolished and schools are provided with sufficient money to cover all the indirect costs of education, access as well as enrolment rates will increase. Education is seen by the coalition to be a prime tool for allowing people to overcome poverty and it is therefore unfortunate that especially poor children cannot access education because of expenses that are related to enrolling. The indirect costs for education especially hinder girls' access to education (Interview Member05, 2009). After the introduction of the Capitation Grant in 2005, enrolment rates for primary and basic schools increased and the enlargement was even more visible in poorer regions and among girls (Adamu-Issa et al, 2007). However, GNECC believed that a grant of three Ghana Cedi per child would still be too little to eliminate all indirect education costs, and decided to track the results of the Grant as well as to advocate for a further increase. The coalition believed that such an increase could be validated when comparing the amount to the amount that neighbouring countries were contributing to schools per student. Other countries in West-Africa were spending between five and ten Cedi per student. According to the coalition, the Government of Ghana should follow their example.

Main strategies

In order to establish an increase of the amount of money allotted per pupil through the Capitation Grant, GNECC used several strategies. Firstly, the coalition conducted research in several districts about the possible impact of the grant, and they did budget tracking on the Capitation Grant in more than 400 schools in the ten different regions (GNECC, 2009II). The District Education for All Teams were responsible for the tracking of the Grant, and the district members involved were trained on how to do budget tracking with funds made available by the WUSC

(GNECC, 2008b). What came forward from the research was that the grant of 3 Ghana Cedi, fell short of the actual user-fees payments in many districts. For example, in the Dangbe East, user-fees at the primary level were ¢37 Ghana Cedi per annum and at the JSS level, ¢72 per annum. GNECC concluded that the introduction of the Capitation Grant would not cover all fees, and would therefore not remove the cost barrier that many poor families are confronted with.

One powerful strategy used by the coalition in elevating government awareness of the difficulties that poor families face if they have to pay school fees was their 'Back to School Campaign'. During this campaign the GNECC stimulated government officials to go back to school, providing the children an opportunity to explain how much money they still had to pay over and above the grant in order to attend school, and the problems that arose as a result of this. Through the campaign politicians gained direct experience of the situation the children face in their classrooms and moreover, the children could explain which other difficulties they endure at school. Finally, the coalition used the opportunity to draw attention to the legal agreements the government has signed, which promised the achievement of fee-free basic education. Throughout the campaign media pressure was also used to convince the government of the importance of the capitation grant, and the right to fee free education. Subsequently, in the monthly Development Partners Meetings, the GNECC advocated for a 200% increase of the grant at the ESAR of 2008. Eventually, the grant was increased by 150%. This increase might seem impressive, but according to GNECC, not much has changed due to rising inflation rate (GNECC 2008c).

Outcome

GNECC advocated heavily for the introduction and further increase of the Capitation Grant by 150%. It received plenty of media attention for the topic, which helped bringing the Grant to the agenda of the government. The coalition was able to contribute to the discussion around the Grant both in the public and in the governmental arena, through giving press releases and by stimulating dialogue with the responsible officials within government. Both benchmarks of the introduction and further increase of the grant were eventually achieved and the coalition rightly took a share of the success in this. The government acknowledged the important role of the GNECC in tracking the grant, as well as advocating for it (Interview Policy-maker01, 2009).

Even though these two successes were achieved, GNECC considers them to be minor steps forward to achieving the EFA goals. Many hurdles are yet to be taken and the coalition continues to advocate for a further increase of the Grant to make education truly fee-free.

DISCUSSING THE COALITION'S IMPACT

As we have seen, the GNECC has gone through several stages since its creation in 1999 and it also had several impacts on the education sector in Ghana. This section will explore the three dimensions of this impact, namely: the procedural, political and symbolic successes of GNECC.

Procedural impact

The coalition has managed to become the prime-negotiating partner from civil society with the government of Ghana. It is interacting in various ways with the Ministry of Education and Ghana Education Service at national level and through its regional and district teams it works with local governance structures. According to an officer of the Ministry of Education, the input of the GNECC is recognized and valued:

> 'We believe in the work the GNECC does. We have to check and be sure that they keep feeding us with the right information; we have our own men on the ground doing this. But we respect all the input the GNECC gives to us, and we use it for our decision-making (Interview Policy-maker03, 2009).'

The appreciation of the MoESS of the participation of GNECC in the education sector becomes clear from the fact that it has recruited an Assistant Planning Officer and Coordinator, whose main task is harmonizing the coalition's activities with the government activities. The officer has good connections with the national secretariat of the GNECC and they share information on regular basis (Interview Policy-maker02, 2009).

According to an evaluation done by the Commonwealth Education Fund, the government recognizes the GNECC as important policy partners, which is demonstrated by the fact that they are invited to play an advisory role at the different meetings at the Ministry of Education (CEF, 2009). Some of these meetings are: the Education Sector Annual Review, the Monthly Development Partners Meeting, the Technical Group Meetings, Education Sector Thematic Advisory Committees (ESTAC), and their cooperation with the Parliamentary Select Committee on Education (GNECC, 2008c).

The government has come to rely, at least partly, on the research findings of the GNECC to get to know what is happening on the ground. For research findings from specific deprived districts they depend largely on the GNECC as reliable evidence based advocacy coalition. The status that the GNECC has obtained at governmental level helps the coalition to attract more funding. As explained by the Education Officer of Actionaid:

> 'Because of the status that the GNECC obtained as an advocacy coalition on education, it is only wise for Actionaid to work with the GNECC. The advocacy that GNECC does is informed by research; the facts are clear and provable. The information is picked directly from the ground. Even the Ministries listen when the GNECC speaks. The GNECC has grown significantly over the past years, they got more organizations and individuals involved who are knowledgeable in the education sector. The voice of the GNECC is accepted by the government. And if Actionaid would not work with the GNECC, it would weaken the voice of civil society organizations on

education. Thus we should cooperate, to not fight within one house, but to create shared goals and statements (Interview Donor05, 2009).'

It is important for the GNECC to keep their positive image, to stay on top of things and to function as the watchdog of the government. Should the coalition falter, they could easily lose their position as the voice of civil society for education in Ghana. An often-heard complaint from the government and donors is that GNECC does not always attend all the monthly meetings at the Ministry of Education, and their credibility among government officials was weakening because of this (Gov01, Accra, March 2009). Or as the director of the Ministry of Education of the Policy, Budgeting, Monitoring and Evaluation Division states:

'We want to promote participation and inclusion of civil society. The GNECC has thus no problem to have their voice heard. The only challenge I see is that the GNECC has to engage more. They have to come and talk to government people, create a learning environment, come face to face with the government, discuss. Sometimes the GNECC does not even come to the meetings. If you do not come to the meetings you cannot blame anybody. If you do not come to the meetings then you do not see how the discussions go. You cannot just complain about the system without engaging (Interview Policy-maker01, 2009).'

In this regard, the case of GNECC is exceptional in the sense that, currently, the coalition does not have to lobby the government for recognition and for being invited in official meetings. The situation is rather quite the opposite and the government is the one asking the civil society coalition to participate more actively in education policy processes.

Political impact

The political impact of the GNECC is dependent on how well they have been able to impose changes in the educational regulations and policies in Ghana. As with all political processes, there is always a variety of actors involved that stimulate policy change to happen and the particular role of GNECC is difficult to isolate. However, the policy changes explained below have been preceded by GNECC's extensive campaigning. Moreover, not only representatives of the coalition, but also government officials and donors acknowledge that GNECC input was accounted for when it came to carry out the policy changes in question (Interview Policy-maker01, 2009).

According to a government official (Interview Policy-maker03, 2009), the role of civil society is especially important when it comes to agenda setting:

'Civil society influences governments by issuing reports. It gets to the government and officers look at these reports and at the issues raised. It helps shaping our perspectives on issues and it helps shaping our policy directions. They are on the ground and they help us to identify what is happening on the ground. Thus they help us in shaping policy.'

One of the most noteworthy policy changes that have occurred after campaigning of the coalition is the introduction of the Capitation Grant, as highlighted earlier. Another major event was the passing of the Education Act in 2008. In 2008 GNECC and the Northern Network for Educational Development joined forces to advocate for the passing of the new Education Bill, before the end of the Kufuor Administration. The Education Act had been at the cabinet level for consideration for over two years already and the coalition did not see any effort from the government to pass the bill (GNECC, 2008). Parliamentary elections were about to be held, and if the bill had not passed before the elections, the coalition believed it could have detrimental effects on the progress of the education sector (NNED01, Tamale, April 2009). At the Education Sector Annual Review the coalition issued a statement on why the bill should be passed, and which aspects of the education sector in Ghana would be improved through accepting the act (GNECC, 2008). Moreover, the coalitions issued position papers and sent their thoughts out through the media. The GNECC presented its statements to the Ministry of Education and they asked from the government to spell out clearly what Free Basic Education means to them. Eventually the Education Act was accepted just before the elections took place (Interview Secretariat01, 2009).

Over the years, GNECC has also advocated heavily for several policy changes concerning teachers. The majority of the coalition members are teachers, which makes this one of the prime subjects on the coalition's agenda. The coalition has successfully advocated for the increase of salaries of teachers who work in rural and deprived areas. A research done by GNECC for the Global Action Week of 2008 showed a 20% raise in teachers' salaries was needed in order to adequately incentivize those working in deprived areas (GNECC, 2008). The GNECC used various strategies to convince the government of their plans, such as the issuing of a position paper, involving the media and publishing their findings in the quarterly edition of the Education Agenda within the newspaper the Public Agenda, and presenting its findings at the ESAR. Eventually, the government included the 20% extra payment in their 2009 budget (Government of Ghana, 2009: 156). Two other policy changes concerning teachers that occurred after fierce campaigning by the GNECC were: the increase of allowances for headmasters and the introduction of tax rebates for teacher salaries. These changes occurred after a similar campaign by the GNECC (Interview Secretariat01, 2009).

Symbolic impact

GNECC does not only want to influence the government and national and international educational policies, but they also try to make the people of Ghana aware of their struggle for EFA as well as raising awareness amongst communities as to their educational rights. When the Capitation Grant was adopted by the government, GNECC and NNED mobilized their District Education for All Teams to organize focus groups to teach communities and teachers about the rights they get through these pieces of legislation. Educational legislation is often too technical or too distant for locals to understand, which frequently means that communities remain unaware of their standing with the law and the District EFA Teams are trained to explain the policies clearly (Interview Member07, 2009). Furthermore, the GNECC strives to win the attention of the media for their case and they try to have their vision and frames portrayed in the national and local media. Over the years the coalition has developed a strong relationship with several local and national media entities in Ghana, such as The Public Agenda, which helps the coalition significantly in spreading their work. The symbolic impact of the coalition is therefore also noteworthy.

CONCLUSION

For more than a decade now, the Ghana National Education Campaign Coalition has fought for the educational rights of the citizens of its country. What started out as a small coalition counting on a few organizations, developed to become Ghana's biggest and most appreciated representative for civil society on educational issues. GNECC has created a strong threshold in Ghana and is invited to all important government meetings on education to represent civil society. The GNECC has been able to achieve various political successes, such as the introduction of the Capitation Grant and the passing of the Education Bill in 2008. These policy changes were established through the interaction of various stakeholders in the education sector and GNECC is most certainly one actor that should not be overlooked. However, the influence of GNECC should also not be overestimated. As stated by a Coordinator of the Ministry of Education Sport and Science:

'The influence of the GNECC is more subtle. The government has competing priorities and limited resources. Civil societies always try to hammer on certain issues. They influence policies, but it has to fit with the strategies of the government (Interview Policy-maker03, 2009).'

The media has not only identified GNECC as being civil society's main spokesperson on education, but it has also partnered on several occasions with the coalition in bringing educational issues to the public attention. What makes the work of GNECC unique is that it has a strong local rooting and is able to carry out evidence-based research right from the ground, through its regional and district teams. Also, it has several international linkages that it makes use of, such as its engagement with the GCE. The main strengths of the coalition are the research it carries out, as well as its budget tracking and monitoring of government spending and policies. The coalition is most likely to find a listening ear at the Ministry of Education when it comes with evidence presented in reports or through campaigns.

The success of GNECC relies heavily on its internal structures, cohesion and stability. Bringing the message forward with one voice, through the right spokesperson has however been problematic. The relationship between the national secretariat and the executive council is not clear cut, which means that different people are often carrying out the same tasks. These frictions cause confusion and it makes the national secretariat feel that it cannot perform at its best. It is therefore important that the coalition makes a clearer division between the roles of the secretariat and of its executive council. Another issue is encouraging the commitment of members to engage in the work of the coalition. Most coalition members have a formal full-time job and some find it difficult to combine their role in GNECC with their official work.

Finding sufficient funding has also been a critical issue for GNECC. Without money, no research can be carried out and staff cannot be hired. For its political influence and campaigning the coalition relies heavily on its evidence based information and field surveys. For its sustainability, GNECC is constantly on the lookout for new sources of funding. Another issue related to funding is the dependence it creates towards donors. Although GNECC sets out its own vision and mission, the coalition often takes part in an earmarked donor in order to get funding. Donors have preferences and conditions that GNECC has to meet before the coalition receives funding. In this way the donors can influence the agenda and the annual plans of the coalition (Interview Member09, 2009).

An important internal achievement of the coalition is the strategic learning they have achieved throughout their evolution. The formal constitution of the GNECC in 2005 was an inflexion point for the coalition, leading to the adoption of different and new strategies to achieve their goals. The General Assembly that is supposed to take place every year is the perfect opportunity for the coalition members to reflect upon the past year and to design new approaches and plans for the future. Furthermore, the GNECC designs a three-year strategic plan and this gives them the opportunity to learn from their past experiences and to create fresh tactics. Strategic learning also takes place through reflection workshops and through writing the annual reports and audits. It has proven to be crucial for the coalition's success that it keeps critically reflecting on its context and own agency to make sure they create innovative ways forward to optimize its impact and, this way, enhance the education opportunities of all Ghanaian children.

LAURA GRANT

CHAPTER 6

National Coalition for Education India: The Second Freedom Struggle Against Illiteracy

INTRODUCTION

Education has always been accorded an honoured place in Indian society. The great leaders of the Indian freedom movement realized the fundamental role of education and throughout the nation's struggle for independence, stressed its unique significance for national development (National Policy on Education, 1968)

India is a rising super-power with a population of over one billion people, and while India is becoming globally competitive in information and communication technologies, business, and manufacturing, it still lags behind in terms of global education standards. With more than a third of its population below the age of 18, India has the largest child population in the world, with an estimated 65 to 85 million not attending school (Census 2001). Establishing a national campaign for education in India was a long process that began in 1996 with the *Bachpan Bachao Andolan* campaign "Education for Liberation and Liberation for Education." During this time several like-minded civil society organizations came together in recognition of the alarming education situation in India. After the *Bachpan Bachao Andolan* campaign, the National Campaign for Education (NCE) became the official representative of the Global Campaign for Education (GCE) in India, and vowed to make significant changes in the education system. The NCE is now a recognized civil society player for the betterment of education in India and has strong representation in the GCE. Along with many other organizations, the NCE strive to achieve Education for All (EFA).

In light of the World Education Conference in Jomtien (1990), education is a globally recognized need. At a local level however, the importance of education has been recognised since India's independence in 1947, specifically in Article 45 of their constitution. Since that time, the political and economic situation has vastly improved, affording the opportunity to get every child in school. With the 2002 93rd Constitutional Amendment making education a fundamental right, paired with the recently passed "Free and Compulsory Education Act 2009," (RTE Act, see Government of India 2009) the legal tools are now available to truly affect change in education in India. However, politically speaking, there is little focus on implementing the act and following through on their 60 year old promise of

Antoni Verger and Mario Novelli (eds.), Campaigning for "Education for All", 83–100.

universal education. At the executive level there is a persistent belief in the beneficial economic trickle-down effect of large scale infrastructure programs, and thus the government's primary focus is on large scale economic endeavours such as mines and dams, and the notion that the revenue garnered from such activities will eventually benefit the social sector has gone unchallenged (Behar and Prakash 2004). While the current government supports civil society efforts for education at a rhetorical level, education is yet to take a higher priority in terms of action (see CMP 2004).

This case study analyses the impact of the NCE in India, taking in factors such as interaction from local to global levels, negotiations on objectives, strategies, and internal and external power relations that have shown to be influential on its impact. The primary data consists of twenty semi-structured interviews with key people within the NCE, GCE, member organizations, academics, and other key informants that were conducted in August to November 2009 in New Delhi, India. Other data includes internal and external publications of the NCE, as well as government documents and media resources.

The following chapter is broken down into five sections. The first one discusses the country context with a focus on the political climate and the education situation. The second section discusses the origins, composition, and goals of the NCE, as well as its relations with other organizations at the supra-national level. The third section covers the collective action repertoires of the NCE and how it has changed through time. The fourth section discusses the political, procedural, and symbolic impact of the NCE. The final section lays out the main conclusions of this case study with lessons learned and recommendations.

Country Context

The Republic of India is located in South Asia. The population as of 2008 is over one billion, making it a significant global player by its size alone. India consists of 28 states and seven union territories with two national languages, Hindi and English, although many more unofficial languages exist. In 1947, India gained independence from the British, and is now the largest democracy in the world. India is remarkable in its conviction that its people are its greatest asset:

> In the Indian way of thinking, a human being is a positive asset and a precious national resource, which needs to be cherished, nurtured, and developed with tenderness, and care, coupled with dynamism. Each individual's growth presents a different range of problems and requirements, at every stage from the womb to the tomb. The catalytic action of education in this complex and dynamic growth process needs to be planned meticulously and executed with great sensitivity (National Policy on Education (1986), revised in 1992)

Even before independence in 1947, the government of India in 1944 prepared a 40-year education plan that promised to provide universal free and compulsory education to all citizens (Tilak 2009). The excerpt from legislation dating back to

1950 demonstrates the long legacy of the Indian government's public commitment to education:

> ... to provide within a period of 10 years from the commencement of the Constitution for free and compulsory education for all children until they complete the age of 14 years. (Article 45).

The majority of India's leaders, especially the first prime minister, Jawaharlal Nehru (1947-1964), agreed that strong economic growth and measures to increase incomes and consumption among the poorest groups were necessary goals for the new nation. This trend continued even through the implementation of the Washington Consensus period of the 1980's onwards, which further increased reliance on market forces for economic growth. This has been carried forward to the current government. However, the current government, despite the positive relationship that exists between education and economic growth (Psacharopoulos and Woodhall 1985), does not place education at the centre of the policy agenda (Rodrik 2006).

The Stigma of Public Education

While there has been an increased recognition of the importance of adequate education in the past decade, the public school system still carries the stigma of being an institution for those living in poverty. This is even true for many of the teachers in the teachers' unions who work within the public system while sending their own children to private institutions because of the poor perception of public facilities. For example, in an informal interview with a headmaster of a public elementary school in New Delhi, he insisted that because of infrastructural inadequacies and poor teacher training the only responsible choice was to send his children to a private school. This was difficult to fathom as the interview took place in his office at the school which had two buildings, a playground, and a full staff of qualified teachers.

The stigma against the education system is one of the main challenges faced by the NCE. The president of the NCE states that "...there has to be one common universal education system providing good quality education to the children" (Interview, September 2009). However, this is challenged by India's reality on the ground and the historically rooted elitism in Indian political culture that in effect resulted in the fragmentation of the education system and its governance.

The educational system is broken down between central government, state government, and local governing bodies, known as *panchayats* (a village council). The vast majority of responsibility for education is placed upon the state governments and local governing bodies, creating a highly decentralized system with minimal opportunities for feedback amongst the differing levels. Overall, educational policies and resources still remain in the hands of the state, resulting in the enforcement of problems, such as corruption, fraud, and poor policy implementation, which runs through India's political system (Tandon and Mohanty 2003). These problems point to a desperate need for educational reform in order to embody what is already legally enshrined; however the stigma against education is perpetrated at the level of government in that education is not a priority nor a vote catching agenda:

If you run in the name of the temple or mosque or in the name of the Hindu Muslim, you will get votes but if you run in the name of education or health or gender, this country is still not sensitive to choose that person because this country does not fight in the name of principles, so it is a very difficult task. (Interview, Convener of NCE, October 2009).

So while there is a space in which the NCE can function, the political atmosphere has never favoured the social policy sectors.

The Big Push Towards EFA in India

Following the formation of the Indian democratic state, nationalist leaders aspired to reverse the adverse effects of colonial subjugation that Indian society had suffered under the British Empire. According to Tandon and Mohanty (2003:14) this aspiration manifested itself in four ways: (1) the framing of a constitution that guaranteed the fundamental rights and freedoms essential for people to live with dignity; (2) the adoption of a multiparty parliamentary democracy that made people sovereign in deciding who they wanted to be governed by; (3) the adoption of a developmental path designed to accelerate economic growth through increase in agricultural productivity and industrialization; and (4) the passing of legislation that would end the unequal distribution of land, the social exclusion of lower castes and the evils of untouchability.

In order for these measures to be realized, expert led centralized planning, as well as moves to protect the domestic economy were all enacted so as to benefit national industry and aggressively pursue a path of development. Various large scale projects were undertaken in the hope of sparking economic prosperity that would have far reaching impact and benefit the lowest rung in the socio-economic hierarchy, thereby resulting in the reduction, if not elimination of, social inequalities (Raychaudhuri et al. 1983). But by the 1960's, a division between state and society was beginning to appear with the state's apparent unwillingness to follow up with policies that were meant to benefit the deprived sections of society (Behar and Prakesh 2004). The states apathetic handling of their people's concerns and issues resulted in the people being unable to practice their democratic rights promised under the constitution, which forced the people to turn to the Supreme Court for support.

The Supreme Court began to permit concerned citizens, public interest advocates, and NGOs to petition on behalf of communities and individuals suffering violations of their constitutionally protected rights in the 1980's. This move opened the door for those who sought to undertake the fight for education, and in 1993, during the well-known *Unnikrishman vs the State of Andhra Pradesh* case, educational rights were brought before the court, which allowed the opportunity to develop a precedent that governed the public provision of elementary education (Alston and Bhuta 2005).. Based on the view that the central and state governments had consistently and systematically failed to apply the Constitution, the Court held that the right to education up to 14 years of age contained in Article 45 amounted to a 'fundamental right' that was enforceable by the courts (Alston and Bhuta, 2005, Sadgopal, 2001).

The Supreme Court's landmark decision in *Unnikrishman vs the State of Andhra Pradesh* gave community activists and NGOs a tool for pushing the executive and legislative toward action on primary education. At the same time it became a catalyst for a number of children's rights groups to form into coalitions demanding government implementation of the fundamental right to education (Alston and Bhuta, 2005, Sadgopal, 2001). Feeding off the Supreme Court decision and other group activities, the NCE and other organizations, based on their experiences with the Global March Against Child Labour[14] and the effectiveness of taking a human right's stance, became the champions of the right to education and pushed for the RTE Act 2009. It is noteworthy that during several interviews, when asked if the current government will listen to civil society advocates, a common reply was that if they did not "they would take it to the courts." With this general erosion of faith of the people in the state, the sphere of civil society began to fill with voluntary associations committed to renewing the Gandhian tradition of social reconstruction and providing basic services to the poor (Otis, 2005).

In recognition of the uprising of civil society advocates the United Progressive Alliance (the current coalition government, UPA) brought forth the Common Minimum Programme (CMP) in 2004. This document outlined the governments minimum objectives with reference to civil society and NGO efforts at educational reform, boldly stating, "the UPA government will fully back and support all NGO efforts in the area of primary education" (CMP 2004:6).

The priorities and the intentions of the government in reference to education are spelt out in the CMP as six points under the section of 'Education and Health', with several other paragraphs in various sections that refer to education. Two of the points are promises referring to achieving the elusive '6% of GDP to education' goal and the full implementation of the Midday Meal Programme (the provision of nutritional midday meals to all school children). Another point refers to the education tax placed on all central taxes "to finance the commitment to universalize access to quality basic education" (CMP 2004:6). This was one of the few points that was immediately acted upon as the first union budget of the UPA levied an education tax of 2% (Tilak 2004). However, there are several other points the UPA is silent about, such as the continued use of para-teachers and the progressive privatization of education. Moreover, there is no reference to the free and compulsory education bill/act.

Overall, because of the increasing reliance on NGO efforts and the welcoming of private companies into the field of education, the government is slowly

---

14 The Global March Against Child Labour began with worldwide march in January 1998 in which it put forth and effort to protect and promote the rights of all children and to eliminate the evils of child labour.

abdicating its own responsibilities. Furthermore, within the CMP there are other initiatives proposed such as strengthening elected *panchayats*, as well as empowering the community and delegating responsibilities and funds to the *panchayats*. This has essentially led to the central and state governments resigning its responsibility towards education:

> It's the cunningness and it's a kind of shirking behaviour of the government...so this is a question of political economy so the government, on the one hand, does not represent the poorest of the poor and secondly education has become now a place for investment of the private sector (Interview, Convener of NCE, Sept 2009).

This is, as I will develop below, the exact opposite of how the NCE accounts for what happened.

Composition, Goals and Scalar Interaction of the NCE

Since its official inception in 2002, the NCE has brought together a varied group of member organizations, uniting teachers unions, non-governmental organizations, and other social movements. At this time, the NCE has seven member organizations that are very well-established nationwide:

- Bachpan Bachao Andolan (Save the Children Movement), a network of more than 760 organizations and 80,000 social activists working on child rights,
- All India Primary Teachers Federation, a union of more than 3 million primary teachers,
- All India Federation of Teachers Organization (AIFTO), a union of 1.2 million teachers,
- All India Secondary Teachers Federation, a union of 0.85 million teachers,
- All India Association for Christian Higher Education, an association of 300 college principals,
- World Vision India, a foundation working for child rights, education and development,

The composition and coordination of the NCE can be broken down into three groups: a) The Board of Trustees that consists of nine members with each member organization having a representative; b) the Steering Committee that consists of board of trustees members, staff, academicians, consultants and financial experts; c) and, finally, the convener who makes the daily routine decisions and is accountable to both the steering committee and the board of trustees.

The entire decision making power of the organization is vested in the Board of Trustees, which meets twice a year to discuss issues and make policy decisions. The board also appoints smaller advisory groups from time to time to look into other more technical issues of everyday activities as well as advising on strategies and how best to proceed.

Strategies and Goals

The NCE has always had a clear vision of the future of education in India, in that "all the children up to 18 years of age are in school and are getting free and good quality education driven by human values to become an empowered and productive citizen" (NCE website).

To make this vision a reality, the NCE has taken a multi-pronged approach with their central strategy being evidence-based advocacy to create political pressure. It is a well-known fact in India that government reports do not necessarily reflect what is actually happening in India, so the NCE draws upon their member organizations expertise and knowledge to create a more holistic picture (Behar and Prakash 2004). There is a firm belief within the NCE that without creating a pool of evidence to present to the government about the ground reality in India, they would have no leverage to push the NCE's agenda. The NCE also draws upon other complimentary strategies like mass mobilization, networking, direct intervention, and communication, all of which are highly dependent on the political climate and resources available at the time. For example, the current focus is on the passed education act and its implementation, monitoring, and ultimately making appropriate amendments to fill in the lacunae found throughout the act. Hence there are five areas in which the NCE demands are focused on:

1. The existing act should be amended so that all children between 0 to 18 years would be covered under the act as defined by the United Nations Convention of the Rights of the Child and Juvenile Justice Act of India.
2. Government expenditure on education should be 6% of GDP, as promised, and half of this public spending should be allocated towards elementary education.
3. To ensure quality of education, fully trained teachers should be recruited in place of untrained para-teachers and given full-time positions.
4. Changes should be carried out in legislation for quality education systems with measurable indicators so that parents and communities can monitor the level of quality (i.e. School Management Committees and budget tracking).
5. The existing act should be amended suitably to minimize privatization opportunities and to focus on implementing a common school system.

However, while these goals are generally agreed upon within the NCE, there is an issue of prioritization and how it is best to proceed, which, as I will elucidate in the following section, has led to some tension amongst the various member organizations.

Working Together in a National Coalition

The member organizations of the NCE stretch the gamut of Indian social advocacy, ranging from government to grass-roots level. There is a general agreement that the political strength of the NCE is drawn from its diversity. However, because of the diversity of its members, and their varying agendas, there are points of contradiction and contestation, which the NCE tries to manoeuvre around by looking at "strategic points of entry:"

> We try to find out what the minimal agreeable terms and issues are, and with teachers unions it was the issue of quality education, and with NGO's it is the government's commitment on the right to education and base our prime agenda around that (Interview, Convener of NCE, September 2009).

Couching the NCE's agenda in such terms does not always eliminate the tensions in and between the member organizations. One of the central sources of tension and conflict is between the teachers unions and the NGO's. Since teachers' unions make up over half of the membership of the NCE, their voice is often louder than others, which creates an "us and them" mentality between the NGO's and teachers unions. Before the passing of the RTE Act of 2009, teachers unions and NGO's kept their dealings separate. When the bill was introduced back in 2002 both groups submitted alternate bills with little or no consultation between them. However, now that the RTE Act 2009 is passed, creating a united front is a recognized necessity. They are now trying to work together on the provision of the School Management Committee (SMC) policy, which has been a source of tension in the past.

The SMC is composed of community members whose duties are to monitor proper policy implementation, proper allocation of funds, as well as the quality of education the teacher is providing to their children. Both NGO's and teachers unions play integral roles in the proper implementation of the SMC policy. However, by making teachers accountable for what they teach, the teacher's union's authority is disrupted, which ultimately threatens the status of teachers. Teachers are invaluable to the education system, but the SMC policy establishes that quality standards are necessary and that those not meeting those standards should be reprimanded in an appropriate way. So to help mitigate the tension between NGO's and teachers unions concerning SMC's, the teachers unions are working with other groups to help amend the constitution of the SMC's, instead of directly opposing it as shown during an interview with the Secretary General of AIFTO:

> Actually most of the teacher's organizations oppose the SMC, well we support it but oppose the constitution of the SMC. We want to know the qualifications of the members, we want the government to decide who is appointed to the SMC with equal position for women, we want the percentage of representation of parents and teachers should be more than government appointees and there should be the possibility of appeal. The teachers should be accountable to someone but they should have the proper qualifications (Interview, August 2009).

At present, one of the NCEs greatest strengths is its communication amongst its member organizations and the ability to find strategic entry points to help create and maintain cohesion. As such, coalition members and affiliates are highly aware of the current situation and the challenges it bears:

When there are discussions, there are a lot of tensions, but in the end we do manage to smooth out our differences…it is very important for the NCE to come together…it's very important we always have a dialogue to sit down and discuss what the issue is and what they are doing. The NCE has managed to do that, to have meetings with all of them so we can tackle those issues and why people are unhappy (Interview, Jawaharlal Nehru University Professor, October 2009).

Maintaining strong relationships internally is essential for a successful coalition, but the NCE also functions on a regional and international scale so those relationships are also key to the development of the coalition.

The International and Regional Scale

In practice, the NCE focuses the majority of its campaigning nationally, but that is not to say that there has been no outside influence. The GCE has had a strong influence on the structure, the strategies, and the coordination of the NCE. The development of the NCE was deeply tied to the creation of the GCE and uses the GCE as a model for its own activities.

The creation of the GCE is often credited to four international civil society groups: Oxfam International, ActionAid, Education International, and the Delhi-based Global March Against Child Labour. The GCE was especially influenced by the Delhi-based Global March that functioned under several principals including, "Exploitation to Education". The Global March being of Indian origin and headed by Kailash Satyarthi[15], brought an Indian perspective into the GCE and highly influenced the campaign framework by drawing from his expansive experience with advocacy. India became the stage for the GCE and several key meetings to discuss the institutionalization and the campaign's framework actually occurred in Delhi.

The GCE's approach is also unique in that it not only unites Northern and Southern NGO's, but also includes other civil society organizations, such as trade unions and campaigners against child labour that have a distinct perspective on education policy. As Kailash Satyarthi was also a founding member of the NCE, this framework is highly reflected in the construction and strategies of the Coalition in India. The NCE takes a very visible approach at the governmental level from a variety of angles because of their diverse membership that includes unions, NGOs, and Northern civil society advocates (i.e. World Vision). In fact, the NCE continues to draw heavily from the experiences and strategies of the GCE for their advocacy work.

While India was at the forefront of the creation of the GCE, its current relationship consists mostly of the sharing of information that can help guide both the GCE and the NCE in future endeavours. However, the NCE itself has little

---

15 Founding member of The Global March Against Child Labour, Bachpan Bachao Andolan and later the NCE as well as being a chairperson of the GCE.

awareness of what else is going on in other coalitions or other global issues surrounding education.

India's international presence in the global education arena has somewhat faded in the past few years, but the NCE is becoming more active at a regional level with their partnership with the Asian South Pacific Association for Basic and Adult Education (ASPBAE)[16]. With this kind of partnership there is a hope of enabling a strong Southern, Asia Pacific civil society voice in local, national, and global education policy forums, as well as in related development processes. In this era of globalization, decisions that bear on states and countries are increasingly framed and, on occasion, even dictated by global (commercial, geopolitical) interests. For this reason, civil society organizations increasingly perceive the need of engaging in regional and globally coordinated mechanisms to respond proactively and effectively.

All in all, the NCE is a national network that focuses on national issues by drawing and learning from regional and international experiences via GCE and ASPBAE. However, this learning process necessitates the transformation of ideas into viable plans of action which I analyze in the following section.

Changing Dialogue into Action

Since their inception in 2002, the NCE has grown and developed in response to changing political opportunities by learning which strategies have shown to be effective over the years. Table 6.1 provides a general overview of the key goals and how they have progressed over the years:

Table 6.1. NCE Goals and Progress

	2002	2003-2007	2008-2009
Central Goal	Passing of "The Right of Children to Free and Compulsory Education Bill 2002" in the Parliament based on rights established in the constitution and other international agreements.	Promote the educational rights defined in the constitution and international agreements. - quality education - proper budgetary allocation - decrease exclusionary	Passing of "The Right of Children to Free and Compulsory Education Bill 2008" into RTE Act 2009, and contribute to proper implementation of said act. -quality education -proper budgetary allocation - decrease exclusionary practices

16 ASPBAE was established n 1964 in Sydney, Australia and now consists of 200 regional organizations that works toward promoting quality education while supporting community organizations, national coalitions, and other civil society groups. The NCE is an active participant in ASPBAE's Real World Strategies Program.

		practices	
Specific Objectives	--	- Empower local monitoring body - Information drive - Preparing alternate bills - Research for evidence based advocacy - Elimination of para-teachers	- Implementation and empowerment of local monitoring body (SMCs) - Amend act to include all children from ages 0-18 - Prevent privatization of elementary school - Creation of Civil Society Education Fund

The central goal of the NCE is primarily based on the assumption that it is the responsibility of the central government to provide education for all. This premise was reinforced with the passing of the education bill in 2002, in which education was made a constitutionally guarded and fundamental right. From 2003 onwards the quality of education became the main focus and the lack of training of teachers and the poor working conditions, as well as poor budgetary allocation were the main impediment to quality education. Another impediment was the prevalence of government reports that often misrepresented the reality on the ground by claiming such things as the gross enrolment of children to be 120% when access to education is still a big problem for many children. As a result, the NCE began to do its own research for use as leverage to fight for better quality education and enlighten the government to the alarming situation of education in India.

However, since the passing of the bill in 2002 and the act in 2009, there is an apparent reneging of commitments by the government which is of great concern to the NCE:

> Now in the current act the government of India decided to unburden this responsibility handing it from central and are giving it to state, and from state they are giving it to local bodies and from local bodies they are giving it to SMCs...it is a political bankruptcy of commitment (Interview, NCE Convener, October 2009).

This called for stronger monitoring systems and feedback loops to increase quality, justice and democracy in education. The implementation of these systems requires the empowerment of civil society, minorities and excluded groups to actively participate in monitoring and ensuring accountability of the government when it comes to policies and practices.

Overall, the demands of the NCE ride on rights and regulations defined by law, research and statistics, and historic claims. The coalition makes use of accountability tactics since there is a long history of the government's inability to follow through in implementing policy. This has resulted in the formulation of the five central goals as mentioned earlier. Table 6.2 collects these central demands accordingly to the three main framing dimensions (diagnosis of the problem, prognosis or solutions to the problem, and motivation for change):

Table 6.2. NCE main frames

	Diagnosis	Prognosis	Motivation
Budgetary Allocation	Current spending of under 4% GDP is not adequate to improve education	Government needs to spend at least 6% of GDP	Promise made by previous and current UPA government.
Inclusion of all children 0-18 years of age	Education is compulsory to children 6-14 years of age	There needs to be provisions for pre-primary and secondary education	Proven effective in other countries also limits child labour opportunities
Elimination of Para-teachers	Government assigning untrained para-teachers to government schools	Para-teachers need to be replaced by full time, trained teachers to improve education quality	Historic demand; teachers invaluable to improving quality education
Common School System	Government is using private public partnerships to make up for "resource crunch'	Government should shoulder responsibility of providing education for all	Risks that educational rights will be undermined
Local Monitoring Body	VECs have become defunct due to lack of interest and motivation	Implementing and empower SMCs to increase accountability for policy and practices	Provision in RTE Act

Since 2002, budgetary allocation has been a main objective, but it has not been achieved for a couple of reasons. The first reason is its lack of tangibility, the target is based on an obscure figure from out-dated governmental reports, and thus it is not indicative or reflective of current needs. Secondly, the Indian economic and political context provided little motivation for the government to follow up on its promise of 6% GDP for education, as other topics such as poverty were more predominant.

The inclusion of all children 0-18 years of age in school has been part of the NCE's agenda since its inception. Different groups in society including teachers, parents and students share this demand, although they often follow different rationales. Placing children in school from an early age provides education, a safe haven, and a place to provide nutrition (via Midday Meal Scheme). Furthermore, if education is only compulsory for children up to 14 years of age, there is a chance they would be forced into child labour at 14 (Interview, Convener of NCE, Oct 2009), which represents a big contradiction in the existing legal frameworks. Several teachers unions have made this one of their central objectives to lobby the government to make a change in the RTE Act to include pre-primary and secondary education in an attempt to also have an effect on the status of teachers.

However, the Coalition's proposals were continually undermined by the government in that they refused to acknowledge international agreements such as UN Convention on the Rights of the Child and the Juvenile Justice Act of India, which defines the child as from 0-18 years of age. The government has thwarted the NCE's efforts by only focusing on providing the minimal amount of education as stated in the Constitution.

The elimination of para-teachers was and still is a strategic entry point in which the teachers unions and other type of organizations unite in the context of NCE for the goal of improving the quality of education. Teachers unions and other groups have made massive strides in improving the teaching profession, making the government provide good salaries, good working conditions and proper training. Yet the allocation of untrained, contractual para-teachers is a common practice, especially in the poorer states such as Bihar. There is no lack in training institutions for teachers, but the government still attempts to get around the responsibility of providing proper funds to get fully trained teachers in every school.

NCE members such as World Vision India and the *Bachpan Bachao Andolan*, who focus on child rights, do not support the elimination of para-teachers strongly enough, because they subordinate the rights of teachers to those of children. Due to the size and power of the teachers unions and their influence on a national level it was necessary for the NCE to make provisions for them to maintain collective action on the topic. However, the fact that not all members are on the same wavelength on this topic gives NCE less force, decreasing the likelihood of it being achieved.

A common school system is the ultimate goal of the NCE, but it is also a mechanism in which the NCE uses to minimize privatization of elementary education. The government has already implemented a voucher system in which they pay private schools to save 25% of seats for underprivileged children (Tilak 2004). However, this is viewed as a gateway to privatization by NCE. Furthermore, the introduction of public-private partnerships (PPP) by the Ministry of Human Resources and Development (see Verger and VanderKaaij 2011) has further confirmed the lack of commitment by the government to improve public education.

A local monitoring body should technically have been in place even before the passing of the RTE Bill in 2002, so their necessity is generally agreed upon, but their effectiveness has been minimal. To enhance their effectiveness, within the RTE Act there is a provision for SMCs to create a better monitoring system. However, this creates a lot of tension between the teachers unions and NGOs by creating a bifurcation of the NCE, even though most of its members support the SMCs and are working to empower them.

The teachers unions are now taking independent steps to rework the SMCs in their favour while the NCE is trying to maintain internal cohesion by promoting a model of SMC that includes the teachers unions without undermining them. Both teacher's unions and NGOs are working towards the same goal of accountability for the implementation of policy and practices, but the tensions are slowing the process down by forcing re-negotiations on the constitution of the SMCs. The NCE had made great strides but the apathy of the government and the difficulty of fostering a united effort with the teachers unions and NGO's have continually eroded the political impact of the NCE in this particular aspect.

The Coalition's Impact Thus Far

While the NCE is far from seeing the realization of its vision for education in India, the NCE and its member organizations have been significant players in a number of political achievements for education. One of the most notable achievements was the NCE's role in establishing the *Parliamentary Forum on Education* in 2002, which was spearheaded by several progressive parliamentarians and former MP and president of the NCE, Ravi P. Verma. The forum has been instrumental in making voices heard on the subject of deteriorating education systems in the National Parliament of India, and thereby forcing the issue onto the political agenda.

The NCE has also made strides towards better funding for education. When external funding was cut back in 2004, one of the hardest hit budgets was social sector spending, the NCE began large scale lobbying and advocacy efforts to levy a 2% education tax on the corporate sector to help fund education. Also, through pressure tactics, the NCE got the government to agree *in principal* to increase public expenditure on education to 6% of the GDP. Other achievements include the NCE's participation in getting the 2002 education bill passed as well as setting up local monitoring bodies at the *panchayat* level.

The impacts at the political level are the most notable, but with the development of the Parliamentary Forum, the procedural impact of the NCE is also significant. While they are not always involved with governmental decision-making processes, there is a voice within the parliament stressing the importance of dealing with educational issues. Furthermore, with the passing of the RTE Act 2009, the NCE has the potential to be very influential at the procedural level because as a civil society movement, the RTE Act 2009 is an essential tool that the NCE can use to empower groups of people to affect change at all levels of government and to become more involved with policy processes.

In terms of symbolic impact, the NCE has played a key role in increasing the dialogue on the topic of educational funding both at state and local levels, as well as creating information programs to increase awareness of the peoples' educational rights. However, this is part of a larger effort in the Indian civil society arena and, consequently, cannot be solely attributed to the efforts of the NCE. Nonetheless, this increased recognition allows for more open discussion and information sharing which can also effect the impact of the coalition.

Overall, the impact of the NCE is highly dependent on the degree of internal and external cohesion. However, this very much depends on the level of knowledge and information sharing about objectives and strategies within the coalition, as well as on the prevailing political opportunity structures in the country.

Unfortunately, the political opportunity structures the NCE are confronted with are based on a corrupt government, making it difficult for advocacy groups to determine which is the best way to proceed (Tilak, 2004). The strong focus on economic improvements from the moment of independence has lead to corrupt elites who made sure the benefits of development stayed with the dominant and influential sections of society rather than those living in poverty (Tandon and Mohanty 2003). The following are some of the characteristics of the political and educational culture in India:

- The historically rooted elitism based on the caste system;
- The low priority on education made by the UPA in the CMP;
- The low valorisation of education on all levels;
- The corruption of the decentralized system;
- The population's lack of interest in education with the prominence of more immediate problems like poverty and unemployment (Tandon and Mohanty, 2003).

Reflecting on the progress the coalition has made since its inception, there was a general consensus that a lack of proper coordination and cohesion between the board and steering committees affected the NCEs ability to have an impact. Back in 2002 the board and committees were still dispersed, and while they were members of the NCE, most were focused on their own agendas, which created a fragmented effort as opposed to a focused and targeted policy drive. While there was a clear objective to focus on the RTE Bill, there was relatively little dialogue concerning how they were going to approach the bill, and little effort to create an alternate bill as a coalition, as opposed to the NGOs and teachers unions that did create an alternate bill. Research was also done on an individual basis, usually resulting in a narrow view of education, either from the teacher's perspective or grass roots perspective with little or no overlap. It was not until there was an effort to improve the management of the NCE with the introduction of a Convener in 2006, that management began to improve and allowed for a dialogue between members to make a more concerted effort.

Furthermore, the coalition's ability to place demands on the government is highly dependent on several factors including, political opportunity structures, the degree of internal cohesion and collective identity between and within the members and stakeholders, international pressures, and adequate financial resources. These factors are constantly changing, and in response the coalition have altered and improved the construction, distribution, and functionality of the goals over the years. Some objectives have faded into the background while others took dominance in accordance with contextual factors, and some new objectives were added all together. In addition, the NCE strives to find new and interesting ways to grab attention which also reveals the understanding of the multifaceted political, social and cultural context of India.

The Importance of Internal Communication and Critical Reflexivity

The NCE as a coalition has developed over the years in such a way that allows for self-critical evaluation, constantly learning from old and new experiences, revising and re-negotiating strategies, as well as formulating new ones all within its ever-changing context. All of those NCE members interviewed displayed high levels of competence and knowledge concerning the historic, social and political context and what it means to be civil society advocates. Since 2002, these reflections and learning processes have facilitated the coalition's ability to gain access to governmental structures, to mitigate internal tensions, and to extend their experiences to the global level.

The nature of transnational advocacy movements requires the ability to function and communicate on different scales, from local to supra-national. A scalar analysis NCE interaction shows that all members have a comprehensive awareness of the challenges and opportunities of functioning on local to global scales. The level of cohesion and the sense of a collective identity among the members of the NCE is highly related to the impact of the NCE:

> In all the coalition building we recognize a few things as fundamental. One is that we do not encourage to dilute or merge the identity of individual partners or members otherwise it would be hard because identity is very important for teachers unions, trade unions and NGO's so we work on a broader platform for common goals but with their own identities and own activities of which we do not interfere (Interview, President of GCE, September 2009).

Whenever the coalition successfully exerted pressure on the government it was a result of good communication with good circulation of information and knowledge as well as a good coordination of activities. On the other hand, whenever tensions occurred around a certain topic or project, the NCE has proven to be less effective.

While many of the tensions within the NCE are not always openly discussed, they are acknowledged, and by couching issues within a certain type of language, the NCE is able to negotiate and, on occasion, solve many of these issues in order to maintain internal cohesion. For example, to maintain a good relationship between the NGO's and teachers unions, the NCE uses the improvement of the quality of education as a uniting goal since it addresses both working conditions of teachers as well as implementing policy. The type of dialogue and rhetoric is designed to facilitate collective decision-making and participatory and critical processes of reflection. Over the years the coalition has successfully learned to combine different views and to negotiate interests. All in all, the critical reflexivity over working in a coalition at different scales alters the strategic action, and thus benefits the NCE both internally and externally.

CONCLUSION

This case study explored the extent to which the NCE has affected India's effort to achieve Education for All by looking at various factors such as India's political context, the NCE's scalar relations, knowledge production, and internal and external power relations. The analysis shows that all these factors are strongly related and that through the complex processes of critical reflexivity and strategic learning, the coalition is able to make strategic choices on how to bring about long-term policy change.

However, while the coalition has played a role in addressing education issues in India, it is important to not overestimate its impact. Due to the robust nature of civil society in India, as well as its size and diversity, it is very difficult to attribute concrete impacts to a single coalition with such a short history. However, without the active participation of the NCE, there would certainly be a less focused effort on education, and educational change would have come about more slowly.

One of the more outstanding achievements that would not have happened but for the NCE was the creation of the Parliamentary Forum. Without the NCE there would have been no space to create a dialogue amongst legislatures and parliamentarians about the educational issues India is facing and how to go about change. Through this, the coalitions managed to get word out to the upper echelons of the government in an attempt to begin a solid effort at educational reform.

Other noted milestones are a little bit more foggy concerning the significance of the role played by the NCE, as other civil society advocates were more than likely involved with pressuring the government to get the 2002 bill passed, as well as the 2% tax levied on all central taxes to fund education. In terms of symbolic impact, the NCE has had an important effect on the governments discourse on education but I hesitate to say that they have reshaped this discourse, changed opinions, or even ideologies. It is however, certainly to the NCE's credit that the topic of budget tracking and allocation are at the forefront of discourse in the educational community.

There is no doubt that the coalition has had an impact on education in India, but to what extent these impacts can be solely attributed to the efforts of the NCE is questionable. It is difficult to use the words "success" or "failure" since both are difficult to define, but the tenacity and the NCE's willingness to continue fighting to improve education will hopefully lead to long-lasting policy change.

From this research, some recommendations to the NCE can be extracted, including the following:

- To continue expanding its membership base;
- To invest in establishing offices throughout India to foster contact at the local level;
- To support better communication to foster mutual projects for both the teachers unions and NGO's to work together on;
- To extend their reach into the private sector to garner more resources and expertise;
- To continue to push the child friendly village model and using direct intervention strategies to help implement the RTE Act 2009;
- To sustain momentum to make a lasting influence on education policy.

ANJA EICKELBERG

CHAPTER 7

Framing, Fighting and Coalitional Building: The Learnings and Teachings of the Brazilian Campaign for the Right to Education

INTRODUCTION

The *Campanha Brasileira pelo Direito à Educação*[17] (CBDE) was created in 1999 as one of the first national coalitions of the Global Campaign for Education (GCE). Today, the CBDE is a recognized political actor and the principal civil society reference for educational funding in Brazil. Furthermore, the coalition occupies an important role as representative of the Latin American continent in the GCE board. The CDBE is the most plural network of its kind in Brazil, uniting more than 200 non-governmental organizations, social movements, teachers unions, education councils and international agencies around the common goal to guarantee free public education of high quality for all Brazilian citizens.

Since the year 2000, primary school enrolment numbers are almost universal in Brazil. However, lack of educational quality leads to high levels of grade repetition and drop-outs, and low learning achievements. The political and economic conditions to improve this situation are, at least formally, established in Brazil. The country is one of the biggest economies in the world. Brazil's head of state, Luiz Inácio Lula da Silva (2003-2010), is a former steel worker turned trade-union leader who went on to become the country's first left-wing president. He belongs to the *Partido dos Trabalhadores*[18] (PT), which has its roots in the social movements, and is Latin America's largest leftist party. However, the government agenda is quite different from the program that many expected after two decades in opposition. In fact, rather than overturn the neo-liberal models for growth of his predecessor, Fernando Henrique Cardoso, Lula instead opted to strengthen them; and further, despite his professed belief in participative democracy, civil society's involvement in Brazil's political decision-making processes remains limited.

The case study assesses the impact of the CBDE in this political context and analyzes factors that account for its success. Primary data consists of twenty in depth semi-structured interviews with key coalition members, affiliates, government officials, academics and journalists, conducted during a fieldwork period from July until September 2008 in the Brazilian cities Rio de Janeiro, São

---

[17] Brazilian Campaign for the Right to Education.
[18] Workers' Party.

Antoni Verger and Mario Novelli (eds.), Campaigning for "Education for All", 101–119.

Paulo and Brasília. Secondary data includes a wide range of coalition, government, and media publications.

The chapter is divided into five sections. The first one analyses the political opportunity structures of the CBDE with an emphasis on the relationship between state and civil society in Brazil, followed by an assessment of the role education plays in the political programs of presidents Cardoso and Lula. The second section depicts the origin, composition, and goals of the CBDE, and explores the benefits and challenges of 'coalitioning' on national and supra-national scales. In the third section, the strategic development of the coalition is analyzed on the basis of its five major campaigns. The fourth section puts in perspective the political, procedural and symbolic impact of the CBDE, and discusses how this impact is related to processes of critical reflection. The final section draws the main conclusions regarding the success of the CBDE, closing with a list of lessons learned and recommendations.

COUNTRY CONTEXT

Brazil is a federal republic that extends over almost half of the South American continent. After 21 years of military dictatorship, Brazil was declared a legal democracy in 1985. Since then, the country developed into one of the biggest economies in the world, based on rich natural resources, a strong industrial sector and vast agriculture. The more than 190 Million Brazilian citizens are spread over 26 states, one federal district and almost 6,000 municipalities, with regional, ethnic and social differences so severe that some live under conditions comparable to those of sub-Saharan Africa, while others benefit from Western European living standards.

Inequalities in Brazil increased with the election of President Cardoso (1994-2002), who introduced an economic growth model inspired by the Washington Consensus. His successor, Lula (2003-2010), was elected with the promise to bring profound changes to neo-liberal politics. However, the new government surprised many observers not only by keeping the pillars of Cardoso's political model intact, but even deepening some aspects:

> "The monetary authorities appointed by President Lula, as those appointed by former President Cardoso, seem to believe inflation stabilization is the only goal of macroeconomic policy. From the fiscal side, all that matters is building credibility with financial agents, leaving out full employment, stable prices, long-term economic growth and social development" (Arestis et al: 2007).

For this reason, and as I will go on to show, education holds a marginalized position in the government's agenda.

Political priorities: The insignificance of universal primary education

The Brazilian education system is highly decentralized. To assure transparency, the federal constitution (*Constituição Federal,* CF/1988) and the national law of education (*Lei de Diretrizes e Bases da Educação Nacional,* LDB/1996[19]) envision the establishment of civic councils in municipalities and schools. In practice, however, the daily struggle for survival is more immediate for the parents of public school students than voluntary participation in the school council. As a consequence, education resources remain in the hands of the local administrative powers, leading to widespread corruption and fraud.

Both president Cardoso and Lula declared education as a political priority, but failed to provide the necessary monetary resources required in order to tackle the many dysfunctions of the decentralized system. Cardoso centered his education reform on primary education, resulting in almost universal access in 2000. Provision and quality of pre-school, secondary, and adult education decreased during his administration. In an attempt to diminish regional inequalities in primary education provision, Cardoso implemented a fund for fundamental education, the *Fundo de Manutenção e Desenvolvimento do Ensino Fundamental e de Valorização do Magistério* (FUNDEF)[20], but failed to comply with his own law and accumulated a US$ 5,4 Billion debt to the poorest states (Pinto 2002). In 2001, Cardoso launched Brazil's Ten-Year Plan for EFA, the *Plano Nacional de Educação* (PNE), but vetoed its most progressive articles, among them the augmentation of educational spending to 7% of the GDP (Campanha Nacional pelo Direto a Educação, 2001).

President Lula came to office with the promise of re-examining the vetoes on the PNE as well as gradually augmenting the education budget (Comissão de programa de governo: 2002). Two months after his inauguration, the education budget fell from 4.6 to 4.3 % of the GDP, and has not since been altered (Doctor 2007). In line with his policy to focus on social inclusion, Lula's educational reform centers on two adult literacy programs, but fails to tackle functional illiteracy within the formal education system. With his popular family stipend program, *Bolsa Familia*[21], Lula invests far more in social assistance than in education (Borges 2003). In April 2007, the Education Minister Fernando Haddad launched the *Plano pelo Desenvolvimento de Educação*[22], which merged existing and new laws into 40 programs for all levels of education (Ministério da Educação, 2007). With its focus on accountability, territoriality, collaboration and social mobilization, the Plan for the Development of Education was generally welcomed

---

[19] The LDB, approved by the government in 1996, articulates the national legal framework regarding education, including governing resource allocation and distribution.

[20] The law of the FUNDEF, introduced in 1998, establishes a national minimum value to be spent per student per year, and obliges the union to complement the budget of those states that lack the means to guarantee this value.

[21] The "Programa Bolsa Familia" provides a monthly monetary stipend to over 11 Mio families and had significant impact on Brazil's poverty level.

[22] Plan for the Development of Education

by the education community[23]. However, its impact is highly dependent on the functioning of the decentralized system.

Political Opportunity Structures: Obstacles for EFA in Brazil

The participation of Brazilian civil society in the political process has advanced with the establishment of constitutional democracy in 1988, but divisions rooted in the country's feudal past have proved a hindrance to the creation of a truly pluralist structure (Wiarda 2003: 90). Until 1888, Brazil's society was officially based on slavery and its "structures and political culture were marked by hierarchical principles that excluded the vast majority of its population" (Silva and Lima 2007: 23). These deeply authoritarian patterns prevailed in populist periods (1945-64) as well as throughout the military dictatorship (1964-1985). Only from the 1980s onwards did social and political forces actively demand the construction of an effective state that recognized universal rights. This impetus resulted in the formation of the Federal Constitution of 1988. However, constitutional democracy has not ameliorated the old vices of Brazilian political culture, namely: elite control of the political process, weak parties, and non-substantive political discourse have been yet to be properly overcome (Slater 1994, Wiarda 2003, Almeida and Johnston 2006).

Under president Cardoso, civic participation in educational policies was strictly limited to corporate foundations, public universities, and selected NGOs[24]. Civil society's access to the government discourse improved significantly with Lula, but the quality of this dialogue leaves cause for concern:

"Progressive civil society is making steps forward, continuously enhancing its discourses and practices. The only one that is not advancing is the Lula government. Its educational policies, discourses, and interaction with civil society are all disappointing." (Interview Director Ação Educativa, São Paulo, August 2008)

Civil society participation in the national congress is permitted, but challenged by the complex composition of legislative and executive. The congress is based on a multi-party system in which Lula's PT is the minority, leading to much tension between government base and opposition. Lula invited a number of former civil society leaders to join his cabinet, but political power is centered on the conservative Finance Minister Antonio Palocci, Foreign Minister Celso Amorin, and "a wider ring of neoliberal senators, governors, and mayors who are deeply allied with business interests and promote privatization policies" (Boito 2003).

The political influence of the Minister of Education, Fernando Haddad, a PT member and Marxist intellectual is limited[25]. Haddad sympathizes with the CBDE,

---

[23] Interview representative Mieib, Rio de Janeiro, July 2008
[24] Interview Journalist Canal Futura, Rio de Janeiro, July 2008
[25] Interview general coordinator CBDE, São Paulo, August 2008

but recently held talks primarily with the members of the campaign *Todos Pela Educação*[26] (TPE). TPE emerged from the Brazilian corporate sector in 2006 with the objective to "help achieve the goal of guaranteeing an education of quality for all Brazilians"[27]. The CBDE is highly critical of TPE, mainly for its business-oriented approach to education, and close collaboration with the Brazilian government and mainstream media[28]. Besides CBDE and TPE, a huge number of NGOs, social movement organizations, education forums and research institutes intervene in educational politics.

> "Education in Brazil is improving principally because of the pressure of civil society. The CBDE is, without doubt, one of the important civil society actors in this process, if not the most. But it would not do justice to our democracy to say that they are alone responsible. The unions, UNDIME[29], the Conselho Nacional de Secretários de Educação (National Council of Education Secretaries) and TPE also play an important role." (Interview Journalist Folha de São Paulo, Rio de Janeiro, August 2008)

COMPOSITION, GOALS AND SCALAR INTERACTION OF THE BRAZILIAN GCE COALITION

The CBDE was launched in Rio de Janeiro on the 5th of October 1999 as an initiative of the Brazilian NGO, Ação Educativa. The coalition builds on the tradition of the *Fórum Nacional em Defesa da Escola Pública*[30], a civil society network that exerted significant influence on the elaboration of the CF/1988, the LDB/1996, and the 'Proposal of Civil Society' for the National Plan for Education. By the end of the 1990s, the network dispersed due to internal tensions[31] (Bollmann 2007). The CBDE was created as a new space for civil society mobilization with the goal to assure that president Cardoso would incorporate civil demands into the final version of the PNE.

Composition

When created, the CBDE had 50 member organizations. Ten years after its foundation, the coalition has over 200 members coordinated by a national executive committee of five permanent employees based in Sao Paulo, a board of

---

[26] All for Education
[27] www.todospelaeducacao.org.br/QuemSomos.aspx [last retrieved: 28/07/2010]
[28] e.g. Interview representative MST, Sao Paulo, September 2008; Interview president CNTE, Sao Paulo, September 2008; Interview communication coordinator CBDE, Sao Paulo, August 2008
[29] União Nacional dos Dirigentes Municipais de Educação (National Union of Municipal Education Secretaries)
[30] National Forum in Defense of the Public School
[31] The Forum was revitalized in February 2011 with the goal to monitor the implementation of the new National Education Plan 2011-2020. http://www.cedes.unicamp.br/manifesto_informativo.pdf [last retrieved: 03/10/2011]

directors of 10 (initially 5) entities, as well as 19 (initially 3) regional committees. Every second year members from all over Brazil meet at the National Assembly.

The CBDE is co-founder of the *Campaña Latinoamericana por el Derecho a la Educación*[32] (CLADE) and board member of the GCE. However, the core issues in the coalition's agenda are explicitly focused on national issues. Its international role is foremost a representative one, intended to establish an increased recognition for Latin America within the global education community (Campanha Nacional pelo Direto a Educação, 1999)

Table 7.1. Organization Diagram CBDE (at October 2008)

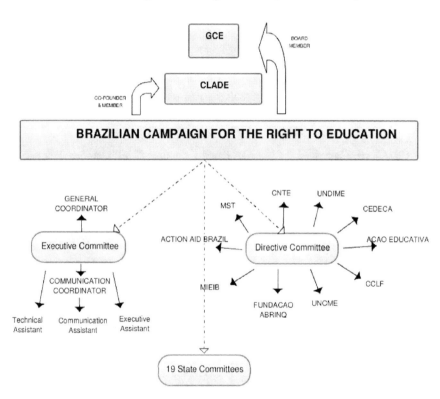

Goals and Strategies

The CBDE defines three main goals in order to improve the quality of public education in Brazil:

- Increase of government spending on education;

---

[32] Latin American Campaign for the Right to Education

- Higher valorization of the public school teacher;
- Democratic management of the public education system.

Based on these goals, the coalition has elaborated a number of concrete objectives that have been followed in campaigns of different size and impact. The five major campaigns will be analyzed in section 4 of this chapter.

In order to achieve its objectives, the CBDE applies five complementary strategies:

- Political Pressure;
- Research and Knowledge Production;
- Social Mobilization;
- Institutional Articulation;
- Communication (ibid).

The national scale: Diversity as strength and challenge

The CBDE states on its website that it is "the most plural and broad articulation in the area of basic education"[33] in Brazil, and its board of directors is representative of this diversity.

"The CBDE has a virtue. It unites very diverse movements from the area of education that rarely dialogued before. It is difficult to reach consent, but whenever the board closes a deal and presents a proposal, she has impact." (Interview parliamentary assessor, Brasília, September 2008)

Despite differing priorities, all board members share a historically rooted progressive view on education, a high level of flexibility, and the belief that lack of adequate government spending is the main factor for the low quality of education in Brazil. In addition, constructive dialogue is facilitated by the existence of an independent general coordinator.

The relationship between NGOs and teacher's unions, traditionally fraught with tension, is trustful and cooperative:

"Brazil is an interesting case because it is one of the few countries in Latin America where the relation between unions and NGOs is not very conflictive because we were united in the fight for democracy and educational rights, first against the military dictatorship and later neoliberal politics." (Interview president CNTE, São Paulo, September 2008)

However, a number of intra-movement disagreements do exist. The election of a left-wing president has led to tensions between government-near organizations like the *Confederação Nacional dos Trabalhadores em Educação*[34] (CNTE) and

---

[33] www.campanhaeducacao.org.br [last retrieved: 28/07/2010]

[34] National Confederation of the Teacher's Unions

UNDIME, and the more critical social movements, such as the landless rural worker's movement MST[35] or the movement for infant education Mieib[36].

"With Presidents Collor, Franco and Cardoso we had the same enemy. When Lula assumed many union leaders went straight into government. So one part of the CNTE is less critical with the government and prefers to present themselves as interlocutor." (Interview director Ação Educativa, São Paulo, August 2008)

As a result, the participation of the CNTE in the coalition depends on the political situation. The role of the MST within the CBDE board is likewise debated. The movement is perceived as too radical within the conservative sectors of Brazilian society and to some extent hinders the coalition's ability to receive financial support from national business foundations. Its political strength is, however, unquestionable:

"If there exists an organization in Brazil that knows how to make politics, it is the MST. They exactly know the political conjuncture, how to radicalize, and how to comport themselves within this conjuncture. They have an excellent feeling for politics." (Interview president CNTE, São Paulo, September 2008)

In addition, concrete interest conflicts arise about political positions, priorities, and strategies. While the MST laments the marginal position of rural education on the CBDE agenda, the members of Mieib's critique is that some board members openly advocate the closing of private community nurseries to secure resources for the public nurseries.

A continuing problem is the disagreement about the weighting of the five different political strategies. The CBDE has changed its action profile over the years, according to the preference of the general coordinator. Denise Carreira (April 2003 – June 2006) fostered a participatory rather than centralized policymaking in order to strengthen the coalition's base, while the current coordinator Daniel Cara has focused on high-impact, centralized advocacy actions at the cost of local level activity. While this research was conducted, the CBDE was planning a participatory reflection and process of restructuring to solve major internal conflicts.

The activity of the 19 regional committees of the CBDE is highly dependent on incentives from the executive committee; only two committees are active throughout the year. Local participation has been much stronger before 2005 when international funding for Brazil was reduced drastically. Today, information exchange between coordination and base happens mainly via the virtual bulletin *Fique por dentro*[37], and direct interaction is limited to major national mobilizations and events.

---

[35] Movimento dos Trabalhadores Rurais Sem Terra
[36] Movimento Interforuns de Educação Infantil do Brasil
[37] Fique por dentro (= Stay informed) was created in 2002, initially published weekly, now monthly

The international scale: Putting Latin America in the loop

The CBDE's membership in both GCE and CLADE does not have much impact on the coalition's national performance and the international contacts of most members are limited. For the general coordinator the participation in the GCE board is an important opportunity to represent Latin America:

"Our continent has always been sidelined from the global agenda. The discourse of the GCE is the same as the one of the international agencies. Africa, Eastern Europe and a part of Asia are prioritized while Latin American problems are rarely recognized." (Interview general coordinator CLADE, September 2008, São Paulo)

In January 2008, the CBDE hosted the Global Assembly of the GCE in São Paulo, which opened strategic opportunities for Latin America in general, and the Brazilian coalition in particular[38].

The relation between Northern and Southern countries within the GCE board is considered respectful, but tensioned. The CBDE coordinator criticizes that the European GCE members "have no idea about what is going on in the South but act as if their model is the right one. There are surely things that we can learn from them but many things are just not adequate here."[39] He also perceives that the African coalitions "usually play the game of the North. [...] They need to evolve their own strategies!"[40]

The relation between African and Latin American GCE board members is considered less problematic[41] and there is agreement that the consolidation of CLADE over the last two years "opened many possibilities to demonstrate who Latin America is"[42]. Although both the GCE and the CBDE agenda are fundamentally based on the Dakar Goals and the Millennium Development Goals, a number of issues that are high on the GCE agenda are not relevant in Brazil[43]. The CBDE disapproves the Global School Report[44] and is critical of the Education for All Fast Track Initiative (FTI) because, despite being "a valuable mechanisms for increasing education funding in some countries, it fails to address the problem of educational quality".[45] Also, the concept of the Global Action Week is criticized in Brazil:

---

[38] E.g. the topic of the Global Action Week 2009 was illiteracy (as suggested by the Latin American coalitions) and the CBDE currently discusses possibilities of technical exchange with Portuguese-speaking African countries.

[39] Interview general coordinator CBDE, August 2008, São Paulo

[40] ibid.

[41] ibid.

[42] Interview communication coordinator CBDE, São Paulo, August 2008

[43] Gender equality in education (Dakar Goal 5) is a topic high on the agenda of the GCE, while it is not a problem in Brazil (in fact girls are slightly advantaged). Universal primary education (MDG 2) and gender equality (MDG 3) are high on the GCE's agenda, but not relevant in Brazil.

[44] Consists of global report cards ranking governments' efforts to achieve Education for All.

[45] Interview general coordinator CBDE, August 2008, São Paulo

"The GCE decides on the topic and gives ideas for action. Their vision is very limited, the stereotypical view of the North on African and Asian reality, without recognizing Latin American much. We always have a national discussion about how to translate this proposal into Brazilian reality, rewriting texts, reworking the images." (Interview coordinator regional committee Rio, Rio de Janeiro, July 2008)

CLADE was formally founded in November 2006 in São Paulo, under significant influence of the first CBDE general coordinator Camilla Croso, who is the first and current CLADE coordinator. The CBDE has a good relationship with the CLADE leadership and its coalitions, but holds a special position due to its 10-year-experience, which stands in sharp contrast to the other CLADE members:

"None of them has a national campaign comparable to the Brazilian one. They are all very dependent on the monitoring of CLADE, whereas the CBDE is a founding member and equal partner of CLADE. We have a very collaborative relationship." (Interview general coordinator CLADE, September 2008, Sao Paulo)

Due to its intense national agenda, the CBDE does not participate much in the activities of CLADE, and there are few serious conflicts.

PROCESS TRACING: THE STRATEGIC DEVELOPMENT OF THE CBDE

Five major campaigns have coined the trajectory of the CBDE in its first decade of life; each of them is analysed in this section. They are (1) the overthrow of the vetoes on the Plan for the Development of Education, (2) the creation of the FUNDEB (as an improvement of the FUNDEF)[46], (3) the definition of a fixed investment per student to assure a minimum of educational quality, (4) the implementation of a national teacher's floor salary, and (5) the realization of a National Conference for Basic Education.

(1) The overthrow of the vetoes on the National Plan for Education became the first concrete coalition objective in 2001, when president Cardoso, immediately after launching the PNE, vetoed nine articles related to funding.

- Diagnosis: The current 4,3% of GDP investment in education is inadequate to improve educational quality.
- Prognosis: The government needs to spend at least 7 % of GDP.
- Motivation: The 7% investment rate has been achieved in other Latin-American countries; it is the rate recommended by UNESCO.

This objective is yet to be achieved, primarily because of the lack of salience and the economical and political tensions: "It was a very fragile objective. Brazil's

---

[46] Both FUNDEB and FUNDEF mean *Fundo de Manutenção e Desenvolvimento da Educação Básica e de Valorização dos Profissionais da Educação Básica* (Fund for the Development of Basic Education and the Valuation of Teachers)

economy at the time was seriously unstable, and there was no social composition to exert pressure to transfer money from the privileged economic areas to education."[47] In 2001 and 2002 the coalition mobilized a broad spectrum of civil society actors, lobbied the parliament with pressure letters, and promoted the topic in events and media. However, the objective was too distant from the lives and experiences of the general population to enable collective actions. In view of the economic context, the credibility among the congressmen was low, hindering the required majority vote against the President's vetoes. The objective remains on the CBDE agenda until the present day.

(2) The Creation of the FUNDEB, a fund that includes all levels of basic education, was the principal focus of the CBDE from 2004 until 2007.

- Diagnosis: The existing fund (FUNDEF) only focuses on primary education, excluding infantile, secondary, adult and special education.
- Prognosis: FUNDEB will improve the provision of basic education.
- Motivation: The creation of a fund for basic education is a historic demand of Brazilian civil society and an electoral promise of President Lula.

In 2004/05 the Ministry of Education (Ministério de Educação, MEC) and the CBDE jointly elaborated a proposal for the creation of the FUNDEB[48]. When President Lula excluded the funding of early childhood education from the final law bill, the CBDE initiated the movement *FUNDEB pra Valer!*[49]. The movement was launched on 31st of August in 2005 with a social mobilization in front of the national congress in the Brazilian capital Brasília, followed by several advocacy actions and local level activities[50]. Although being a very specific topic it appeals to a broad spectrum of civil society actors, from feminist movements to business foundations, councils of the social area, and parents associations. In addition, the issue has a high salience among the general population because the underfunding (and lack of) nurseries is a problem congruent with the life experience of many Brazilians. Popular participation was encouraged by the strategic use of elements of the Brazilian popular culture, resulting into unconventional action repertoires. Prime examples are the *Carrinhata* (protest march with baby buggies) and the *Fraldas pintadas* (painted diapers)[51] at the launch of the FUNDEB movement, as well as numerous *cirandas* (traditional children's circle dance) in and around government buildings, and the delivery of a football with the motto 'Make a goal

---

[47] Interview general coordinator CBDE, São Paulo, August 2008
[48] Public statement: Sociedade civil entrega emendas à Comissão Especial do Fundeb em audiência pública. October 26th, 2005.
[49] FUNDEB for Real!
[50] Various public statements, e.g.: Esforço concentrado do Fundeb é pautado pelo movimento "Fundeb pra Valer!". March 6th, 2006.
[51] With this name, the CBDE gave the "Caras Pintadas" (painted faces) movement a wink. The "Caras Pintadas" entered the Brazilian political scene in the beginning of the nineties to protest against the corrupt government of president Fernando Collor de Mello. These protests, which had the main national students union behind, characterized by the students painting their faces, usually with the colours of the Brazilian flag.

for education – FUNDEB now!' to the senators when the FUNDEB proposal was stuck in the congress during the Football World Cup 2006. At the same time, evidence-based advocacy gave the movement a high credibility within the Brazilian government. The movement activists presented themselves as both militant – sending pressure letters and mobilizing on the streets – and analytical, delivering technical documents elaborated with financial experts. Accountability politics and moral leverage proved successful on a government that is highly dependent on and interested in a favorable international reputation[52]. However, in several key moments the CBDE and its allies were sharply attacked by the Minister of Finance Antoni Palocci who tried to interfere in the approval of the FUNDEB. This provoked the activists to extend their pressure to the whole federal executive power. The movement's actions were picked up by a number of quality newspapers, which reported favorably about the activists, and the coalition's press releases were distributed by numerous agencies.

After almost three years of intense advocacy and mobilization, President Lula signed a FUNDEB bill that incorporated the majority of the demands presented by the social movement. The fund was implemented in January 2007 and is until today the biggest success of the CBDE. It established the coalition's role as the primary source on the topic of educational funding for both government and media representatives[53]. In addition, the CBDE gained a significant support base in the national congress and a stable interlocution with key decision makers in the MEC. The National Congress honored the CBDE with the award *Prêmio Darcy Ribeiro 2007* which aims to encourage outstanding initiatives in the area of education. The monitoring of the FUNDEB implementation remains a key focus of the coalition.

(3) The definition of a fixed investment per student to assure a minimum of educational quality (CAQi[54]) has been on the CBDE agenda since the beginning.

- Diagnosis: The current government spending per student is so low that it hinders quality.
- Prognosis: The definition of a minimum investment per student is necessary to improve educational quality in Brazil.
- Motivation: The necessity to define a fixed investment per student is mentioned in CF/1988, LDB/1996, FUNDEF and FUNDEB.

In 2002, the CBDE initiated a process of calculating the required investment for all educational levels on a yearly basis at a continuous level of quality. Between 2003

---

[52] Various public statements, e.g.: PEC do Fundeb: Morosidade em Meio à Urgência. Posicionamento publico. August 30th. 2006; Regulamentacao do Fundeb: o processo democrático para a efetiva consagração dos direitos educacionais. Posicionamento publico. December 7th. 2006.; Regulamentacao do Fundeb: O respeito a educacao no congresso nacional. Posicionamento publico. February 8th, 2007; Regulamentação do Fundeb no Senado: da rede pública que temos à rede pública que queremos. Posicionamento publico. May 21st, 2007

[53] Interview Secretary of Basic Education, Brasília, September 2008; Interview representative Ministry of Education, Rio de Janeiro, August 2009; Interview journalist Canal Futura, Rio de Janeiro, July 2008

[54] Custo Aluno Qualidade Inicial = Initial Student-Quality-Cost

and 2005 the CAQi was discussed in three highly strategic and contested expert workshops.

> "The challenge was not the numeric calculation, but to define the ingredients of the quality school. Of course there are very different understandings, but we managed to define everything collectively; it was a long but very rich process." (Interview ex-coordinator CBDE, August 2008, Sao Paulo)

In addition, the CBDE initiated popular participation consultations about the topic, for example at the World Education Forum in Porto Alegre 2003. The final product – the book *Custo Aluno Qualidade Inicial: rumo à educação pública de qualidade no Brasil*[55] (Carreira and Rezende, 2007) – was published in 2008 and gained high credibility. It has been mentioned in a number of newspapers, and one national magazine dedicated a detailed article on the study. According to the responsible journalist, "it is an amazing study. I guard the book in my computer as a reference."[56]

In November 2008, the CBDE and the *Conselho Nacional de Educação*[57] (CNE), a sub-agency of the MEC, signed an inter-institutional cooperation (the first one ever signed between the CNE and a civil society entity) in order to discuss the possibility of transforming the CAQi into a reference for the financing of public education in Brazil. In May 2010 the CNE approved a resolution which establishes the CAQi values as the national minimum measure for the quality of basic education in Brazil. In addition, the CAQi will be used as a base for similar studies in countries such as Nigeria, Peru, Argentina, Columbia and India[58].

(4) The definition of a national teacher's base salary has been on the CBDE agenda since the first day.

- Diagnosis: Brazilian teachers are de-valorized and underpaid.
- Prognosis: A base salary will improve performance and stimulates formation.
- Motivation: The base salary is a historic demand of Brazilian civil society

Although all CBDE board members support a higher valorization of the teacher's profession, the objective has not been inclusive enough to support a collective action. E.g. for the MST, with its focus on rural and popular education the teachers base salary is a very distant issue.

In April 2008, after intense advocacy of the CNTE, the minimum base salary was fixed at 950 R$ (~410 US$) per month. The negotiation process generated intense frame disputes within the CBDE board, particularly between UNDIME and CNTE. The president of the teacher's unions explains:

---

[55] English Title: "Cost of Initial Quality Education per Student: a Brazilian Campaign' proposal for the financing of public quality education for all"

[56] Interview journalist Revista Epoca, São Paulo, September 2008

[57] National Education Council

[58] www.campanhaeducacao.org.br/?pg=Conquistas&pgs=CustoAlunoQualidadeInicial [last retrieved 28/07/2010]

"The CNTE has been fighting for the base salary for thirty years. UNDIME generally supports it, but we don't agree about the way it should be constituted. This dispute involves our visions on the role of the state and how it should treat its employees." (Interview president CNTE, São Paulo, September 2008)

The issue proves the importance of internal cohesion for framing purposes. As one CBDE member highlights, "the board reached consent, but it was divided badly. UNDIME did not really agree, the unity broke, so the campaign had less force."

(5) The realization of a National Conference for Basic Education (Conferência Nacional de Educação Básica, CONEB) with civil society participation was defined as a political priority in 2004.

- Diagnosis: Civil society is rarely involved in educational policies, leading to low government transparency and accountability and a weak democracy
- Prognosis: A national conference is an important space to present and discuss popular demands and ideas on education
- Motivation: The federal government is based on participatory democracy; Education is the only social area without a national conference

The realization of a CONEB with civil society participation was approved by the MEC in 2006, as a result of intense pressure by the CBDE[59]. The coalition conquered 38 (out of 1463) seats at the CONEB held in April 2008. Beforehand, the CBDE brought together its conference delegates and educational experts to collectively analyze the CONEB documents and define the political positioning of the CBDE (Campanha Nacional pelo Direto a Educação, 2007). The comprehensive preparation led to a high credibility of the coalition's demands at the CONEB.

"The campaign came to the plenary to lead the discussion, especially on the topics of educational funding and democratic management. More than 90% of its amendments have been approved."[60]

The two most important conquests of the CBDE are the implementation of the CAQ and the realization of a national conference for basic, higher and professional education, to be prepared in municipal and state conferences, every two years from 2010 onwards[61]. Furthermore, the CONEB was "a moment where all members demonstrated their commitment."[62] This mobilization capacity reveals a high salience among CBDE members all over Brazil, based on their awareness that the conference is a unique opportunity to take their proposals to the federal level. The implementation of the conference resolutions remains an important objective.

---

[59] Various public statements, e.g.: Da Conferência Nacional de Educação Básica que temos à Conferência de Educação que queremos. Posicionamento Público. October 7th, 2007; Por uma Conferência Nacional de Educação ampla e plural. Posicionamento publico. December 19th, 2007.

[60] Interview representative Ministry of Education, Rio de Janeiro, August 2009

[61] Interview representative ActionAid, Rio de Janeiro, July 2008

[62] Interview coordinator regional committee Rio, Rio de Janeiro, July 2008

DISCUSSION

What is the impact?

Although the CBDE did not succeed in pressuring the Brazilian government to increase the educational budget, there are a number of concrete achievements which did or will contribute to the improvement of public education in Brazil.

The coalition had significant influence on the approval of the FUNDEB which, if implemented correctly, means a significant change towards regional equality in education provision and enhanced quality on all educational levels. The definition of a minimum government investment per student is an important contribution to the institutionalization of the link between educational funding and quality. The definition of a minimum teacher's floor salary, although being relatively low, is a first step to the higher valorization of the teacher's profession in Brazil. The CBDE played an important role in bringing the issue on the government agenda (through FUNDEB and CONEB), but the final definition is fore and foremost the merit of the teacher's unions. Furthermore, the coalition played an important role in the approval and realization of the CONEB.

Despite these successes, the CBDE so far falls short on its goal to improve the democratic management of the educational system. In addition, the coalition fails to establish regular dialogue with schools, youth groups, parents and student organizations.

At a procedural level, the CBDE's recent political influence has facilitated the interlocution with the MEC and the Brazilian Congress. The invitation of the National Education Council to discuss the CAQ-study proves an enhanced recognition for the efforts of the CBDE. Although educational topics are rarely discussed in the Brazilian media, one government representative observed that "the CBDE is often consulted by the media. When there is an educational debate they first consult the government, and then the campaign."[63] A journalist from the national magazine "Epoch" confirmed this view:

> "The CBDE is an important source for me, either to give ideas for new topics or information about what is going on in congress. Whenever I need someone to explain something to me in detail, Daniel [Cara] is the one that knows everything." (Interview journalist *Revista Epoca*, São Paulo, September 2008)

Also in terms of symbolic impact, it is certainly a merit of the CBDE that the topic of educational funding is more central within the education community and the governmental discourse on education. However, it is doubtful that the coalition shaped this discourse, or even changed policy-makers opinions on education issues. The public consciousness for education has increased in recent years, but *Todos pela Educação* is more present in the public domain than the CBDE, due to the resources and the organic links with mainstream media TPE counts on.

---

[63] Interview secretary of basic education, Brasília, September 2008

However, the fact that education is more central in the public discourse certainly opens more space for the actions of the CBDE.

Internationally, the coalition is a respected co-founder and member of CLADE and board member of the GCE, where it struggles to establish an increased recognition for Latin American demands.

How impact is possible?

The ability of the CBDE to exert political influence is dependent on the combination of a range of factors, such as the political opportunity structures, the degree of internal cohesion between and within the different constituencies, and the way knowledge is produced and translated into objectives and strategies.

The political opportunity structures in which the CBDE operates are highly unstable due to a complex and volatile government system. The change of government in 2003 from the conservative rule of president Cardoso to the 'people's president' Lula led to a relative democratization between state and civil society, but the challenges, in essence remain the same. Some of these are related to entrenched characteristics of the Brazilian government and political culture:

- The lack of a clear line in the political orientation of the federal government, leading to severe tensions within the political left.
- The complex composition of the legislature.
- Corporatist structures at the state and municipal level.
- A political culture of subordination in many regions.

Others challenges are unique to the area of education:

- The low value placed on education at all administrative levels.
- The various dysfunctions of the decentralized system.
- The relative powerlessness of the MEC in light of the neoliberal government agenda.
- The population's disinterest in education in view of more immediate problems like poverty and violence.

The level of cohesion between executive, directive, and regional committees on the national scale is highly related to the political impact of the CBDE. Whenever the coalition exerts successful pressure on the national government, the circulation of knowledge, the coordination of activities, and the division of responsibilities have been high. Whenever tensions occurred, impact was limited.

There are three main phases that can be distinguished. From 1999 to 2002 the CBDE was lead almost exclusively by the general coordinator who was primarily concerned with the composition of the leadership, and regional committees, and the definition of the coalition objectives and principles. From 2002 onwards, cohesion between the different campaign members and scales increased, with peaks in key moments of the FUNDEB process, which have been strongest in terms of political impact. Since the approval of the FUNDEB in June 2007, regional participation has slowed down extremely due to a number of reasons: disagreements about the Lula government; lack of funding; the change of the general coordinator; and conflicts between the key member organizations. The coordination's incentives for a strong participation at the CONEB have been effective, but the conference generated further internal tensions. This lack of internal cohesion has led to a de-mobilization on national and regional levels.

The production and functionality of collective action frames (Benford and Snow, 2000) of the CBDE is highly related to the political success of the coalition. Well elaborated and articulated objectives foster cohesion on national and regional scales. However, the extent to which certain strategies become efficient advocacy tools is highly related to the political context and the opportunities it offers for intervention. Counter-framing can diminish the strength of a frame, but may be outbalanced by a reformulation of strategies. More recently, the maintenance of a 'collective identity' within the CBDE board is increasingly challenged by framing disputes.

The current demobilization of the local movement is highly related to the managerial style of the general coordinator who focuses on political advocacy at the cost of social mobilization. Furthermore, successful collective action is hindered by the lack of financial resources.

The central role of critical reflexivity

The CBDE has developed itself in a self-critical fashion, constantly evaluating and learning from past experiences, revising strategies, and formulating new ones according to contextual changes. All interviewed coalition members and affiliates demonstrated a high level of competence and knowledge about the historic, social and political context of the CBDE, and the reasons why actions are succeed or fail. This is not surprising, given the fact that many of them are academics and/or long-term civil society activists.

New political opportunities have been opened for the CBDE over the years as a result of the broader political context, but also of the coalition strategic action. The CBDE and its members have continuously reflected about the political context and about their own actions in relation to the context. And, on the basis of this reflexivity, they have had the capacity to open certain political opportunities to advance their demands. Failed strategies have diminished over the years, mirroring an improved understanding of the context. The following are some of many 'lessons learned' in relation to the Lula government: The importance to address advocacy to all three levels of government; the significance of alliances with key parliamentarians; and the impact of moral leverage and accountability politics.

Today the CBDE makes use of a wide range of means and vehicles to advance its agenda: traditional civil society strategies like research and advocacy are complemented by participatory consultations, legal actions, and the use of the mass media, amongst others. In different spaces and occasions, both formally and informally, coalition members reflect upon and thus improve and modify these methods. Moreover, demands are framed in different and often innovative ways for different audiences, revealing a comprehensive understanding of the complex social and cultural context the coalition is embedded in.

However, the members of the CBDE do not always manage to translate their knowledge into successful strategies. There is, for instance, a high awareness of the importance of citizens' mobilization and formation, but actions towards it are limited. This failure reflects that high levels of reflexivity do not necessarily translate into influence.

Reflection and learning about internal cohesion and conflicts is crucial for the functioning of the CBDE. All interviewed members demonstrated a comprehensive awareness of the challenges and opportunities of working together within and beyond scales, and the analysis of this scalar interaction is crucial to build strength as a network. The internal organization of the CBDE is designed to facilitate collective decision-making and non-hierarchical processes of critical reflection and knowledge construction. More recently, however, formal reflection processes are carried out mainly between and within the executive and directive committees and their cohesion has been challenged by framing disputes and other interest conflicts, while the local committees are disarticulated in the majority. All these factors hamper the political strength of the CBDE.

Reflection processes about supranational scalar interaction are rather informal and limited to those members that take part in the CLADE and GCE meetings. The main observation over the years is that the GCE does not incorporate yet what the CBDE is built on, which is the importance of respecting the differences between its members, rather than attempting to develop universal, centralized solutions that deny the diversity of identities. Notwithstanding, the CBDE will continue to participate in global meetings and events, because the GCE is seen as an important platform to promote Latin American demands.

Some of the main lessons learned by CBDE with the passage of time, as reflected by their members themselves are: the need to invest in a strong social base; foster a diverse membership to strengthen legitimacy; exert different strategies in a balanced fashion; formulate clear and realistic goals that appeal to a broad range of actors; strengthen expertise on central goals; invest in high-quality knowledge production and elaborate strategies to strategically use this knowledge; follow objectives in well grounded and continuing political dialogue; do not limit advocacy actions to the education community, but include the head of state and the Ministry of Finance, national media and the general public

CONCLUSION

Based on the assumption that the performance of the CBDE is dependent on a variety of internal and external factors, the case study has looked at the coalition's strategic scalar intervention, its knowledge production and dissemination, as well as political opportunity structures and internal organization. The analysis reveals how all these factors relate to each other in complex processes of critical reflexivity and strategic learning.

Given the complexity of the political context, the density of Brazilian civil society actors concerned with education, and the fact that educational change usually happens over a long time period, it is difficult to attribute concrete impacts to a single coalition with a history of ten years. However, contra-factual analysis and process tracing have shown that a number of education-related issues would be different or non-existent in Brazil if the CBDE had not have intervened.

Without the coalition, there would be no federal fund for basic education and the student quality cost would not be on its way to becoming the principal reference for the federal education budget. There would also not have been a national conference of basic education in April 2008, at least not one with such broad civil society participation, and the last Global GCE Assembly would have happened anywhere, but not in Latin America. The creation of the FUNDEB has certainly been the key process, both in terms of coalition learning and political impact of the CBDE. It established the coalition as recognized political actor and has opened doors for other conquests.

I want to distance myself from speaking of 'success' or 'failure' of the CBDE because it is hard to define what constitutes success, primarily because the broad goal of quality in education will never be reached, since improvements will always be possible. When I asked the first general coordinator of the CBDE about her expectations for the campaign in 2009, she replied:

"My hope was that I would become what it became: A strong civil society movement that is able to think and backup its lobby positions with good arguments, that is autonomous and recognized, that inspires people and makes them mobilize." (Interview general coordinator CLADE, September 2008, Sao Paulo)

Departing from this perspective, the campaign certainly lived up to its ambitions.

FELICE VAN DER PLAAT

CHAPTER 8

Advocating EFA in Zambia: A Case Study of Civil Society's Struggle for Equal Rights for Education

INTRODUCTION

Zambia is a landlocked country in Southern Africa with a population of eleven million people. 44% of Zambia's citizens live in urban areas (FTI, 2007). Zambia is highly ethnically heterogeneous and has over seventy different tribes. The country's economy is vastly dependent on its copious natural resources, including copper, cobalt, zinc, lead, coal, emeralds, gold, silver, uranium, water and fertile land. The falling prices of copper led to a major economic crisis in the 1970's that lasted until the 1990's. During this period, government expenditure on social services decreased dramatically, hindering the development of the education sector and other social services. In 2005, Zambia saw the elimination of most of its debt under the Highly Indebted Poor Countries initiative and the Multilateral Debt Relief by the G8. This provided space to breathe and the possibility to envision a way forward. It is Zambia's vision to be a "Prosperous Middle Income Nation by 2030" (Republic of Zambia, 2006). In contrast to this encouraging goal, Zambia is currently still one of the poorest nations in the world. In 2007 65% of the citizens lived below the poverty line and unemployment rates are still obscenely high. Also, social indicators continue to decline. According to the 2010 edition of the United Nations Human Development Index, the quality of life in Zambia has been falling. If the government of Zambia aims to become a middle-income country by 2030, then progress needs to be made to improve the welfare and wellbeing of its population. One of the ways to develop the nation, as the government identifies in a strategic document (MoE, 2007), is through educating its citizens. Education is seen as a way to spearhead the economic and social development of Zambia both in a national and in an international context (Republic of Zambia, 2006).

In this chapter, the efforts of the Zambia National Education Campaign coalition (ZANEC) in working for the achievement of the Education for All (EFA) goals in Zambia are analysed. ZANEC is operating in a country that is still thwarted by high poverty levels and where education was not a key priority for the government until the end of the 1990's. The chapter will first describe the structure and development of the education sector in Zambia, with a focus on the specific education problems in the country. Subsequently, the state-civil society relationship will be analysed. After this, the historical development of ZANEC is depicted, with a specific focus on the strategies used to influence educational

Antoni Verger and Mario Novelli (eds.), Campaigning for "Education for All", 121–139.
© *2012 Sense Publishers. All rights reserved.*

discourses and policies in Zambia. In the subsequent section, an example of a campaign is explored, to illustrate how ZANEC works to influence policies. Finally, the impact of ZANEC on procedural, political and symbolic levels will be discussed.

The fieldwork for this research took place from October to December 2009. In total, 33 people were interviewed. These persons were selected because of their role within ZANEC or their function in the education sector. Most interviews took place in Lusaka, but a few happened with provincial coalition members in the North-Western province of Zambia where ZANEC organized several workshops. Besides the interviews, the most important ways of obtaining information were through participant observation at ZANEC headquarters, analysing relevant documents and documentaries and through a participatory-workshop at the end of the fieldwork period. During this workshop, the preliminary findings were presented and a big share of ZANEC members was given the possibility to react and comment.

COUNTRY CONTEXT

Before gaining independence from Great Britain in 1964, education in Zambia was under the control of missionaries. The education system was highly underdeveloped at that time, with less than 0.5% of the population estimated to have completed primary education (Mutangadura, 2003). Education was seen as a way to achieve Zambia's aspirations for the fruits of independence. However, chiefly due to the lack of economic developments, progress in the education sector lagged behind. In the 1980's and 1990's a debt burden forced the government to cut the budget of education, which resulted in the deterioration of the education sector. As a consequence, enrolment rates faltered and literacy rates fell (Minbuza, 2008). It was not only the education sector that was suffering, the whole of Zambia's wellbeing and social conditions were faltering. A striking statistic is the value of the Human Development Index (HDI). Zambia is the only country whose HDI value at the end of the 1990's was lower than in 1975 (Economic Commission for Africa, 2002).

The development of new strategic plans and guiding documents was critical for the progress and development of the education sector. The current ruling legislation in the education sector in Zambia is the Education Act of 1966. As can be predicted, a major complaint from civil society is that this act is outdated and not adequate for the developments that the education sector in Zambia has undergone over the past decades. The 1966 Education Act governs the provision of education in Zambia (interview secretariat01, 2009). Amendments such as 'Focus on Learning' (1992) and 'Educating our Future' (1996) played a structural role in reshaping the education sector (Stateuniversity.com, 2009). Despite the many amendments however, the Commonwealth Education fund still claims that the Act does not adequately provide for the needs of the education system in Zambia and the achievement of the MDGs and the EFA Goals (Muunga et al, 2008).

An important step forward was the development of the Basic Education Sub-Sector Plan (BESSIP) for 1999-2002 that went hand in hand with the Sector Wide Approach (SWAP) in the development of basic education. The BESSIP programme was an immediate offspring of Educating our Future, which focused on increasing enrolment at the primary level and eventually up to High Schools (10-12). To enhance access, the Free Middle Basic Education policy (Grades 1-7) was announced in February 2002, a policy that the Zambia National Education Coalition heavily advocated for. The policy abolished all user fees as well as removing the requirement that children should wear school uniforms. In 2003, BESSIP was followed up by the Ministry of Education Strategic Plan for 2003-2007; which was followed up by major achievements in improving access to basic education.

Other important policies guiding developments in the education sector are Vision 2030, and related to this the Fifth National Development Plan (FNDP) and the National Implementation Framework (NIF) for the education sector. In Vision 2030 the government of Zambia states that Zambia should become a "Prosperous Middle Income Nation by 2030" (Republic of Zambia, 2006). The vision is operationalized through implementing five National Development Plans until 2030, the first one being the Fifth National Development Plan (2008-2010), following up the Fourth National Development Plan (1989-1993). The Fifth National Development was written to obtain a more holistic approach to development in Zambia, dealing with cross-sectoral issues. Central to the development of the FNDP was the involvement of civil society. The Civil Society for Poverty Reduction in Zambia, a platform of CSOs of which ZANEC is a member, delivered a version of the FNDP and presented that to the government who considered the input for the writing of the final document. Some of the suggestions of the civil society version are reflected in the official version.

What should be noted from the latest policy developments in the education sector is that policies are to a great extent directed towards the international donor audience. The different Cooperating Partners of Zambia, notably the IMF and the World Bank, play a big role in dialogues concerning the adoption of new policies (Economic Commission for Africa, 2002). In addition, policies are under the influence of international commitments such as the MDG's and the EFA goals, as well as the right to education as signed by Zambia under the Convention of the Rights of the Child (1989). However, although Zambia signed this Convention, education still has no legal status in Zambia. The Ministry of Education states that its broader policy principle, as guided by the MDGs and EFA goals, is that basic education is an integral part of social and economic development and that it is a fundamental human right (MoE, 2007). However, in the National Constitution this right is not clearly guaranteed; it is rather said: "The State shall endeavour to provide equal and adequate educational opportunities in all fields and at all levels for all." In this way, the state does not guarantee the right to education to its citizens. Since the state can only be judged or challenged on its central text on the right to education, whether this is the Constitution, the laws or the policies, it cannot be held accountable for providing education to all its citizens. Precisely, one of the main goals of ZANEC is to make an amendment to the National Constitution, to ensure that education becomes a guaranteed right for every child (Muunga et al, 2008).

PROBLEMS IN THE EDUCATION SECTOR IN ZAMBIA

The problems of the education sector in Zambia are wide ranging and can primarily be divided into problems of access and problems of quality. In terms of access the main problems are: large percentage of out of school children and drop-outs; children of incorrect age are often highly represented in lower and middle basic classes; gender and social issues that hinder girls for attending education; teacher absenteeism and a lack of productivity of teachers due to illness; unequal opportunities for marginalized, orphaned and disabled children; societal problems such as child labour; and the growing number of orphans and child-headed households because of HIV/ AIDS, to name but some of the issues, all influence the demand for education. In terms of quality the main problems are: high pupil-teacher ratios; large class sizes (especially in urban areas); low quality of education, the curriculum, and of educational facilities. Although participation and access have improved, issues of quality and explicitly learning achievements are still troublesome. Compared to other countries in the Southern Africa sub-region, in terms of learning achievement, Zambia has comparatively low scores. The recent increase in enrolment rates in Zambia has caused some new problems, which is in no small part due to the increase in rates of enrolment at the same time that infrastructural development and teacher employment have lagged behind. Further, in line with the expansion of enrolment in education has stretched the available resources, resulting in a reduction of schooling hours per student in parallel with an increase in hours per teacher; a shortage of teachers and teaching materials; and overcrowded classrooms and schools. The National Implementation Framework labels quality of education as its key area of focus, especially because of the low learning outcomes experienced in Zambia.

The amount and diversity of problems that can be identified in the education sector is a problem in itself, because they are not likely to be resolved all at once. Due to financial restrictions, the government focuses on certain issues, which inevitably lead to other areas being neglected. Over the past years the government has been focusing on making improvements to basic education. A little over 50% of the education budget is allocated to this subsector, which has led to improved access and participation. Another 23% of the budget goes to the MoE headquarters and 11% to high schools. The lowest funded area is the Distance Education Directorate, which covers adult education and literacy, and receives only 0.2% of the budget. When assigning the biggest share of the budget to basic education, other subsectors remain underdeveloped, such as secondary, tertiary and adult education. Nowhere is this trend clearer than in the bottom-weighted graduation rates that take on the shape of a pyramid: which is to say that the bulk of graduations occur at primary level, and with each subsequent year there is a sharp and evident drop off.

THE STATE AND CIVIL SOCIETY

Civil society has played an important, but highly restricted, role in Zambia ever since its independence. Civil society has a history of protesting against government structures and policies. An example of this can be found in the civil unrest and protest in the 1970's against the one party regime of President Kaunda. Conversely, the government structures that civil society protested against also held them back; civil society in Zambia is heavily influenced by the country's history of authoritarian traditions. For several decades civil society mobilization was largely restricted to activities within the agendas and control of the state (Maitra, 2009). Even in the current era, the government seems eager to restrict civil society actions, with the NGO bill of 2008 being a prime example. In this Bill the government demands from NGOs to register and reregister themselves frequently and the government gives itself the right to prohibit any NGO from continuing its existence. According to a government advisor (Policy advisor01, 2009) this allows the state to weaken oppositional NGOs, while at the same time it gives the government the opportunity to start supporting NGOs that also support the state's vision and work. As a diplomat from the Royal Netherlands embassy notes:

"The big danger is that on the one hand the government needs civil society, but on the other hand they are afraid because many civil society organizations criticize government. The new NGO bill is a very clear example that the government is really trying to hinder the functioning of especially the critical NGOs, which is I think a big blow for any type of development. This issue should be high on the agenda of the NGOs. The problem is as far as I know and I heard that most of the NGOs are afraid to speak out against the NGO bill. Only a few are willing and able to speak out, because they fear that the government can really tackle them in any way they want because of the NGO bill." (Interview Donor01, 2009)

Civil society has always been particularly prevalent in urban areas in Zambia, with Lusaka being the main hub for civil action. Their presence has been growing significantly since the 1990's, when Zambia became once again a multiparty system. Civil society engagement became especially apparent during the writing of Zambia's Poverty Reduction Strategy Paper (PRSP) and the FNDP. However, although civil society engagement with the state and politics has been growing steadily, its impact and participation are still not as forceful as possible. An important issue is the lack of institutionalised mechanisms for civil society participation in policy processes. Government and administrative structures are highly centralised (Maitra, 2009). Furthermore, both civil society and the government itself are dependent on donors. Consequently, government seems to listen more to donors and their Cooperating Partners than to civil society. Another issue is that although civil society has a strong background in policy implementation, their technical capacity required for advocating and lobbying is still lagging behind. Related to this is the fact that most technical civil society actors are located in Lusaka, which often leads to a lack of local knowledge of other parts of the country (Interview Donor02, 2009). And importantly: the government is often willing to listen to civil society, but translating their message into policy change is something that the government is still reluctant to do.

According to ZANEC, a recent 'Ministry of Education Strategic Plan' Review Report confirmed the continuing weak linkage between government and civil society. Instead of engaging civil society, the government has been compelled to responding to Cooperating Partners' concerns. Civil society has the challenge to demand and ensure that the system is accountable to the recipients of the services, who are primarily the citizens of Zambia (ZANEC, 2007).

HISTORY AND DEVELOPMENT OF ZANEC

Just as with most national coalitions advocating for EFA, the constitution of ZANEC is related to the World Education Forum (WEF) in Dakar in 2000. While ZANEC was formally established after the WEF, the first initiatives were put in place in 1998 when a group of NGOs were brought together by UNESCO to build their capacity in basic education. Additionally, Oxfam supported the NGOs in making an input to the WEF preparatory process and five representatives from Zambia were sent to Dakar. After Dakar, the different organizations joined forces to come up with an evaluation of the conference and of their input more specifically. As one of the initiators of the coalition mentioned at the workshop:

"ZANEC is truly a baby of the EFA movement because the establishment of the coalition came to being almost immediately after the World Education Forum which was held in 2000 in Dakar, Senegal." (Interview member01, 2009)

The coalition started off with an interim committee of five member organisations namely; the People Action Forum, Adult Education Association of Zambia, Pamuka, Forum for African Women Educationalists of Zambia, Zambia Pre-school Association and the Zambia Open Community Schools, which designed the legal and administrative documents that guided the initial coalition. The interim committee also tried to attract more members to strengthen the voice of the coalition and to increase their combined knowledge on different themes and areas. The coalition was composed of civil society organizations, NGOs, teacher unions, faith based organizations, and grassroots organizations. The first donors to ZANEC were Oxfam and the Commonwealth Education Fund. The functions of the coalition were centred on three objectives that the Commonwealth Education Fund put on the table: capacity building of members in advocacy and policy formulation; budget tracking; and creating innovative ideas to achieve the EFA goals.

Although ZANEC was unofficially established in 2001, the official launch of ZANEC took place in 2003, when it joined the Global Campaign for Education. Since 2003 ZANEC worked with a draft constitution, which was reaffirmed after elections in 2004. It was also in 2004 that the first secretariat of ZANEC was established. The coalition was then divided into four main organs: the annual general assembly, the executive council, the thematic committees, and the national secretariat.

The highest decision making body is the Annual General Assembly (AGM). At the AGM all final decisions are made and the policies and functioning of the coalition are reviewed. The AGM takes place biannually and at the event the board members for the executive committee are chosen. The executive committee has the power to implement the aims of ZANEC and to provide overall policy guidelines, and it recruits the staff members. Furthermore it cooperates with the secretariat to monitor its functioning. The secretariat is the coordinating and implementing body of the coalition. It is concerned with the day to day running of ZANEC. There is thus a clear division of tasks between the different organs, and although the daily business of ZANEC is in the hands of the secretariat the members have the biggest say.

ZANEC relies heavily on their charismatic executive director and on a couple of highly respected and influential persons in their thematic committees and executive committee. The executive committee consist of people with a strong history in the education sector in Zambia, both in political terms as in advocacy. ZANEC has done a smart job by attracting these persons for their advocacy work. As one member puts it:

> "ZANEC's main strength is the capacity of human resource that they have. There are quite knowledgeable characters within the coalition that are highly courageous and that are able to talk about things. They are able to say what should be addressed. They have the human resource that is required" (Interview Member02, 2009).

Another internal achievement for the coalition is that it has been able to increase its membership base significantly. While starting with only five organizations, for the past years ZANEC had a membership base between 40 and 50 member organizations. These have all been divided into the thematic committees. ZANEC's members and activities are essentially focused in Lusaka. Until now, only three other provincial focal points have been established in the Northwestern, Luapula, and Eastern Province. Some of the member organizations are however from elsewhere in the country, and some of the bigger member organizations such as the Forum for African Women Educationalists of Zambia (FAWEZA) have different branches throughout Zambia. These local linkages are crucial for the coalition to spread their message to the communities, the parents, teachers, and the District Education Boards as well as being instrumental in obtaining local knowledge that can be used in their evidence based advocacy campaigns. It is important for the coalition to expand and strengthen their local linkages to make sure that the organization does not become too centralized and Lusaka oriented.

STRATEGIC DIRECTION OF THE COALITION

For ZANEC to operate successfully it needs to have effective institutional frameworks, functioning operation systems, and strategies in place. These have to promote the accountability and transparency of the coalition to strengthen its credibility, and to facilitate collaboration with donors, partners and the government. The development of the First and Second Strategic Framework have been crucial in guiding the operations, processes, and expenditures of the coalition. The first strategic plan was effective between 2004 and 2007. The coalition is currently working with its second strategic plan which will end in 2011.

To develop their strategic framework ZANEC uses inputs from its members derived from pre-strategic planning meetings, ZANEC further assimilates input from the secretariat, consultants, donors, the government, the cooperating partners and other stakeholders in the education sector with whom ZANEC established partnerships. The goal of ZANEC as spelled out in its second strategic plan is:

"To contribute towards creating a learning environment that promotes quality and relevant education to all learners in the education system through effective engagement with Government and other stakeholders whilst building the capacity of ZANEC to effectively fulfil its mandate" (ZANEC, 2007).

Its key strategic considerations to achieve this goal are: 1) to focus on evidence-based advocacy and lobbying, 2) to use the Fifth National Development Plan and the National Implementation Framework of the government, 3) to strengthen member participation in planning and implementation of programmes, 4) to work more with other government agencies besides the MoE and 5) to enhance the resource mobilization for both the activities of the secretariat as for the member organizations. The two strategic directions that ZANEC takes are the Education Development Strategy (EDS) and the Organization Development Strategy (ODS). The EDS addresses the external goals of the coalition, while the ODS looks to the internal ambitions. ZANEC has developed a broad range of strategies over the years to achieve its goals. The main ones for the EDS are lobbying for increased support to the education sector, and for effective monitoring processes in education institutions. Part of this lobbying involves a public relations strategy that combines the holding of press conferences; the issuing of press releases; undertaking, conducting, and publishing research; documentation and tracking of budget; engaging with government over terms of legal and policy making processes; initiating and overseeing proper planning, monitoring and review processes; and finally, implementing monitoring and evaluation systems for the communication and advocacy strategy.

A strategy to be highlighted here is the networking of ZANEC with international bodies, partners, donors, and the media. The coalition benefits through engaging and interacting, at the supra-national level, with the Africa Network Campaign on Education for All (ANCEFA) and the Global Campaign for Education (GCE). A big advantage for ZANEC is that the office of the regional division for Southern Africa is located in Lusaka, which allows them to work closely with the ANCEFA staff on certain projects, as well as providing ample opportunity for the staff of ANCEFA to assist them in more effective lobbying. ANCEFA also tries to fill up the capacity gaps for the national coalitions and because their involvement with ZANEC is so direct they are able to identify challenges and the necessary steps to be taken to overcome them quickly. The coalition also benefits from their membership with the GCE, although these benefits are less apparent then their involvement with ANCEFA. ZANEC participates in certain GCE activities such as the Global Action Week, and they also attend meetings. Their involvement with the GCE gives them a global voice during the GAW, which opens windows of opportunity for engaging directly with the government.

The impact of ZANEC can also be linked to their networking with donors and partners. Especially Irish Aid, which is an important linkage, because it is one of the leading Cooperating Partners in the education sector. ZANEC often brings educational issues to Irish Aid with the question to help them advocate for improvements with the government, although some consider that these exchanges could be more frequent. As one officer and advisor of Irish Aid noted:

> "The way we help them to network is that we as Lead sit on most of the key committees of the MoE and we lobby for ZANEC's involvement in these committees. We do help them in that way, we connect them to other people, and we connect them to opportunities. We connect them also to other donors. (Interview Donor03, 2009)"

Furthermore, ZANEC has a strong relationship with the media in Zambia. ZANEC's main media partner is the *Media Network on Child Rights and Development*, which is a network of individuals and organizations involved with the media. This network is also a member organization of ZANEC and it helps the coalition in creating and strengthening its relationships with the different media houses in Zambia.

A problem with the Strategic Framework of ZANEC is that it is has proven to be overambitious. The average budget ZANEC calculates per year is around one million US Dollars, but the funding attracted has never been able to cover more than half of this (Interview Secretariat01, 2009). This can cause disillusionment among members and donors about the plans and outcomes of the coalition, and it can also affect the credibility of ZANEC.

SCALAR INTERACTION AND INTERNAL COHESION

Working in a coalition has several advantages: firstly, it is a tool to familiarize CSOs in Zambia on education issues. Secondly, it was felt that by joining forces, it would become easier to push the government to honour its promises towards the EFA goals and to advocate for related policy changes. Thirdly, ZANEC aims to supplement and complement the work of the government by using the different strengths, skills and knowledge of its various members. Most members were primarily concerned with implementation and service delivery on the ground, and ZANEC could use their information for evidence based advocacy. By training these implementation oriented NGOs in advocacy, research, budget tracking, and resource mobilization, the Zambian civil society's efforts could have more impact. A further advantage is that duplication of activities could be prevented when combining efforts, and the NGOs involved could learn from each other through sharing experiences and information, and through cooperating on certain issues.

'Coalitions of civil society organizations involved in education are a strong avenue to advocate for the realization of the EFA goals because they represent a larger constituency by pulling together several agencies in the country with different specific needs and mandates but whose aggregate scope fall within the EFA goals.' (Interview Member03, 2009)

Teacher unions form an important part of the coalition. However, as is often the case with unions, the large membership base and attendant political tensions could threaten ZANEC's efficacy by making it subject to the demands of a larger organisation, which could jeopardize the coalition. Currently there is no evidence that this is taking place, but inevitably within ZANEC the larger organisations have a greater impact on the coalition's affairs than the smaller, grassroots organizations. This is simply because they have more resources and staff available, they are better engaged in research and advocacy and they are better engaged with the government. Examples of highly influential organizations are FAWEZA, the Zambia National Union of Teachers and CAMFED. Especially FAWEZA has a strong role to play. It has offices throughout the country and therewith forms ZANEC's main connection to the field. Also, FAWEZA cooperates separately from ZANEC with the government and with the Development Partners in the Education sector and it has been able in the past to establish certain political successes, such as the Re-Entry Policy for girls.

Internal cohesion is needed to make sure that members are committed and dedicated to the cause of the coalition and to smoothen the operational processes of ZANEC. A sense of unity and belonging is crucial for the functioning of the coalition. Within ZANEC, some members feel their expectations of becoming part of the coalition have not been met. Reasons for this are for example that they anticipated obtaining financial resources through their membership, or because they expected to play a different role within the coalition than they are doing now. There are specifically misunderstandings about what is to be the role of the secretariat and of the members.

"The idea of a coalition and a small secretariat is that really your strength should be in your member organizations coming together. The secretariat should coordinate what the members do; you support what they do, instead of trying to do what they are doing. There is not enough cohesion between the member organizations and that is partly because many member organizations think they do not get enough from their membership with ZANEC (Interview Policy advisor01, 2009)."

In the current situation, the secretariat takes up most of the responsibilities of the coalition. They organize events, meetings, workshops and press conferences, advocate with the government, attend international conferences, and try to contract donors for the funding of their budget. Some members would like the secretariat to take up a more coordinating role, while the member organizations take part in the implementation of programs and in advocacy meetings with the government. These mixed expectations harm the adequateness of the coalition and the level of commitment of its members. The secretariat has responded to these challenges by handing over more responsibilities to its members, for example by sending thematic committee members to the government. By doing this, ZANEC experienced several advantages. Firstly, members are specialized in their area of interest, which meant that they could provide valuable contributions to these meetings. Secondly, the core staff of ZANEC would have more time to spend on other issues. And thirdly, members would feel more tied to the coalition.

In terms of scalar interaction, ZANEC still needs to make significant improvements. In the current situation, almost all actions take place in the capital Lusaka, and there are only two other provincial focal points in place. It is therefore difficult for the coalition to obtain country-wide information about educational issues. The coalition is working towards setting up provincial focal points in all its provinces, but until this time, the coalition is quite top down with few connections to the field.

ADULT LITERACY CAMPAIGN: A CROSS CUTTING ISSUE

In this section the aim of ZANEC and specifically the thematic committee on Adult Education towards realizing an Adult Literacy policy in Zambia will be analyzed to show in more detail the different processes that lay behind the campaign. This particular example is chosen because adult education and adult literacy more explicitly is identified by ZANEC as a crucial issue, but the importance of this topic is not yet universally accepted or put into being by the different stakeholders within Zambia. This unfavourable context provides a fruitful soil to distinguish the tactics and framing strategies used by the coalition to achieve a positive result.

Problem identification

The thematic committee on Adult Education was established to advocate for the achievement of Goal 4 of the EFA action framework: increase adult literacy by 50 per cent. According to ZANEC, increasing literacy is one of the most neglected of the six EFA goals (ZANEC, 2009). In Zambia, the adult literacy rate for the period 2003-2008 as measured by UNICEF was 63% (UNICEF, 2009). Illiteracy rates have even seen an increase since the 1990s and if the government is serious about achieving a 50% increase of the literacy rates a lot more work needs to be done. Although working documents such as the National Implementation Framework for Education make avowals on improving the literacy rates in Zambia; the right to education is not legally binding yet in Zambia. Therefore, the government is not indebted to guarantee the various forms of education to the citizens of Zambia. Subsectors such as adult education seem to suffer from this. The fact that adult education is one of the most neglected themes in the education sector in Zambia is shown from the amount of money that goes to the directorate of Distance Education, no more than 0.2% from the total budget on education (Machila, 2009).

The coalition thinks that the high illiteracy rates and the lack of opportunities for adult education in Zambia pose a serious threat to the development of the country and its citizens. Illiteracy seems to have a strong link with poverty and the coalition believes that by combating illiteracy levels individual and country-wide economic standards can be raised. Furthermore, literacy brings access to information and knowledge, which can be of help in the daily life of the Zambian citizens. Also, research has shown that parents who are literate seem to encourage their children more to complete education. Additionally, people who are illiterate seem to be less aware of their civic and political rights. According to Machila (2009) who conducted a research adult literacy in Zambia for ZANEC:

> "With literacy comes awareness and ability to be critical to issues such as budgets, corruption and other areas requiring government accountability. They (the government) know and realize that empowerment of its youths and adults is the key to real change; change which will not only promote participatory and accountable governance but also bring about real and genuine change to the untold miseries of the youth and adults in Zambia, the region and globally. Empowerment through youth and adult literacy has been known in history: the era of enlightenment and the role it played and continues playing in Europe and other societies."

Problem attribution

Several cultural, contextual, economic, and political aspects influence the high rates of illiteracy in Zambia. And although ZANEC acknowledges that there are more stakeholders who carry responsibilities to improve the results on Adult Education, they primarily put the blame on the government's plate. The coalition does not think that the government takes this subsector seriously. Until now, Zambia has not had a policy on adult education; there has been no overall curriculum; and the latest learning guides for adult education are more than 20 years old. These factors have led to fragmentation in the way adult education is delivered by the different stakeholders (the government, churches, NGOs, CBOs and other civil society actors). Considering the minimal budget that is available for the Directorate of Distance Education, as well as the fact that this money has to be shared among the different provinces and districts in Zambia, it is clear that a lot of work lays ahead for ZANEC's thematic committee on Adult Education.

Prognostic framing

The thematic committee of Adult Education under ZANEC has come up with several ways forward to overcome the problems in the adult education sector. Firstly, the coalition advocated for the introduction of a policy on Adult Literacy. Secondly, the coalition lobbied for a curriculum for adult education. And thirdly, an increase in budget for Adult Education is asked for.

However, what ZANEC really wants to combat is the current lack of political will in Zambia in order to overcome the challenge of adult education, and to establish a regulatory policy framework that can help to mainstream the actions in the sector. The lack of interest for adult education seems to be a universal problem, which does not only lie with the Government of Zambia. When looking at education and the EFA goals, the primary focus worldwide seems to be on achieving universal education for all. The focus is on children and primarily on children between six and twelve years old. Adults that have not enjoyed primary education are frequently overlooked.

Motivational framing

ZANEC believes that by merely focusing on basic education and not on improving the literacy rates of adults, the government makes a crucial mistake by leaving out an important group of citizens. If Zambia truly aims to develop into a middle income country any time soon, the coalition believes that the government should focus on improving the literacy levels of its citizens, and the level of education of its adults. According to both ZANEC and the government, development rests on education. The coalition links its own goals of improving adult education and literacy levels, to the government's goals of economic and societal development. Both parties find common ground here, and this is one of the reasons why ZANEC is progressing quite well in the establishment of an Adult Education policy in Zambia.

In order to bring their message out to the public, ZANEC claims that "literacy is power". It is power for the citizens to develop themselves personally and economically, but also to the nation as a whole. Through youth and adult literacy programmes, participants will be empowered to critically analyze the various contexts in which they find themselves, as well as to have the tools to take appropriate actions to transform situations for personal and societal development. As such, the rights based approach to adult literacy is critical to the transformation of any society. ZANEC's position is that education is a fundamental right regardless of age or nationality.

> "Literacy is a basic human right and a crucial asset for overcoming poverty,
> improving health and reducing human rights abuses" (ZANEC, 2009).

They use this frame to convince the government of Zambia about its responsibility for providing literacy to its citizens.

ZANEC believes that it must be possible to increase the literacy rates in Zambia. As stated before, the adult literacy rate for the period 2003-2008 as measured by UNICEF was 63%. This is a rather low percentage compared to its neighbouring countries, of which only Mozambique is scoring worse. The adult literacy rate in these countries was as follows: Zimbabwe 91%, Mozambique 44%, Angola 67%, Namibia 88%, Malawi 72%, Botswana 83% and Tanzania 72% (no statistics available for the Democratic Republic of Congo) (UNICEF, 2009).

Therefore, ZANEC believes that it is possible to take their neighbouring countries as a positive example and that change is possible.

Main strategies

In order to ensure that adult education becomes higher on the agenda of the government of Zambia, leading to an Adult Literacy Policy, an increase in budget and a new curriculum; ZANEC uses several strategies. First and foremost, the coalition tried to recruit all civil society organizations in Zambia working with Adult Education to join forces in the thematic committee. By doing this, the different members hoped to be able to present their concerns and proposals as one voice. Secondly, as the thematic committee, the members designed a clear strategy to approach the government. An important step was to design shared goals and strategies to meet the desired results. Thirdly, the members carried out a research on adult literacy in Zambia, to highlight the problem areas and to give suggestions for the way forward.

As part of its strategy, ZANEC built a support network that would back up their lobbying and advocacy work. ZANEC invested in community mobilization and linking the agenda to various constituencies of Youth and Adult Literacy providers. Also, ZANEC stimulated the different Youth and Adult Literacy providers to share institutional knowledge about effective strategies that enhance and sustain literacy and used this information for its advocacy agenda. Jointly, ZANEC started an intense mobilization, advocacy and lobbying campaign to establish a policy on Adult Literacy within Zambia. ZANEC, lobbied by members of parliament, attended meetings of the Adult Literacy Technical Committee of the Ministry of Education, gave press statements to the media, tracked the budget on adult education, and participated in the drafting of a policy on Adult Literacy with the MoE. By doing this, ZANEC was identified as one of the key stakeholders in helping to design Adult Literacy policy draft, and as the most important actor of civil society.

The GCE global action week (GAW) of 2009 was dedicated to Youth and Adult Literacy and Life Long Learning" (ZANEC, 2009). ZANEC organized activities in the four provinces: Lusaka, Eastern, Luapula and Northwestern Provinces. The GAW is a very important happening each year for ZANEC, because it is backed by international support, and it comes with a lot of attention, which makes it the perfect opportunity to advocate for certain issues. It was therefore very helpful for the thematic committee on adult education that the GAW of 2009 was dedicated to their topic. The GAW campaign was launched by the Minister of Education, Professor Geoffrey Lungwangwa on the Zambia National Broadcasting Television (ZNBC). During the launch, the Minister acknowledged the various challenges that still remain to be addressed in the literacy education subsector, such as the need for the speedy enactment of the adult literacy policy, the need for allocating more resources to the subsector, and the need for an effective adult literacy coordination mechanism. Herewith, he expressed government commitment to address these challenges (ZANEC, 2009). Engaging directly with politicians and political matters over the course of this week is an important part of ZANEC's strategy. Also, engaging with media is very important to reach the wider public. During this GAW, ZANEC aired six discussions about Adult Education and Literacy on national television. The programmes were broadcasted in the six local languages spoken in Zambia. Also, radio programmes were developed. The media was used to bring ZANEC's message to the people of Zambia and to lobby the government.

OUTCOME

Although the government paid attention to adult literacy during the GAW, and rhetorically committed itself to sharpen its focus on the subsector, this has not led to any effective results. Although promises might be made, there is still a problem with having the government putting their promises into practice. This is shown from the fact that the Policy on Adult Literacy has been in process since 2004 and a draft has long since been ready but the government has failed to put it into action. According to a staff member of ZANEC:

> "The process of responding is very slow, especially on matters related to policy formulation processes. But there are things that we can point at, advocacy issues that we have pushed that have really worked very well."
> (Interview Secretariat03, 2009)

ZANEC is used to having to advocate persistently before any real changes are put into being, but in the past advocacy work has resulted in policy changes. Therefore, ZANEC keeps its hopes up that the draft policy will be enacted any time soon. And small improvements have already been made: for a long time literacy matters were left out of government policies and statements, but in the FNDP the Government for the first time mentions the importance of adult literacy (Republic of Zambia, 2006).

In all, the most noteworthy impact of ZANEC considering adult education is the fact that they have been able to bring the topic on the agenda of the government. Now ZANEC will have to wait for their efforts to bear fruit.

DISCUSSION

Although the existence and input of ZANEC in the education sector has been apparent for quite some time, a clear understanding about its impact is still lacking. Questions remain about what it really means to be the education sector's most acknowledged civil society actor and about what impact the work of ZANEC truly has. This section will look at the external impact of ZANEC that can be divided into procedural, political and symbolic impact.

Procedural impact

The procedural success deals with to what extent ZANEC has been able to create a negotiating space within the education sector in Zambia. It is important for the coalition to gain recognition from the government, the Cooperating Partners, donors, the media, and other actors in the education sector. This recognition can be measured by analyzing in which processes, meetings and decision-making summits ZANEC is involved in and what their role in these meetings ultimately is.

ZANEC has been involved in meetings and procedures, preparing for important overarching policy documents for the education sector in Zambia. Examples of this are ZANEC's involvement in the preparation of the National Implementation Framework and the Fifth National Development Plan. Currently ZANEC is also in cooperation with other civil society stakeholders in the education sector in preparing a civil society version of the Sixth National Development Plan. The appreciation of the government for the contribution of ZANEC to the National Implementation Framework can be noticed by the fact that the MoE mentions ZANEC in their acknowledgment section of the Framework for their input. For the coalition this was a big incentive (Interview Secretariat01, 2009).

"It doesn't get any better than that basically. When someone appreciates your input it means they know the significance of your input."

Through its national coordinator ZANEC participated in the committee that revised the Education Act and in the Constitution Review Committee, which are both not yet enacted. Furthermore, ZANEC participates in one of the most important decision-making meetings in the education sector in Zambia, namely the Sector Advisory Groups. The credit that ZANEC has obtained throughout the years also ensures that they are approached by the government to participate and give a civil society statement in the Joint Annual Review (Donor04, 2009). It is however not simply important that ZANEC gets the opportunity to participate: its involvement should also be meaningful. One of the biggest challenges for the coalition is to make better use of the political opportunities presented to them. Some commentators noted that some do not attend decision-making meetings to which they are invited or they come insufficiently prepared which negatively affects its impact.

"The opportunities are there it is just how clever you are taking advantage of them. I can't see that the MoE does not recognize ZANEC if they have a clear voice. If you do have an open door to a place then you have to be prepared and utilize this opportunity (Interview Donor02, 2009)."

According to other stakeholders in the education sector it is important that ZANEC upgrades its proficiency and preparedness for important meetings. Suggestions from donors are that ZANEC should conduct more research and invest more time in keeping themselves informed. Monitoring and budget tracking are suggested to become more important strategies of the coalition, in order to improve their evidence-based advocacy. According to one of the main donors of ZANEC it is important that ZANEC strengthens their campaigns and arguments with proven knowledge of the sector. Facts are often more convincing for politics than emotions. As said by an educational advisor:

"Their participation could be much stronger than it is now. They could be better prepared to make a full input at the meetings. ZANEC should spend more time before meetings to look at the issues that will be discussed and to prepare properly, in order to have an input that is based on proper research and discussion. So that when they speak, they speak from an informed position (Interview Policy Advisor01, 2009)."

Another issue is that, according to some sources, civil society impact during meetings and on policies is minimal compared to the impact of government, the Cooperating Partners, and the donors. The reason for this is that the technical knowledge of civil society is often lagging behind in comparison to other stakeholders and also, civil society misses the power of financial resources.

"You can not talk about any policy change that can be mostly linked to ZANEC. ZANEC has made contributions. ZANEC thinks they had a lot to do with the increase of the allocation to the education sector. I told them that you need to be able to illustrate that with convincing evidence. What I know is that there are other forces at play (Interview Policy Advisor01, 2009)."

Policy impact

While ZANEC has evolved into the main spokesperson for civil society on education during government meetings and decision-making processes, the impact of ZANEC at the policy level is somehow more difficult to measure. The reasoning behind this is that there are not necessarily linear causalities to be determined between the coalition's advocacy and concrete actions and policy changes. Or, as Robert Chambers (2002) notes:

"For policy makers to be informed is one thing. For them to listen is another. For them to change policy is yet another. And for that policy to be implemented and to make a difference for the better for poor people is a further and often weak link. All those along the chain of policy and implementation need to be influenced and then committed".

Although it might not be possible to fully attribute policy changes to the work of ZANEC; it is possible to point out some policy changes that ZANEC has contributed to. As said earlier, ZANEC has been involved in the drafting of a new Education Act, a new constitution and policies considering Adult Literacy, and Early Childhood Care, Development and Education. None of these policy documents have been enacted yet. This seems to be a big problem in the education sector in Zambia: the government is rather slow in creating or changing regulation. However, one important policy change that ZANEC has contributed to has been the introduction of the Free Middle Basic Education policy (Grades 1-7) in 2002. The policy abolishes all user fees and makes uniforms no longer compulsory. ZANEC had been advocating for this policy ever since its institution, using the EFA goals as their backing motive. It believed that Free Education could help bringing more children into school.

On occasion, the member organizations achieved successes in their areas of work, with a more or less direct support of the coalition. An outstanding achievement at the policy level is the introduction of the Re-Entry Policy, which allows young female students re-entry to school after dropping out because of pregnancy. This can in part be attributed to the advocacy and campaigning that its member FAWEZA has been doing, backed by ZANEC. Also, ZANEC has been successful in campaigning for abolishing the cut-off point from grade 9 to 10. Through this measure, more students are able to proceed to grade 10.

Symbolic successes

The symbolic success of ZANEC is primarily related to their good relationship with the press. By way of example ZANEC has organized several workshops for journalists and editors in order to increase their knowledge about education issues. For instance, in 2008 ZANEC conducted media training for journalists in reporting Early Childhood Care and Development Education issues, drawn from various media institutions across Zambia. The training helped increase awareness and reporting on such sensitive issues. In 2009, because ZANEC has the belief editorial appreciation for the importance and nature of education issues is key to valuable coverage, they undertook a training program that focussed on editor and specifically set out to improve their knowledge of issues pertinent to education. This strong linkage with media linkage has been key to ZANEC having their message spread to the MoE, and the other stakeholders in the education sector and to show that they are a vibrant player in the sector. The media is also important to create awareness among Zambian citizens about their rights concerning education and new educational policies. ZANEC and its members work closely with local radio stations which can carry their message to far off communities that would otherwise not be reached. The media see ZANEC as one of the most important civil society spokespersons in the education sector and will therefore contact the coalition to give statements about issues that are taking place in the education sector (Interview Journalist01, 2009).

CONCLUSIONS

After one decade of advocating and campaigning, it is difficult to think about the education sector in Zambia without ZANEC representing the voice of civil society. And what is certain, the members of ZANEC will not stop their work on education for all in Zambia until it has reached its goal:

> To contribute towards creating a learning environment that promotes quality and relevant education to all learners in the education system through effective engagement with Government and other stakeholders whilst building the capacity of ZANEC to effectively fulfil its mandate" (ZANEC, 2007)

ZANEC's main internal successes are that it has increased its membership base significantly; it has spread itself to three provinces in Zambia; it has improved the proficiency of its members through capacity building; it has been able to attract charismatic staff and it has been able to react to internal challenges. Challenges of internal cohesion have been countered with handing over more responsibilities from the secretariat to the member organizations. The added value of a coalition should be more than just the sum of its members; ZANEC should be able to achieve higher aims than the separate members and in the best situation members would experience certain gains from participating within ZANEC. What is important for the sustainability and further success of the coalition is to get a wider stretch throughout Zambia, and to get more connections on the ground. Currently, the functioning of the coalition is quite top down, with a focus on Lusaka.

The tactics of the coalition to achieve external successes have shifted throughout their existence, which is linked to changes in the political climate. Without being able to react to the constant change in the political and societal context of Zambia, ZANEC would lose its legitimacy and influence capacity. At first, the coalition mainly lobbied for political commitment and awareness for the EFA goals, now it has adopted a strategy of pointing out ways forward to achieve the EFA goals. ZANEC has been especially successful in getting involved in policy-making processes and government meetings. They are invited as the representative for civil society to practically every meeting in the education sector. ZANEC functions as a watchdog, monitoring policies and expenditure of the government on education. The main success of ZANEC has been agenda setting. The coalition has been able to bring certain topics to the table of the government, but also the media in Zambia. A challenge remains on how to move beyond agenda setting, towards policy-making. Policy-making processes in Zambia happen slowly and are under the influence of many other actors and factors. And although ZANEC has been part of the drafting of several new policies and acts, only the Free Middle Basic Education Policy has really been enacted.

An important success that should not be neglected, is the fact that ZANEC has been able to improve the voice of civil society in the education sector in terms of lobbying and advocacy, being a prime example for other civil society actors in Zambia. For the coalition to improve its voice, it is recommendable to improve the lobbying capacity of not only its staff, but also its members. Also, ZANEC should focus more on evidence-based campaigns such as monitoring of policies and budgets. To adopt these changes, more financial resources are required. Increasing these resources remains one of the biggest challenges for the coalition.

In sum, ZANEC has evolved itself over the past decade into Zambia's most important civil society representative on educational issues. However, a number of challenges still remain for the coalition. Responsiveness of the government towards civil society remains a test. Government engagement with civil society is one thing, but putting their suggestions into actual policy change requires a lot of time, especially seeing as many of the promises made are verbal and not backed up with any physical documentation. Internally, the coalition should invest in getting a wider network outside Lusaka to make itself a truly nationwide coalition. Expanding its membership base can improve the coalition's voice and it can help to become an actor in Zambia's education sector that cannot be overlooked.

SELMA HILGERSOM

CHAPTER 9

Advocating Public Education in Indonesia. The Role of Organizational
Processes and Critical Reflection within E-net for Justice

INTRODUCTION

E-net for Justice was established on May 14, 2004, by thirty Indonesian Civil Society Organizations concerned with the situation of education in the country. The coalition is an emergent movement still within its formative state and therefore, the analysis of its impact included in this chapter needs to be interpreted taking into account its youth. E-net focuses on a broad range of education levels, from early development through to adult education. Its main objective is building and strengthening a social network to advocate critical, innovative, and transformative education. The most critical problem the network is trying to address is the upcoming privatization of the educational system in Indonesia, which threatens to exclude certain groups of Indonesian society from the right to education. The need to confront this issue led to the founding of the coalition. Therefore, advocating education reform policies which ensure access to educational opportunities for everyone is an important role of the network.

Before the establishment of E-net for Justice, some members were already working closely together to advance systemic reform, but its founding was the first step towards the creation of a formal education network in Indonesia. E-net for Justice currently consists of 34 members, the majority of which are non-governmental organizations (NGOs) and grassroots organizations. Currently, there are no teacher unions participating in the education network.

Although Indonesia is moving towards the education standards set forth by the Education For All framework (EFA) (World Bank, 2003), there are still many issues to be resolved (Kristiansen and Pratikno, 2006). In the mid-eighties, universal primary education was achieved. While many would consider this to be a big achievement for the advancement of Indonesia's schooling system, enrolment statistics indicate many problems still exist. Dropout rates remain to be a cause for concern, and only 80% of children who enrol actually complete their course. Nevertheless, after the perceived success of achieving universal primary education, the government shifted its attention towards junior and secondary schools. Current challenges being faced by the Indonesian government today concerning education include ensuring access, raising quality standards, and coping with marginalized populations. Although the government in Indonesia does acknowledge these problems (Jalal *et al*, 2007), it is widely stated that education is not considered to

Antoni Verger and Mario Novelli (eds.), Campaigning for "Education for All", 141–156.

be a 'hot topic' in the public agenda, and therefore advocacy could make a difference in this field.

This case analyses the impact of E-net for Justice in Indonesia as an advocacy organization. The political context of Indonesia is taken into account when describing the role and impact of the education network. Primary data was gathered in the four-month period from February to May 2010 at several locations in Indonesia. The majority of the research took place in the capital, Jakarta, due to the fact that most of the actors involved in this research are based in this city. However, actors located in the East-Java and West-Sumatra regions, acting both within and alongside the coalition, have been interviewed as well. In total, twenty-two members of the network were interviewed, as well as seven key informants (including international NGO staff, journalists and policy-makers) who are working independently of E-Net for Justice within the field of Indonesian education. Documents provided by E-net for Justice, media publications, and governmental data are analysed as well.

This chapter will start with an analysis of the contextual aspects of the educational system in Indonesia, with a focus on the opportunity structures to influence the government. Secondly, the origin and evolution of the current state of affairs surrounding E-net for Justice will be addressed. The focus of the third part is on the internal cohesiveness within the coalition, and how this is affecting the coalition's actions. The role of critical reflection within E-net for Justice will also be addressed in this part. Fourthly, the impact of the education network is analysed. The chapter will end with an overview of the main conclusions of the research, and will present recommendations for the future development of the network.

Country Context

Indonesia's education system has a tumultuous and turbulent history, which is in part related to a long history of military invasions accompanied by political meddling, which has inevitably had negative knock-on effects for their system of education. Before the 1611 establishment of the Dutch colonies, the Indonesian education system was virtually non-existent (Kristiansen and Pratikno, 2006). In the late nineteenth century, the Dutch recruited indigenous people to work for them, which required the education of young Indonesians. Although the Dutch forced many Indonesians to work for them and exploited the country, especially Java, the Dutch also introduced a new education system in the country. Beginning in 1906, the Dutch began to establish schools in the nation's villages. At that time, only a select few Javanese natives were permitted to study alongside Dutch descendants and reach university level. By 1945, less than 6% of the indigenous population was literate. Structural means to establish a comprehensive educational system were largely absent, due to a lack of political authority, insufficient financial means, language barriers, and the reluctance of Dutch colonists to include native populations in its educational system.

Seven years after Indonesia gained its independence in 1942, the development of a formal educational system by the government had been labelled as a priority. This was in accordance with the 1945 National Constitution which held the government responsible for providing all of its citizens with a quality education. Despite these public vows, the development of a functioning state-founded education system never materialized. Financial limitations were cited by the government as the main limitation for doing so. Therefore, most new schools that were established were privately funded and nearly always founded on Christian or Islamic religious beliefs.

In the last decades, Indonesia followed a disciplined, linear approach in achieving the EFA goals. From 1973, with increasing oil revenues leading to an expanding government budget, attendance at primary schools doubled due to the creation of new primary schools. By the mid-eighties, universal primary education structures had been implemented, although the availability of this system did not ensure that all children who enrolled actually finished. Following this achievement in primary schooling attendance, the government shifted the attention to secondary school enrolment.

In 1994, nine years of education became compulsory for every child in Indonesia. From the mid-seventies until 1997, junior secondary enrolment increased from 17% to 70% (Kristiansen and Pratikno, 2006). In July 1997, Indonesia was hit hard by the Asian financial crisis, and junior secondary school enrolment targets were postponed. However, it is not evident that the goals would have been met whether or not the crisis had occurred. The secondary school enrolment ratio of 2005-2009 was 75% for male students and 74% for female students (Unicef, n.d.). Currently, two prevailing developments in the educational sector characterize the overall situation: privatization and decentralization.

PRIVATIZATION

E-net for Justice perceives the ongoing transfer of activities, assets and responsibilities from governmental and public institutions to the private sector as a threat to education. Although privatization is advancing in primary and secondary educational spheres, the shift is more prevalent at the higher level. Government policy *'explicitly commits to private schools'* (Bangay, 2010:168). The government is increasingly pushing the responsibility of education down to the school level, which is encouraging the privatization trend. Public funding is also channelled to the private sector. According to the government, the purpose of this strategy is to make schools more accountable and effective, not to shift responsibility away from the state (Interview Vice Minister of Education, 2010). Privatization is also perceived by the government as a way to increase resources available for teaching, to use existing funds more efficiently, and to provide more flexibility within the education sector.

Overall, privatization is approached as a way to improve education in the country. In regards to primary education, the Indonesian government focuses on increasing the availability of public schools and subsidizing private schools (James *et al.*, 1996). Although the emphasis on better access and expanding the number of schools has resulted in lower public expenditures per student and higher enrolment rates, students often lack books or other necessary teaching materials. Private funding is seen as one of the solutions to this dilemma.

According to E-net for Justice and other actors in the Indonesian educational field, privatizing education leads to profit-based schools which wrongly place the financial burden on students and their families, thereby depriving them of their constitutionally guaranteed right to a free education. The fear for increasing costs does not only apply to private education, but also to public schools where the increasing influence of private interests in the education sphere poses a perceived threat to the provision of free education by the government:

> "Though government schools are funded by government and managed by civil servants, they still raise funds (often at significant levels) from various levies exacted from parents". (Bangay, 2010:168)

One of the findings of the Education Watch research (hereafter referred to as Edwatch), performed by E-net for Justice in cooperation with the Asia South Pacific Association of Basic and Adult Education (ASPBAE), showed that one of the consequences of the ongoing privatization of education at the community level is that 100% of the surveyed households are faced with relatively high education costs. The increase of private influence into education is seen to have led to an increase in the number of dropouts, and therefore higher illiteracy rates among poorer communities. Additional arguments are made that 'poor but bright' students will not be able to succeed in higher education due to financial restrictions. Therefore, it is considered important that civil society *'seriously advocates the efforts that oppose the privatization of education policies in Indonesia.'* (ASPBAE, 2007:14).

DECENTRALIZATION

The organization of the educational system in Indonesia is not restricted to one centralized national department, making the overall education system landscape and its governance much more complex. The need to improve the delivery of services has driven substantial changes in the political structure of Indonesia in the past decades. After years of highly centralized and autocratic rule, political and economic power was shifted away from the national government. After the highly centralized regime of Suharto, the second President of Indonesia holding the office from 1967 to 1998, decentralization was introduced by the national 'Law 22', which effectively dissolved political and economic power from the national government. Differing from other countries where decentralization was implemented alongside the need for better service delivery, decentralization in Indonesia largely resulted from a general frustration toward the centralization of power (Ahmad and Mansoor 2001:3). Distinct ethnic and geographical factions contending for control over resources and the need for political and legal autonomy led to the demand for a more decentralized government. However, the primary objective behind the decentralization process was that of increased efficiency and reduction of public spending.

In 1994, after years of informal discussion, the Indonesian Ministry of Education and Culture required *"all elementary and junior high schools in the country to allocate 20 percent of total instructional hours to locally designed subjects"* (Bjork, 2003:184). This represented a significant departure from previous highly centralized top-down education policy. Not only because of the change in curricular content, but also in the roles and responsibilities of teachers. Schools were not obliged to implement a standard curriculum constructed by experts in Jakarta. However, following the requirements of the Indonesian Ministry of Education and Culture, friction between the objectives of decentralization and a sociopolitical context that has traditionally defined teachers as dutiful civil servants has led to the maintenance of the status quo (Bjork, 2003). Indonesian teachers are reluctant to adopt the role of autonomous teacher. Consequently, the redistribution of authority to the school level has been hindered by a resistance on the part of the teachers.

The service delivery and quality of education can be negatively affected in the short run, and even long-term advantages are uncertain because of the increased risk of corruption, and the negative effects of downsizing administrative units. Decentralization is of current an ongoing process and the full scope of its long-term consequences is yet to be determined.

E-Net for Justice: goals, activities and internal cohesion

E-net for Justice was founded on May 14, 2004 by thirty Indonesian NGOs who share concerns about the privatization of education and its implications for free universal primary education. The network grew spectacularly and, in the first year, seventy-two organizations held membership. At the time of research, the organization consisted of thirty-four organizations located on the islands of Java, Sumatra, and Kalimantan. The network consists of relatively small Indonesian NGOs and grassroots organizations. There are no big (international) NGOs among the members. As stated before, there are no teacher unions affiliated with the coalition, but in the past, the teacher union Persatuan Guru Republik Indonesia[64] (PGRI) had held membership. The coalition does not have members present in all parts of Indonesia. The Eastern part of Indonesia is the most noticeably underrepresented. Before covering how E-net for Justice expanded its membership base, there are some organizational issues within the current coalition that need to be addressed.

Goals & Organization

E-net for Justice is connected to two international organizations: the Global Campaign for Education (GCE) and the regional network of GCE in Southeast

---

[64] In English: Teachers' Association of the Republic of Indonesia

Asia: the Asia South Pacific Association of Basic and Adult Education (ASPBAE). The cooperation with GCE is mainly focused on cooperation with the Global Action Week (GAW). The connection with ASPBAE has been worked out through the Real World Strategies (RWS) project and in partnerships that the two coalitions share. The national coordinator of E-net for Justice attends activities organized by GCE and ASPBAE. Although E-net for Justice works closely together with these organizations, the network is free to collectively determine which issues they address in their campaigns. The country-specific problems that have arisen around privatization in Indonesia, ascertained by E-net for Justice, have been acknowledged by ASPBAE, and this led to awareness about similar issues in other countries.

E-net for Justice has one national coordinator whose purpose is to 'execute the program of E-net for Justice in cooperation with the planning of the organization' as well as to function similarly to an administrative organization for the larger network. Three executive board members are responsible for the organizational matters within E-net, and three members of the supervisory board monitor the day-to-day activities of the executive board. Persons from member organizations who were elected to the national congress occupy all positions within the executive and supervisory boards.

E-net for Justice can be conceived as the core of an emergent anti-privatisation movement in the education field. The ongoing resistance of privatization in the name of protecting the right to free education was part of the organisation's establishing principles, and to this day continues to be at the heart of the mission of the network. E-net for Justice has four main goals that were established in the first congress[65]:

1. Building and strengthening social groups to advocate critical, innovative, and transformative education.
2. Developing alternative education that promotes critical thinking based on humanism, pluralism, gender justice, and liberation values.
3. Advocating education policies to ensure the access of education for all, especially poor, marginalized, and disadvantaged women and children.
4. Developing a multi-stakeholder education coalition on a local, national, regional, and international level.

These goals were formulated at the first congress when the coalition was originally established. Interestingly, the push to meet the EFA's international educational standards is not stated as a high priority within all the goals. Although the coalition goals are strongly related to the EFA goals and the Millennium Development Goals, the education situation in Indonesia is not totally captured by these global frameworks. Thus, the coalition interprets that issues such as secondary education and the problem of privatization needs to be addressed as well. According to one of E-Net's statutes for Justice, *"EFA goals do not work in Indonesia (in part because of...) the privatization of education."* (Interview E-Net member 02, 2010)

---

[65] Statutes E-net for Justice, 23 October 2009

The collective goals of E-net for Justice are not all primarily concerned with educational reform. Member organizations maintain private agendas and some work only indirectly on educational issues. Some members therefore disclose that their goals are not necessarily similar to the larger network, but all members do recognize the importance of improving education, as one of the members working with domestic workers states:

> "I think education is very important, for all humans, for all people, for all domestic workers" (Interview E-Net member 01, 2010).

Nevertheless, the focus on strengthening weaker social groups, as explicitly stated in E-net's agenda, could be interpreted as a political tool to empower people in society in order to influence the state indirectly. It would therefore be misleading to portray activities to strengthen communities only as "*actions designed to confront power structures or capture the levers of governmental power as 'political'*" (Eldridge, 1990:505). Instead, the betterment of society by NGOs for self-managing and enabling grassroots to deal with governmental agencies serve to "*strengthen civil society vis á vis the state*" (Eldridge, 1990:505). The importance of influencing and empowering communities is frequently emphasized by a majority of the member organizations of E-net for Justice (Interview E-Net member 02, 2010).

E-net for Justice's members and management characterize the organisation's structure as 'democratic', and 'transparent'. Emphasis is given to procedural due diligence within the organization to ensure that it lives up to its ambitions of being a democratic structure. Transparency is also high-up on the agenda as the board has to report to all members on their operations and actions, as well as disclose all details regarding the organization. Organizational structure has become a core topic of E-net for Justice and is frequently addressed during sessions of congress where important decisions are formally made. For these reasons, E-net for Justice is best described as a 'flat hierarchical organization with a decentralized decision-making processes and a high level of transparency'.

Most members value the flat nature of the network's organization. However, the non-hierarchical structure has not prevented internal power struggles. In one notable instance, the teacher's union, PGRI, once took E-Net to task by trying to claim a position on the board on the basis of their large membership base, which they asserted warranted a position of more power than some it its smaller counterparts.:

> "If we will come to the E-net for Justice, it means that we must have a role in decision-making because it is very important, because behind us are so many members." (Interview E-net member 04, 2010)

However, despite their assertive stance, despite their broad membership base, PGRI was not given a place on the board. The prominence of PGRI as an influential teacher's union in Indonesia was not considered as a significant reason to elect their representative to serve on the board because all E-net for Justice members are considered equal regardless of their size and clout:

"In our organization, all members are equal. In our congress [...] all the members are equally elected. So maybe the teacher unions did not only resign because of the ideology but maybe they also wanted to be elected, to become a member of the board. But the members didn't choose them." (Interview E-Net board 01, 2010).

Due to this conflict over the role of PGRI within the network, PGRI decided to withdraw. One interpretation of this turn in events could be that PGRI's desire for a controlling stake in E-Net, together with E-Net's firmly principled position of not giving preference in the name of equilibrium for all members presented E-Net as an unacceptable threat to PGRI. This is a clear instance of the political clashes and conflicts civil society organisations become open to.

The national coordinator was elected during the last congressional session. The national coordinator had no previous experience in leading a coalition. Although the network has an official leader, there is still no physical office space available for running the network. The role of national coordinator, a full-time occupation, is executed from the National Secretariat based in offices of member organizations in Jakarta. The guidance of the national coordinator, who is active both internally and externally, is considered important for the effective functioning of the network and its successes. The national coordinator is supported by three members of the board of trustees and three members of the governing council.

Although not all members were aware of the severity of privatization before their involvement with E-net for Justice, the coalition has now come to a consensus that this is one of the key issues in Indonesia's educational sector. In the first congress, the participants discussed the problems in the educational field. The conviction of the founders that privatization is indeed the main problem was accepted by all the other members and –if not already the case- incorporated in their organization:

> "We define common strategies when we feel this is felt widely, like the issue of privatization, it does not only occur in Solo or Yogja, but in the whole country so it's something we can commonly do together." (Interview E-Net member 06, 2010)

The consensus about the main goals did not involve much struggle among the members. The basic principles of the network were shared by all the members before its establishment. Members have joined the network on a voluntary basis and because they agree with the vision of E-net for Justice. However, within the first two years, twenty-four organizations left the network. A possible explanation for this is that some organizations did not share the views and priorities as initially expected. [66]

The threat of privatization was held up as the main rationale for establishing the coalition, and during the first congress, when discussing the implications and consequences of surrounding privatization, all members agreed that the process of

---

[66] "E-net for Justice as a network", presentation at the second congress, Jakarta, 21 oktober 2009

privatization should be acknowledged as the organization's chief concern. The primary directive of E-net for Justice is creating awareness and fostering public opinion around the full implications of privatization trends, as well as raising community awareness in societies around concerns related to ongoing privatization.

In accordance with this belief, the organization does not cooperate with other organizations that support privatization in any manner. For example, the World Bank is viewed as an opponent because, according to E-net for Justice, they support different forms of privatization. For this reason, funds for civil society that are channeled through this organization are refused by E-net for Justice:

> "We cannot work with the World Bank because, according to us, the World Bank is the main source of privatization, not only in education. So we think that if we work with the World Bank this means we also get involved in the process of privatization" (Interview E-Net member 02, 2010)

The strong consensus on the problems plaguing Indonesia's education system, and the fact that members all share these common values, supports the feeling of unity in the network.

Influencing the state

Since the governing political structure in Indonesia is decentralized, the E-Net's activities take place at multiple levels. Consequently, the organization's effectiveness is difficult to perceive. According to many members of E-net for Justice, outlets for civil society organizations to be influential in political decisions are mostly ignored when it comes to national government policy-making. Although some formal space is provided to citizens to participate in the political process through seminars and discussions, the national government tends to adhere to their own policy. Data from civil society opposing governmental data, such as Edwatch's research performed by E-net for Justice, are not taken seriously by Indonesia's national government, even though E-net for Justice claims to include more respondents in their research than government commissioned data.

The national government tries to be impervious to the criticism and influence of E-net for Justice. However, other Indonesian NGO's experience similar difficulties in influencing the state. A highly remarkable example is the difficulty that several NGOs and the largest teacher union of Indonesia experienced in their legal proceedings against the state. These organizations filed a motion to force the government to set the annual educational budget on the national, provincial, and district levels to at least 20% of the national budget, in order to conform with the 2002 amendment to Indonesia's constitution, which also conform with the objectives of E-net for Justice. Even though the legal challenges proved successful in the constitutional court, and in the Supreme Court, the government still refuses to comply with the amendment. The refusal to honor this decision leaves civil society, the judiciary, and the legislature powerless to effect change in the face of a stubborn executive, which creates an understandable feeling of frustration:

"So even if you are trying to influence the government by law and you win, they still aren't listening" (Interview E-Net member 04, 2010).

As the above scenarios indicate, influencing Indonesia's national government is a nigh impossible task. To achieve some level of impact, long-term investments of resources are required that can be potentially derailed or complicated by changes within the political bureaucracy, which often act to slow down advocacy efforts.

At lower levels of government, NGOs and grassroots organizations have more opportunities to accomplish their mission. According to the vice Education Minister, interviewed in the context of this research, the decentralization of government has provided opportunities for citizens to speak up through bottom-up channels. The national coordinator of E-net for Justice also refers to the opportunities of operating at the local level when it comes to influence national or regional level policies:

"At the local level the government is more welcoming and happy. (...) That's different from the national government." (Interview E-Net secretariat 01, 2010)

Although the opportunities to engage with and influence political matters differ from place to place, some NGOs do feel their political voice is being heard and that they are able to effectively contribute to local policies. There are few indications that local organizations have actually achieved concrete results, but governments at this level acknowledge that they consult all constituency groups before making policy (Interview Vice Minister of Education, 2010).

E-net for Justice operates with limited funds and consequently there are not many opportunities to undertake large-scale coordinated initiatives. The two main activities that all members cite as core business of the network are: 1) the Edwatch research, a study initiated by E-net for Justice to provide alternative data about education in Indonesia, and 2) the participation in the yearly Global Action Week. However, activities concerning the Global Action Week were perceived differently among the members, and collective action undertaken by a great deal of the members was absent.

The Edwatch research was carried out by E-net for Justice because there is a lack of uniform data available for public review in the country, a shortcoming that greatly stifles advocacy efforts and public opinion of the issue. The provision of data is considered a big step and necessary tool towards educating the public and legitimizing their efforts. Creating data sets of their own is highly important for E-net for Justice to legitimize their own motives. Edwatch does not represent the overall educational situation in Indonesia, but rather focuses on equity issues. Its main objective is to *highlight the education gaps and problems particularly among disadvantaged groups* (ASPBAE, 2007:2). During the research, mixed methods have been used that were both quantitative and qualitative in nature: a total of 6,241 respondents were involved in a household survey and another 8,244 participants were involved in a literacy test. In addition to standardized questionnaires and tests, ethnographic observation was used as an additional data collection method. Problems in the education field in Indonesia that came up in the Edwatch research were included in the program of E-net for Justice.

After the main findings of the research were finished, the research was presented at a press conference, and a seminar was conducted together with the National Commission on Human Rights. A summary of the report has been published online as well. The results of the Edwatch initiative were presented to the government, but officials rejected the data. According to one interview candidate, government officials rejected E-net's findings because they contradicted the government's own data (Interview E-Net secretariat 01, 2010).

The national coordinator and some of the E-net members in Jakarta have also been involved in seminars and discussions with the government regarding the publication of the Edwatch research, but there is no evidence found in this research for follow-ups to those meetings. However, E-net for Justice has been invited to give inputs on the National millennium development goals report on account of the research. E-net for Justice is planning to do more research to strengthen their advocacy, especially when it comes to the problem of privatization:

"Political parties and the parliament members say that NGOs and civil society always work without data. So I think that if E-net for Justice wants to influence them, E-net should do new research on privatization" (Interview E-Net member 02, 2010)

Internal cohesion

Although there is a huge amount of commitment among the members, some factors hinder their actual involvement in the network. First, the fact that some of the members are participating in many other existing networks in Indonesia, shifts part of its attention away from E-net for Justice. Second, the voluntary character of membership hinders the urgency to actively participate. Although this 'on-a-voluntary-basis' is an important characteristic of the network, some of the members feel that the agenda could be led more intensively and that there is a lack of coordinated activities. Although there is internal communication through a mailing list, information flows within the network are often experienced as one-way traffic: information is sent to willing recipients but there is no incentive for any follow-up action or response. This lack of urgency to follow-up actions is mentioned by several members as a factor that reinforces their passive attitude. A difference in the level of involvement was found between members living in or close to Jakarta or members that are located further from the capital but who occupy an important leadership position within the network, and 'regular members' who live further away and are not involved in the board. Overall engagement in the network seems to be significantly lower from members that are located far from the national secretariat and routinely miss out on board functions.

Another reason for the limited involvement in the network stated by many members is related to internal organization. All members acknowledge that the network is led by the secretariat in Jakarta, and therefore the national coordinator is expected to generate internal cohesion. However, except for the Global Action Week and the Edwatch research, there are few other tangible activities organized, nor does the network function as a base for public collective strategic actions. The low frequency of events is often mentioned as a barrier to internal cohesion. In general, membership is often described as a networking tool for gathering information and establishing contact with other organizations in order to assist in setting up individual campaigns, leaving advocacy-related activities as less important. Strengthening the coordination and active use of the mailing list has been proposed to boost the strength of the network[67].

Media

The media are one of the most important tools in advocacy work in Indonesia. Members as well as external players frequently state that media is a tool to reach the people, influence public opinion, and pressure the government. Media can function as an outlet to communicate the activities and agenda of E-Net. However, one of the problems experienced by E-net for Justice is a general lack of interest from the media on educational affairs. This might be due to the current emphasis on environmental issues and other popular topics that are prevailing in the media. Due to the fact that there is not much collective action undertaken by individual members, E-net for Justice fails to gain significant popularity through its members' individual efforts. This could be explained by the fact that the network consists of relatively few organizations, but media ties could also be boosted and intensified:

> "If E-net for Justice has research to monitor education, they conduct many seminars and on that seminar E-net for Justice also invites the media to cover the results (…) But maybe E-net for Justice has to collaborate more with the media to continue their publishing… Because until now it is only incidental. There's some publication in the media but E-net for Justice is not regularly heard about that issue." (Interview E-Net member 05, 2010)

E-net's low profile is a two-pronged result of poor media relations and weak internal effectiveness. Consequently, E-net for Justice is generally unknown to the public outside of their direct circles of contact through media channels.

The national secretariat is aware of opportunities present through working with the media. That is why one of the next steps in improving the network is to enhance public media relations (Interview E-Net secretariat 01, 2010). The creation of an online blog is one intended method to strengthen its media profile and keep members informed about the activities of the network[68].

The inner evaluation: An Opportunity for Reflexivity?

Evaluation of the program of E-net for Justice takes place every four years, in the context of the coalition's Congress. This is the main opportunity given to members to change the inner structure of the organization, its vision, and stated mission. During the congress, experiences of the network, ideas, and thoughts about the

---

[67] Logical Framework of E-net for Justice
[68] Logical Framework of E-net for Justice

state of education in Indonesia are shared and discussed. Concrete (planned) campaigns and activities of E-net for Justice are not major topics at the congress. Reflection upon these issues through evaluations is an integral part of the congress[69]. There are also evaluations of specific activities of the network, attended by the taskforces involved. These evaluations take place more regularly. For example, evaluations about the Edwatch research were organized every three months. All members involved have access to the results of these evaluations.

Intra-congress evaluations present the only opportunity to change the inner structure of the network. During the first congress in Manado, the focus was mainly on building the network and defining the vision and mission of E-net for Justice. Evaluations performed in more recent congressional meetings do not directly address the established strategies and vision of the network, which remain unchanged, but focuses more on practical issues. For instance, as a result of one of these intra-congress evaluations, E-Net for Justice moved the secretariat to Jakarta. The former secretariat was based in Surabaya to prevent a concentration of power in the capital of Indonesia, but this led to logistical difficulties in advocacy work due to not being in close proximity to the capital where the national government is seated.

However, the intra-congress evaluations do not focus on concrete activities and their outcomes, but on broader ideas and agendas. Evaluations of specific campaigns or activities such as the Edwatch research are different; these evaluations do focus on concrete activities and their outcomes. During this research, regular evaluations have been organized according to the national coordinator, who was part of the research team. This project, beyond its external input, has helped to build research skills of members within the network and to strengthen the research capacity of the coalition.

Contrary to the benefits of the evaluations related to the Edwatch research, the results of the intra-congresses are limited. Although outcomes are shared, the outcomes of the evaluations are generally documented in 'formal' notes, structural changes related to the outcomes or concrete actions based upon the findings are absent. The fact that many new members have joined the network recently and attended the four-year congress for the first time made the evaluations complicated because, for the greater part, the congress focused on the introduction of these members. New members could not participate in evaluations of past events they were not part of.

Many members state that they are not informed about results of evaluation proceedings or any concrete actions to modify structural changes identified as necessary within the network:

"After the E-net congress we have not met each other yet. So the outcomes have not been used yet..." (Interview E-Net member 07, 2010)

The communication shortcomings within the network, and the limitations of member participation mentioned above, could explain the fact that the evaluation's outcomes haven not been used for the improvement of the network. It seems that

---

[69] Declaration at the second congress, 21-23 October 2009, Jakarta

the outcomes of evaluations have not been 'put into reality' yet. The lack of a national secretariat and a leader of the network could be an explanation for this. In the future, the establishment of the national coordinator could lead to more follow-ups after evaluations, and increase the quality of information within these evaluations, allowing for implementable improvements. The current ambiguous state of the national secretariat could be an aggravating factor, not to mention the difficulties to follow-up with internal self-reflection since evaluations take place only every four years. Overall, it seems that internal evaluations, if organized in another way, could substantially contribute to the development of the network.

The effectiveness of E-net for Justice to impact educational policy reforms is being influenced by the lack of reflection and self-evaluation of the network. The missed opportunity to plan advocacy activities both on the national as well as the local level, negatively effects the amount of collective action within the network.

THE IMPACT OF E-NET FOR JUSTICE

Impact redefined

Defining the impact of E-net for Justice on Indonesia's educational policy landscape is not easy for a number of reasons. First, due to the limited activities organized by E-net for Justice and the difficulties in measuring outcomes of the Global Action Week, and the Edwatch research. Second, encouraging change within Indonesian society is not only achieved by advocacy related activities, but also by community strengthening. Community strengthening is perceivable, but difficult to fully quantify since the network brings together different member organizations, but does not get involved in their individual local-level activities. In this research, the impact of the larger network is to be defined, not the impact of individual member organizations engaged in their respective work. It should be remembered that the activities and achievements of member organizations are not to be regarded as activities and achievements done in the name of E-net for Justice - unless this is explicitly mentioned. Therefore, the impact of these specific activities cannot be accredited to the efforts of the network.

The activities of E-Net for Justice at the national level are acknowledged by the national government, and the Vice Minister of Education himself has praised the network as being a player in the domain of civil society. Some of the events that are organized by E-net for Justice (such as workshops on education policy, budget tracking, etc.) are recognized and even attended by the government, but substantial tangible influence of E-net for Justice on government matters cannot be substantiated. However, it is widely recognized by NGOs and grassroots organizations that the government does give the appearance that it takes civil society initiatives into account when devising policy. But actionable influence is hardly accepted at all, confirmed by the considerable difficulties faced by those fighting through litigation channels, as illustrated by the legal action undertaken by, among others, the PGRI. For the reasons explained above, there are some players in the educational field who do not know of the existence of the network and its operations yet. The reach of the network is restricted to communities where E-net for Justice is active and is therefore not highly influential beyond this level:

> "We have to admit that our advocacy is maybe not very much effective. I mean, our activity is only limited, we don't mobilize people or we have something like a meeting with the division in the local level, not that far. We only give ideas to the people in our area." (Interview E-Net member 01, 2010)

On the local level, the impact of the network is rather vague. Although some of the members do participate in the Global Action Week, local governments that have been interviewed in this research were not familiar with E-net for Justice. The data of the Edwatch research is known by all the members of the coalition and considered as an important tool for advocacy, but there is no evidence for any purposeful application of the data on the local level. In this sense, the network could be more proactive on providing advice and data to some of its members.

The Vice Education Minister acknowledged E-net for Justice as a player in civil society, and has recognized that the network has called political attention to the gender issue through its Edwatch research. However, in relation to actual policy making, the network is not considered very influential. One of the members talks about 'paradise win': the government states that they are agreeing with the proposals from citizens but when it comes to putting the input of civil society to practice, they do not:

> "Sometimes the government gives.... we call it paradise win. They say 'yes we know it and we try to make the policy you want' (....) but mostly they don't do it. (...). They don't want to accept our proposal to them." (Interview E-Net member 02, 2010)

Following E-net for Justice, its existence has also raised attention and awareness to the problems concerning privatization, as well as within the communities where it operates. This is considered one of the biggest achievements of the network. The network considers it important to make Indonesian people aware about the fact that the government is responsible for their education and that they should not have to pay for that. The question of whether the ideas of E-net have been picked up in communities and spread outside them goes beyond the scope of this research.

So, E-net for Justice does raise awareness concerning the privatization problem, although still at a small scale, in Indonesia. However, through its participation in regional networks, the impact of its awareness work has acquired an international dimension. For instance, the coalition from The Philippines has started working on this subject due to E-net for Justice's efforts:

> "We quarrel with E-net Philippines because in the Philippines they didn't agree that privatization is a problem. But we kept working on this issue and right now, the Philippines do actually agree." (Interview E-Net member 02, 2010)

Through the incorporation of the ideas concerning privatization by other members of ASPBAE E-net for Justice is already influencing the GCE to be more oppositional to the privatization of education. To strengthen the advocacy on privatization, E-net for Justice plans to commission a number of research studies around this topic in the future. The mapping of privatization as well as the cooperation with the Global Campaign for Education through the integration with the Global Action Week are aiming to strengthen advocacy against privatization[70].

Conclusion

The aim of this study was to describe the impact of the E-net for Justice on educational policy in Indonesia. The political structure in Indonesia, as illustrated by the absence of a follow-up on the litigation process mentioned above, is not encouraging civil society organizations participation and influence. Although the government seems to accept that, to some extent, they benefit from E-net's influence, structural changes are hard to achieve. Since education is not prioritized in Indonesia at this moment, there is not much emphasis on this topic, which makes advocacy difficult. In this research, no evidence was found on the impact of E-net for Justice on the national level.

The internal factors tugging from within at the coalition bring light to the importance of internal cohesion. Although the coalition consists of members with shared values who are all very much dedicated to the improvement of (alternative) education, the amount of collective action is still limited. E-net for Justice is also almost a completely unknown entity to many people in society, in fact to nearly everyone who does not share their presence inside their own communities. The limited media coverage is one of the explanations that the impact on society in general is also limited.

However, the fact that the national secretariat of E-net for Justice is acknowledged by the government gives the opportunity to be heard through workshops and seminars. The time frame of the organization is to be considered when discussing the impact of the national coalition: E-net for Justice is a relatively new coalition and the national secretariat was established only one year ago. Before, there was one leading organization performing a similar function, but there was no full-time availability. The constitution of the coalition is still 'a work in progress', internal as well as external issues are being addressed at the moment. To achieve a stronger political position in Indonesia, the internal coordination and visibility of the coalition needs to be improved, and it is likely that this will positively effect the achievements and overall impact of E-net for Justice. Many of the issues addressed in this research have been acknowledged by the national coordinator and are taken into account in the logical framework for the upcoming period. Member organizations of the network have high hopes for the future. Although the network is still in the process of development, the network future trajectory is seen to be headed in a positive direction. As stated convincingly by one of its key organizers: *"There is a long way to go, but in the end there will be results"* (Interview Secretariat, February, 2010).

---

[70] E-net for Justice Logical Framework

ANTONI VERGER AND MARIO NOVELLI

CHAPTER 10

Understanding the Outcomes of Advocacy Coalitions in Education. A Comparative Perspective

In this chapter, we use comparative analysis lenses to better understand the nature of civil society coalitions and their impact in the educational field. The arguments provide a synthesis of core issues that have emerged from the case studies presented in earlier chapters. In particular, this chapter looks at different aspects of education advocacy coalitions (EACs or coalitions): the coalition's profile; the agenda of the coalitions; their strategies and actions; the impact dimensions of advocacy, the levels of internal cohesion of EACs; and the opportunity structures that are conducive to impact. Finally, we conclude with some core reflections on the outcomes of the research and some key suggestions for coalition building.

PROFILE

The notion of "civil society" is open to multiple and contested definitions that encompass a range of organizations of a very different nature, organizational structure, size, priorities, etc. (Scholte 2007). The existing diversity within the category of civil society is clearly reflected within the civil society coalitions that operate in the field of education that we have explored. These coalitions can be very different when it comes to variables such as their composition, origins, availability of resources, level of professionalization, and so on.

Most civil society coalitions operating in the educational field include NGOs, teachers unions, and grassroots movements. On occasion, certain coalitions may also count on the participation of scholars and other people coming from the academy, as well as journalists, or youth organizations, and even international organization staff. The "standard configuration" of most coalitions consists of NGOs and teachers unions. However, the participation of teachers unions in EACs cannot be taken for granted. Most coalitions, from their creation, have included teacher union participation as a core component. However, with the passage of time, and in a number of countries, the relationship between teachers' union representatives and NGOs has deteriorated to the point that some teachers' organizations have even left national coalitions. Towards the end of this chapter, we will explore in more detail the reasons behind the tensions and disagreements between teachers and other constituencies.

Antoni Verger and Mario Novelli (eds.), Campaigning for "Education for All", 157–173.

Coalitions vary significantly, in accordance with their origins. For instance, the creation of some EACs has been promoted externally by international donors or the GCE itself in the context of the global movement for Education for All (including, for instance, funding from the Commonwealth Education Fund). This is the case for many coalitions in Africa, whereas other coalitions have a much more endogenous origin. The latter, for instance, is the case of the *Contrato Social por la Educación* in Ecuador, that was created in 2002, and became a member of the GCE four years later, in 2006. For the Ecuadorian coalition, being part of the GCE was a way to raise their international profile as well as their legitimacy within national education politics. However, its *raison d'être* and the factors that explain its origin and existence are clearly grounded at the national level.

The level of internationalization of EACs does not only rely on their origin, but also on their composition. In relation to the latter, it should be acknowledged that some national coalitions are open to the direct participation of international actors (like INGOs, donors, and international organizations), while others, such as the Indian NCE, only allow national organizations to become members. This type of option may impede the construction of broader coalitions, and it may even generate some tensions with international civil society groups operating in the country. On the other hand, this allows advocacy processes to be more locally rooted, and ensures that international agendas do not steamroll national ones.

The form and structure of the coalitions is very diverse as well. The organization of some EACs is distinctly horizontal; while others are more nebulous and incorporate hundreds of organizations of very different sizes (as in the case of Indonesia and the Philippines); and others are an umbrella of a few very big organizations (as in India, where the national coalition is composed of seven huge organizations including the biggest teachers unions and social movements, each of them representing hundreds of thousands of members).

The level of resources and, specifically, the funding of the coalitions does not correspond to a common pattern either. The sources of this funding can be external (for instance, the donations of aid agencies as in the case of most African coalitions), or it may be of a more internal nature (for instance, fees paid by members). Just as an indicator of funding differences, some coalitions included in the study have a secretariat with seven members, while others have only one. Resources do not necessarily explain the level of success of EACs, but, of course, the capacities of a secretariat to operate and coordinate the coalitions may vary substantially according to the size of their staff.[71]

Finally, at the individual level, the profile of people participating in EACs can be very different as well. Most coalitions count on a more professionalized, urban and highly educated profile of participants, similar to what Boaventura de Sousa Santos (2005) calls the 'intimate civil society', i.e. a section of civil society made

---

[71] There is a growing concern that the civil society fund provided to the GCE coalitions that operate in countries that are part of the Fast Track Initiative (FTI) may accentuate this level of inequality between the coalitions as only certain countries can gain access to the resources available.

up of people that enjoy social and economic rights that fight for the rights of other social groups. However, other coalitions count on participants coming from rural areas and grassroots movements that do not necessarily reproduce the previous schema. It is rare to see a coalition with a balance between both profiles of participants. E-Net in The Philippines and, to some extent, the Brazilian Campaign for the Right to Education, are exceptional in this respect.

AGENDA

Different civil society organizations come together into an advocacy coalition in order to push for a common education agenda, and for common demands. In this respect, "Education For All" works as a global action framework in all the coalitions that are part of the GCE. However, the Education for All agenda is usually adapted and translated to different realities according to the prevailing educational needs within them. Thus, in less developed countries with more burning education necessities, the topics and demands of EACs are quite concrete. They focus on a *thin* EFA agenda, which is very similar to the objectives of the Millennium Development Goals (basic education for all, and gender parity). While this agenda is less ambitious, this does not mean that it is easier to achieve. On the other hand, in countries with better socio-economic indicators, coalitions construct wider and more complex agendas that include themes such as alternative pedagogies, teachers' labour policies, education management ideas, etc. While these different agendas might be a product of the particular level of economic development and educational needs, they also reflect the areas of expertise and interests of members, and competing priorities within the coalitions on thin versus thicker versions of the Education For All agenda.

However, independently of whether coalition agendas are more or less busy with themes and claims, or more or less sophisticated when discussing education policy, there is a common topic that unites them. All coalitions demand an increase in public spending on education. In this sense, all coalitions coincide when it comes to the central argument that improving access and quality in education depends on increasing the levels of public educational funding. This does not mean that the struggle of the GCE in education is reduced to 'numbers and dollars', since most EACs engage in much broader debates, but that inputs are a necessary condition for the achievement of gains in education outcomes, such as student learning or education equity.

STRATEGIES

Most education coalitions analysed deploy a range of common action repertoires including: a) Lobbying decision-makers (by, for instance, arranging meetings and sending letters/emails to decision-makers); b) public awareness through public speeches, information campaigns and media releases; c) mobilization and street action; d) activist research, including budget tracking, studies on the state of education in the country, etc.

Most of these actions repertoires are, in one way or another, interlinked. For instance, street action is a way of reaching decision-makers or the media, and budget-tracking can support the organization's arguments in the context of public speeches or lobbying initiatives.

The effectiveness of the repertoires of action adopted is context sensitive. This means that an action that may be very effective at a certain moment and in a certain place may not be so effective within other time-space coordinates. While being aware of the limitations and dangers of generalization, we have identified through our case studies a number of strategies that may contribute positively to EACs achieving their policy objectives.

The first strategy concerns the *framing action of the coalitions*. As we explained in the methodological section in the introduction to this volume, we employ the term 'framing' in reference to the way in which civil society groups build and transmit their message to society. Such message could be constituted by three main dimensions, namely explanatory, prognostic and motivational (Benford and Snow 2000). Through 'explanatory' frames, civil society groups construct a situation as problematic (i.e., the situation is not "natural" and things could be different) and identify the main causes and agents behind the problematic situation. Through 'prognosis', they identify and communicate their alternatives and solutions to the problems, as well as their demands to governmental bodies. Finally, through 'motivation', they encourage people and decision-makers to contribute to changing the problematic situation; they do so by explaining that change is possible and that, more importantly, they count on the contribution of various agent's capacities as a necessary tool to make change happen. Successful strategies in the framing action terrain require a balance between the three described dimensions. In other words, in order for a campaign to be successful, it needs to succeed in explaining the reality of a given situation, and it then needs to pose alternatives to that reality so as to motivate the audience and create the impetus for action. Thus, those coalitions that provide very convincing and sophisticated explanations of problems, but do not provide alternatives and solutions (or the alternatives and solutions are not consistent enough with the diagnosis) will not be as persuasive or convincing as those that spread their framing efforts between the three dimensions.

On the other hand, from the framing point of view, it is important that the messages of the coalition are grounded in a combination of beliefs that are both evidence based and principled. Arguably, all social movements are driven by principled beliefs because people ultimately come together in social movements to fight against a situation that is unfair (Keck and Sikkink 1998). However, if movements want policy makers to listen, it is important that they support their claims on more evidence based ideas or causal beliefs. That is why a balance between these two types of beliefs is very important. A message that is framed on the basis of principled ideas (for instance, "early childhood education is a right and must be available for all") and, supported by evidence ("research done by X in countries Y and Z shows that early childhood education comes at a crucial moment for children's development and correlates significantly with higher levels of enrolment and learning") is more powerful and persuasive than a message that is only based on one of the two aspects.

A second collective action strategy for EACs consists of *taking advantage of electoral junctures*. The ambition of influencing decision-makers and political parties is embedded in the *ethos* of advocacy coalitions and, specifically, electoral conjunctures open many windows of political opportunity for coalitions to put their message and demands firmly in the political arena. This is the consequence of political parties being more sensitive to citizens' demands (and opinion polls) in the run up to elections. The Ecuadorian coalition is a good example of a coalition skilfully using the 2002 presidential elections to organize a campaign with the slogan "if your candidate does not know how to change education, change your candidate". The Coalition successfully spread this campaign through conventional and nonconventional media, and most political parties ended up emphasizing their ideas to improve education in their electoral programmes.

The third strategy identified is that of having a *systematic communication plan*. Coalitions benefit from having an explicit working programme to engage with the media. Media sources are a key instrument to amplify the messages of civil society campaigns and, in this way, to transmit them to public opinion and decision-makers (McAdam 2001). Some coalitions benefit from having direct links with journalists or media representatives. Having an informative and up-to-date website also contributes to this purpose. Most EACs are aware of the importance of the media and count on a communication strategy. However, due to the urgency and demand of their everyday work, not all of them apply this idea systematically and relate to the media in a rather ad hoc manner, i.e. "when something happens".

The fourth strategy is *justiciability*. This consists of taking the government to court to denounce its lack of fulfilment of its legal obligation of providing/guaranteeing education to all its citizens. This strategy seems highly appropriate in countries with a legal framework and constitution that clearly guarantees the right to education. This strategy appears to work most successfully in a political system in which there exists an effective separation of powers. The coalitions in India and Indonesia have successfully participated in this type of initiative. For instance, through justiciability, the Indian NCE championed the "Child's Right to Free and Compulsory Education" bill. For its part, CLADE, the Latin American campaign for education, has initiated a process with the Inter-American Commission of Human Rights in relation to the violations of the right to education in Chile, Haiti and Colombia. They expect that the decision of this Commission will contribute to the government of these countries having to implement concrete financing mechanisms to guarantee the quality education for all in their territories.[72] The latter is a good example of a 'boomerang effect' strategy, as described by Keck and Sikkink (1998), whereby a civil society organization (whose claims are not usually listened to by the national government; or whose access to consultation spaces is blocked) activates an international

---

72 See: http://www.campanaderechoeducacion.org/financiacion/?p=320 [last retrieved: 09/10/11]

organization or an international agreement to exercise political pressure at the national level in a more effective way.

The fifth strategy identified consists of *targeting the Ministry of Finance*. All EACs, as mentioned earlier, aim at getting more public investment in education. Many times, they bring this funding claim to the Ministry of Education, whose representatives may not have all the decision-making powers on funding issues and, most probably, are generally sympathetic to the claim.[73] However, the Ministry of Finance usually takes important decisions concerning education-funding affairs. Moreover, ministers of finance in most countries tend to give priority to the control of macro-economic variables rather than to spending on public services such as education. For these reasons, education advocacy campaigns benefit greatly from targeting the Ministry of Finance more directly. A good example of the benefits of this strategy can be found in Brazil. The Brazilian coalition organized a campaign to lobby for the Fundeb (a huge basic education fund to guarantee education for the poorest in the country). One famous publicity stunt carried out in the context of this campaign consisted of waiting for the minister of finance to exit a governmental meeting, and putting a young child in his arms with a t-shirt with the slogan "Funded for real!". Many journalists were present during the event, due to the high profile nature of the meeting. As a result, the media covered the publicity stunt widely, and the image of the child carried in the Minister's arms was such a powerful image, that the message travelled around the whole country. In 2007, the Brazilian Parliament approved the Fundeb Law with an annual budget of 30 billion dollars.

However, in relation to the latter strategy, it should be pointed out that, currently, politics and economics are more globalized than ever and, as a consequence, many decisions affecting the education funding of countries are taken (or influenced) at the supra-national level (Dale and Robertson 2007). For this reason, targeting the minister of finance alone, may not be enough. International organizations such as the World Bank and, even more importantly, the International Monetary Fund should be taken into account by the advocacy work of the coalitions as well (GCE, 2009). Coalitions could develop this strategy both directly, through the GCE itself or through the regional coalitions. However, most EACs still have quite a nationalistic understanding of the educational problems in their country and, as a consequence, they often fail to incorporate international actors and processes within their meaning repertoires and agendas of struggle.

Finally, related to the latter, the sixth strategy identified is that of the importance of *re-scaling advocacy politics*. The national coalitions studied adopt this strategy and are part of broader regional and global networks, such as the GCE itself. Operating at a supra-national scale contributes to the building of economies of scale when it comes to organizing workshops and seminars or to producing

---

73 We should take into account that bureaucracies, by default, are happy with having more resources for them to manage and with their topic being more central in the public policy agenda. Ministries of education may not be an exception to this rule.

knowledge, reports or other types of resources. But, more importantly, working at the international level allows them to exchange and learn from the experiences of other coalitions. It also allows national coalitions to be, more or less directly, represented in international *fora* such as the Fast Track Initiative or the regional meetings of UNESCO on EFA. Supra-national initiatives like the Real World Strategies have contributed to promoting interesting advocacy initiatives at the national levels such as budget tracking (Ghana, The Philippines), or Eduwatch (Indonesia, The Philippines). Moreover, being part of an international network empowers EACs in the national political terrain and contributes to the national government perceiving coalitions as a more legitimate political actor.

However, it should be also pointed out that not all members of national EACs are aware of the advantage of operating at different political scales. We have also observed that the connection between the different levels (national-regional-global) relies more often on 'personal politics' than on established procedures (for instance, those coalitions with a member in the board of the GCE feel more connected to the global than in conjunctures in which this person is not a member any more). Finally, a number of coalitions participate reluctantly in *global* campaigns such as the 'Global Action Week' or the 'One Goal Campaign', which they perceive as externally driven and not always aligned with their own priorities. In this debate, it should be emphasized that we are not arguing for a shift in strategy to the global scale, but more so for a recognition of the possibilities of acting on a range of geographical scales from the local, national, regional, and global, according to the specific objectives of the campaign. In an increasingly globalised world, power and decision making operates across and through a complex geography of spaces, and national coalitions need to reflect on how and at what scales they can best push forward their objectives, with which allies, and with what resources.

IMPACT

The impact achieved by EACs has a multidimensional nature. As other social movement scholars have observed before (see Giugni et al 1999), at least three impact dimensions can be identified: symbolic, procedural, and political.

Symbolic impact refers to changes in public opinion, values, and beliefs in society. Most coalitions are very active in the symbolic terrain or, in what some call, the "battle of ideas" (Blyth 2002). They produce and disseminate knowledge by doing research or through initiatives such as EduWatch, they are invited to public debates on educational policy in their countries, and try to influence public opinion through appearing and writing in the media. However, symbolic impact is the impact dimension that is more difficult to measure with precision since ideas and ideational change in particular are very abstract concepts in nature (Hay 2002). We have observed that most coalitions organize the necessary actions, generate the conditions, and have access to the appropriate spaces to make symbolic impact possible (see Table 10.1 for more details on specific outputs). In any case, for coalitions, it is important to invest time and resources in achieving symbolic impact because, even if it is not so tangible in the short term, it may cultivate the terrain to help substantive or procedural impact happen.

Procedural impact consists of advocacy coalitions being recognized as political interlocutors, and gaining access to consultative governmental bodies and decision-makers in a systematic and regular way. This is probably the terrain that education coalitions have been more clearly successful in, within all the cases analysed. It should be acknowledge that, in contrast to the symbolic impact, procedural impact is more easily observable, since being invited to a meeting or being part of a consultative committee of the Ministry of Education (or not) are very tangible indicators.

In some countries, national coalitions have gained procedural impact thanks to the prevailing external conditions. The global consensus around the importance of "civil society participation" in the aid for development field has benefited the coalitions operating in aid dependent countries. This is the case, for instance, of FTI countries, where civil society participation has been institutionalized within the procedures for the elaboration of a national education plan. Thus, on occasion, even if a government would like to go ahead with top-down politics as usual and, thus, ignore civil society claims, they may not be able to do so because of aid conditionality. This is what happened in Ghana, where the World Bank representative forced the government to invite GNECC (the education advocacy coalition in the country) to the Development Partners meeting arguing that civil society has an important role to fulfil in the education sector in Ghana (see van der Plaat in this volume). However, in analysing and reflecting on the impact of procedural impact we should be cautious about not directly conflating this with decision-making power. Some of the evidence emerging from the case studies might suggest that the presence of civil society representatives in high level committees might be more spin than substance, and that participation needs to be accompanied with efforts to improve the impact of attendance on policy change in education. While this does not detract from acknowledging the importance of EACs success in gaining entrance to high-level government meetings, it does emphasise the importance of seeing participation not as an end goal, but as a means to an end.

Political impact consists of tangible changes in different areas of education policy, such as an increase of education funding, changes in education regulation, the introduction of new pedagogical practices, etc. Analyzing political impact is methodologically challenging due to the so-called attribution problem in social movement studies. As pointed out in the introduction, it is very difficult to assert that a certain policy change is the consequence of an advocacy coalition action, or that the preferences of decision-makers have been directly influenced by the coalition. Policy change may come as a consequence of the political pressure exercised by another civil society actor (different to the one we are studying). It should be acknowledged that there are countries, such as Brazil or The Philippines, where more than one civil society coalition is organized in the field of education. It could also happen that the government preferences (A) may coincide with the preferences of the coalition (B), which is very different to assuming that A is the consequence of B. There are a few cases in which attribution doubts can be clearly dispelled. For instance, in 2007, the *Conselho Nacional* of the Brazilian Parliament awarded a prize to the Campanha pelo Dereito a la Educaçao – the Brazilian EAC - due to their role in the creation and implementation of FUNDEB. In this case, there is an official public recognition of the role and impact of the civil society coalition. However, this was a rather exceptional case, while with other cases we can at best attribute that the EAC was a factor in the change.

Because of this attribution problem, on occasion, it is more accurate to say that coalition X has *contributed* to policy change Y (rather than asserting a direct causal link between X and Y). As observed in our case studies, the way most EACs have contributed to policy change in their countries consists of obtaining new funding commitments by the government in the education sector. Some examples are the creation of new education funds and capitation grants, improvements in teachers' salaries, or the elimination of education fees and related costs. However, the funding commitments achieved have not always represented an increase in the total spending in education in the countries analysed. For instance, in The Philippines, the public expenditure on education as a percentage of the GDP has decreased from 3.5% in 2000 to 2.8% in the year 2008, in India the same indicator has decreased from 4.46% in 1999 to 3% in 2006 and in Zambia from 1.92% in 1999 to 1.34% in 2008.[74]

In the following table (Table 10.1) we detail the symbolic, procedural and political impact achieved by the coalitions that were part of our study.

Table 10.1. EACs multi-dimensional impact

EAC	SYMBOLIC	PROCEDURAL	POLITICAL
Brazil	High media profile	National Conference for Basic Education Interlocutor of National Congress and National Education Council	FUNDEB bill Capitation grant Definition of teachers floor salaries
Ecuador	High media profile (regular presence in *El Comercio*, biggest newspaper in the country)	Put a New Education Bill (they put a full proposal; only two education stakeholders did it)	Abolishment of the 25$ school fee Proposals on education accepted in the new Constitution Free books and meals in schools
Zambia		Invited to meetings in the Parliament	More attention to adult education in

---

[74] See UNESCO Institute for Statistics at www.uis.unesco.org/ [last time consulted: 05/02/11]. It should be acknowledged that, in The Philippines, real spending on education increased by 0.2% annually from 1999 to 2008. However, this is a relatively low increase due to the fact that the country economy grew by 5% a year in the same period (UNESCO 2011).

			the policy agenda
Ghana	High media profile	Seat at the Development Partner meetings, Technical Group meeting and Education Sector Thematic Advisory Committees	Capitation grant (2005) Passing of new education bill (2008) Increase in salary for rural teachers
The Philippines	Moderate media presence EduWatch	Chair of National EFA Committee Seat at the government table over education Invited to budget hearings and technical governmental meetings	Alternative budget initiative Community-base projects
India		Establishment of Parliamentary Forum on Education	Passing of new education bill (focus on the right to free compulsory education)
Indonesia	EduWatch	Attends seminars and workshops organized by the government	Put privatization in the education agenda

Source: authors

To conclude this section, we would like to point out two elements that are highly related to the positive impact of advocacy coalitions. The first one refers to the level of internal cohesion within the coalition, and the second one to political opportunity structures. We will now talk about these in detail below.

INTERNAL COHESION

It is not surprising to expect a positive relationship between the internal success (or internal cohesion) of an advocacy coalition and its external success (or impact). However, "internal success", beyond a simple explanatory factor, is something that needs to be explained. Our research identifies a set of elements that contribute to making EACs more internally cohesive. These elements are very different in nature and go from the micro level (for instance, the role of the national coordinator) to macro (civil society having a common history of struggle in the country). Other elements identified are related to the way the coalitions operate and take decisions, and others to the role, characteristics and preferences of the members of the coalition, especially teachers unions and NGOs. Again, we are cautious about making generalizations across contexts, and the findings below are meant to promote discussion by coalitions rather than replication.

In the context of advocacy coalitions, *sharing core beliefs* appears to work as coalitional glue. There are, at least, two core beliefs that are present in all EACs and that are widely shared by their members, namely 'education is a human right' and 'the state is the key institution responsible for guaranteeing education rights to its citizens.' Most coalitions are composed of dozens of organizations and it cannot be presumed or expected that all of them will share all the ideas, values, and preferences concerning education policy and other educational issues. However, they should share a set of core beliefs such as the two mentioned above. These beliefs need to be stable and cannot be challenged by members constantly (Sabatier 2007). Members can have healthy and beneficial discussions about secondary ideas, and even change their perceptions and opinions on certain topics by learning from each other. But when the core beliefs are directly challenged, the coalition could lose its cohesion and even its *raison d'etre*.

For coalitions to be cohesive, it is also important that they *build their agenda through consensus*. The more successful coalitions are those that build their agenda by taking into account all members by setting topics for the agenda by way of mutual consensus and deliberating about why these and not other topics should be selected. This type of procedure is very democratic, but may imply more time and conflict than other ways of building agendas. For instance, the "collage" system is apparently easier and less conflictive because it consists in building agendas by simply adding the different preferences and interests of the member organizations. Collage agendas are usually very long and it is very difficult for all members to appropriate themselves of the complete agenda. Through consensus, however, EACs may be able to construct narrower agendas (with a concrete set of themes and objectives) and the efforts of the members will be much more focused. As a consequence of this, the chances of achieving political impact will be higher.

We have also observed that building cohesive EACs is easier in those countries where there is a *common history of struggle in the civil society sphere*. This is the case of countries such as Brazil and The Philippines where social movements and civil society organizations have come together in intense struggles against dictatorial regimes. These struggles have happened relatively recently and as a result, the complicity and trust between activists coming from different organizations, and the memory of working together among them is still alive. Thus, there is a political culture in the civil society arena that benefits building transversal and cross-sectoral coalitions such as those emerging in the educational field.

The *relationship between teachers unions and education NGOs* is, potentially, a contentious issue that is susceptible to affecting the internal cohesion and level of inclusiveness of EACs. As observed in the case studies, the coexistence between these two types of organizations is smoother in countries that do not have a single or very dominant teachers' union. In a country with such a big teachers' organization, which is usually the case in Latin American countries, the union may feel that the coalition is challenging their hegemony in the field of education. It is also difficult for very big unions to work with other social organizations in a totally horizontal way. They feel, often quite justifiably, that they represent a big constituency (thousands of teachers, even millions in the case of some Indian unions) and that it is not fair that they share an equal place at the table with a small but very professionalized NGO in the context of a coalition. At the same time, we have also observed that the level of inclusiveness of teachers' unions is higher in countries where there are various organizations representing teachers (and none of them is clearly hegemonic) because working in coalitions can clearly benefit them when it comes to increasing their visibility, to defend teachers rights and to bargain with the government to advance other educational objectives. Furthermore, in countries where teachers' unions are prosecuted or repressed, such as in the Philippines, unions receive signs of solidarity from other social organizations which is conducive to coexistence.

Finally, teachers unions are often not happy with working with organizations that bring sensitive issues into the agenda of the coalition such as school accountability, teacher evaluation, and other issues that may undermine teacher professionalism and labour conditions. Since teacher unions are usually very supportive of public education, they are also reluctant about working together with NGO members that are private education services providers in their daily activity. For obvious reasons, the presence of such NGOs in the context of coalitions may generate tensions and contradictions when it comes to organizing advocacy campaigns against the privatization of education.

EACs benefit enormously from having a *skilled broker as the coordinator* of the coalition. Of course, the individual attributes of all members in a coalition are important. It is well known by social movement participants that personal interests or big egos affect collective actions processes very negatively. However, the attributes of the coordinator may be crucial to understanding the level of internal cohesion within a civil society coalition, but may also be reason why member organizations participate more or less enthusiastically within the context of the coalition. The coordinator needs to be sensitive to the different interests and needs of the members, avoid taking part when a conflict emerges, and make sure that members do not lose the focus of the advocacy agenda. Coalitions also benefit from having a coordinator that knows when he/she should take the lead or stay in the background, and who does not seek to be a protagonist in the process. On many occasions, the coordinator also needs to convince members that they should invest more time and resources in doing advocacy work, which often means having to persuade – and even teach - them about the comparative advantage of advocacy work. This is due to the fact that many organizations became members of EACs by inertia, but not necessarily because they have strong ideas on why and how they should raise their advocacy profile.

Another element that explains internal cohesion in EACs, which is closely related to the tasks and skills of the coordinator mentioned above, consists on counting on clear mechanisms, procedures and spaces for *information circulation within the coalition*. Member organizations need to be constantly informed about the work of the secretariat, important meetings and events, decisions taken by the board, and so on. If this kind of information does not circulate properly or is not distributed in a systematic way some members will be easily left behind. Paying attention to information aspects is especially important in coalitions that have members spread all around the territory and where it is not easy for them to meet regularly in person. In fact, with a few exceptions, many members in the different countries analyzed complain about the fact that the coalition dynamic is too often centralized in the capital of the country, where the secretariat usually has its headquarters. However, more and more EACs are taking advantage of the Internet, but also other ICT technologies such as mobile phones, in order to circulate information among all their members at lower costs, which to some extent neutralizes the problem of a centralized organizational structure.

Finally, many EACs have what we call a *collective identity* problem, which is rooted in many members not feeling enough ownership over the coalition and not identifying themselves "as" the coalition. Often, the members' discourse generates a sort of alterity (or "otherness") that decouples them from the coalition entity. In fact, some members' discourse identifies and restricts the coalition to the coalition's secretariat. This is usually the consequence of members not being sufficiently involved in the coalition, although this should not be, a priori, a problem because most EACs allow members have different levels of involvement: from taking part in occasional initiatives (attending workshops, signing statements,...) to participating actively in working commissions or on the board. Again, the role of the coordinator and the secretariat can be key when opening spaces for members' participation and to make their voices heard through different channels. This way, through the day-to-day praxis, identification and loyalty to the coalition can be built.

Political Opportunity Structures

The outcomes and impact of coalitions is very often mediated by contextual conditions and circumstances that the coalitions themselves do not have control over. Social movement scholars usually introduce this idea by referring to political opportunity structures (POSs) (Tarrow 1994). We have identified a set of contextual opportunities that are conducive to the impact of EACs. Some of them are very similar to those identified in the POSs literature such as: a) a clear division of powers within the state, which, for instance, is an important condition for justiciability strategies to be successful; b) a political culture in the country that is sensitive to civil society participation; and c) access to political elites. We have observed that the latter happens more frequently when a progressive political party is in power. In such a political juncture with progressive governments, it is more likely the EAC members know people personally that occupy key decision-making positions (see Hoop in this volume).

In fact, the presence of progressive governments, but also governments with an economic competitiveness agenda, opens many windows of opportunity for EACs. This is due to the fact that these types of governments are often open and willing to invest more resources in education, although they may do so by following different rationales. Progressive governments consider that investing in public education is important because they usually adopt a rights-based approach to education. Pro-competition governments conceive of education as being a key asset to developing the country economically, politically, and socially. Thus, these types of government are more sensitive to education investment than, for instance, governments that subscribe to a neoliberal doctrine whose main aim is to control public spending and make the state thinner.

In the last decade, there has been a progressive shift in Latin American politics, rooted in a number of left-wing political parties that have often come to power with the support of social movements. This has been the case of the two Latin American countries in our sample: Brazil and Ecuador. In Brazil, with President Lula, public spending in education grew from 10% in 2002 to 16,2% in 2006. Something similar has happened in Ecuador with President Correa who has doubled teachers' salaries and put education at the centre of his 'Citizen Revolution'. In both countries, EACs enjoy very beneficial, structurally selective contexts for their claims, especially for those claims involving an increase in educational spending. That is why, with the passage of time, both coalitions have needed to re-define their agendas strategically accordingly to their new context. For instance, the coalition in Ecuador counted on a very 'materialistic' agenda at the beginning (basically, asking for more resources in education) and, currently, given the fact that there are more resources for education in the country than ever before, it has adopted a more complex and ambitious agenda. Their new agenda is not so focused on resources and rather advocates for radical changes in the governance of the education systems, and for making Ecuador an "educational society".

Our case studies also show that coalitions advocating for 'Education For All' can be affected, beneficially or detrimentally, by a new wave of opportunity structures, which are not so usually taken into account in the social movements literature. We refer to global political opportunity structures, media opportunity structures, and public opinion/sentiments on education.

Let us start with *global POSs*. As shown in the *Impact* section in this chapter, some EACs benefit from the new global norms on international aid delivery that promote civil society participation. These norms have benefited especially those coalitions operating in FTI countries and other aid dependent countries, because they mean that donors push governments to invite civil society to sit on the policy-dialogue table. Furthermore, and perhaps more importantly, the global push by the major international donors and UN agencies towards achieving EFA has meant that EACs are knocking at a door that has already been opened, at least partially, by the global education agenda. However, as noted earlier in the chapter, we should not overestimate the importance of 'procedural' success. Being present in discussions does not necessarily equate with decision-making influence, and on the contrary may be a way to neutralise and co-opt civil society actors: giving them a sense of power without any commensurate change in their influence. However, overall we feel that the global push for civil society participation needs to be further explored.

Media opportunity structures are very important as well, above all when it comes to understanding the level of the symbolic impact of coalitions. Regardless of the quality of the communication strategy of EACs, their impact in the media is very much mediated by the attention that the mass media give to educational affairs. As observed, there are countries where 'education' is an issue very much present in media agendas and where, for instance, most important newspapers have a journalist or a section specialized on the topic (this would be the case, for instance, for Ghana, Brazil, and Ecuador). However, in other countries, education is a topic that is often marginalized by the media (and the political agenda in general). This would be the case of Indonesia and India. Of course, in the latter countries, it is much more difficult for the coalitions to count on the media to transmit their message to society, even if they invest large amounts of resources and count on enough expertise in media affairs.

Finally, *public opinion* and *public sentiments* on education issues (and particularly, on public education) can also help to advance the EACs demands, and alternatively, to hinder them. Again, India is a good example of how these conditions can work against the objectives of the coalition. In this country, there is a lack of strong public sentiment in support of 'public education'. This appears to be partly a result of an historically rooted elitism in society (see Grant in this volume). In contrast, in most Latin American countries, there is a 'common sense' conception of education as a human right that is historically embedded within society. Thus, 'Education for All', and related slogans, resonate much more positively in this region, and the education demands that coalitions pose can be potentially even more ambitious than in contexts where these conditions are not met.

CONCLUSIONS

Talking about "conclusions" perhaps sounds too premature when reflecting on civil society education coalitions that remain in their early stages (most of them having been in existence for less than ten years). However, in this section we will synthesize some of the insights above, make some suggestions for future strategy development, and raise some final comments about where the EFA agenda is currently headed today, and the associated challenges.

Insights

As we have seen from the myriad of case studies presented in this book, national civil society coalitions affiliated to the Global Campaign for Education have made significant symbolic, procedural and political impacts on their respective national educational landscapes over the last decade. EAC's are making a difference and they are doing this in a variety of innovative and imaginative ways. While many national coalitions have their ups and downs, civil society advocacy in the field of education appears to have embedded itself firmly inside the national education debate. Similarly, the commonalities in action repertoires of these movements reflects the ongoing transmission of ideas and strategies between local, national, regional and global scales, not in some top-down transmission belt way, but in a much more symbiotic and organic way. While we believe that much more could be potentially done by many national coalitions to improve their strategic activities on different scales, beyond the national, the case studies in this book provide clear evidence of the emergence of a genuinely multi-scalar advocacy coalition network for education whose potential remains great.

Suggestions for action

- *EAC's need to address the territorial imbalances within their coalitions.* While capital cities are often inevitably and necessarily the central location of national campaigns, it is important to build and strengthen networks and branches that reach out across the geographical terrain of the state to those regions that are often faced with the most difficult education and social conditions. This can not only strengthen political power and influence, but also enrich the diversity of the national coalitions and improve their knowledge base.
- *Socio-economic and gender imbalances need to be reduced if national coalitions are to effectively represent the different educational aspirations of national civil society.* Mechanisms need to be developed to enable participation of marginalized groups in the coalitions work and strategies (workshops, training, capacity building, etc.) so as to ensure that their participation is meaningful.
- *More awareness needs to be raised amongst members about what advocacy means, and how the coalitions objectives can be achieved.* Related to this is the importance of organizing action at a multiplicity of scales, from the local to the global, and how coalitions can pool resources and plan common actions across borders to address national priorities and objectives.
- *Care needs to be taken on managing the relationship between teachers' unions and other civil society components of education coalitions, nurturing commonalities and working together to address differences.* The relationship between education trade unions and NGOs is an important one. While there are apparently differences between the main drivers of both organizations - unions were created to defend the rights of teachers and education staff, and many NGOs emerge to defend and support ideals of improving education - there are also many commonalities. Both have an interest in the central role of public education and demanding better educational funding. Both also have a strong interest in improving the quality of education, albeit with different emphasis on the core strategy to do this (for instance, improving teachers' salaries in the case of unions, and improving teacher accountability in the case of NGOs).
- *More investment should be made in sharing information, experiences, and best practices both within and between coalitions.* Critical reflection on where coalitions have come from, what they can learn from their experiences, and reflecting on how they can improve their strategies and the efficacy of their activities are vital tasks that can ensure the longevity and future success of campaigns. We modestly hope that the research presented in this volume has contributed to this final objective.
- *Guarantee the plurality of the coalitions.* With the passage of time, some coalitions tend to be commanded by (and consequently identified with) one single organization and/or with the secretariat. To avoid this to happen good

leadership, democratic internal rules and appropriate communications systems are key. Coalitions can also benefit from incorporating or establishing partnerships with organizations that are usually under-represented (such as students organizations) or other organizations that do not have an explicit focus in education (anti-poverty networks, women movements, youth organizations, etc.).

Future Directions

Finally as a call to action for EACs we conclude this book by raising concern that while the global opportunity structures since the 1990 Education For All conference in Jomtien have been fairly favourable for the commitment to achieving quality public education for all, these may not be with us for much longer.

The winds of austerity are blowing across the world, and while the global economic crisis since 2008 is geographically uneven, it is placing pressure both on national education budgets and on the international development assistance budgets of the major bi-lateral and international agency donors. In these processes education financing appears to be facing a double attack. On the one hand, the overall pool of national government funding is being reduced due to economic contraction, and, on the other hand, the relative importance of education vis. a vis. other state and bi-lateral donor sectoral priorities is also coming under threat.

While it is too early to be certain, it may well be the case that we will reflect upon the last two decades as a golden period for the commitment of the international community to education (despite its failure to deliver all the promised resources). If this is indeed the case, then the conditions under which EACs operate and the national and global political opportunity structures may be much less enabling than before, and this will require major strategic rethinking for the GCE and other civil society networks advocating education betterment. While a difficult battle appears to lie ahead, the magnificent growth of EACs and the strengthening of the GCE over the last decade mean that much better tools are available with which to pressure the national and international community to not give up on its commitments to EFA, and to continue to fight for a quality, well funded public education system for all, regardless of geography, race, ethnicity and gender. A cause that remains both unfulfilled and absolutely necessary.

REFERENCES

Abetti, P., S. Beardmore, Tapp, C. and R. Winthrop. (2011). *Prospects for Aid to Basic Education Put Students at Risk*. Washington DC: Centre for Universal Education, Brookings Institute.

Adamu-Issa, M. L. Elden, M. Forson and T. Schrofer. (2007). Achieving Universal Primary Education in Ghana by 2015: A Reality or a Dream? UNICEF, Division of Policy and Planning Working Paper.

Ahadzie, W. (2007). RAO Engagement With The GPRS Framework 2005-2006, RAO Convention, November 22-23, 2007 Accra.

Ahmad, E., Mansoor, A. (2000). Indonesia: Managing Decentralisation. Paper At *IMF Conference On Fiscal Decentralisation*, Washington D.C. November 20-21 2000. Retrieved August 13, 2010 from: http://www.imf.org/external/pubs/ft/wp/2002/wp02136.pdf

Akyeampong, K. (2007). *50 Years of Educational Progress and Challenge in Ghana*, Brighton: Centre For International Education, University Of Sussex.

Akyeampong, K. (2009)' Revisiting Free Compulsory Universal Basic Education (FCUBE) In Ghana', Comparative Education, *45*(2): 175–195.

Almeida, P. and Johnston, H. (2006). Neoliberal Globalization and Popular Movements in Latin America. In: Almeida, P. and Johnston, H. (Eds.) *Latin American Social Movements: Globalization, Democratization, and Transnational Networks*, Oxford: Rowman & Littlefield.

Alston, P. and Nehal, B. (2005). Human Rights and Public Goods: Education as a Fundamental Human Right in India. In P. Alston and M. Robinson (Eds.) *Human Rights and Development: Towards Mutual Reinforcement*. Oxford: Oxford University Press.

Ampiah, J. G. and C. Adu-Yeboah. (2009). Mapping The Incidence Of School Dropouts: A Case Study Of Communities In Northern Ghana, *Comparative Education, 45*(2): 219–232.

Archer, D. (2007). *Building Strategic Partnerships Between Teachers' Unions and NGOs*. Brussels & London: EI & Action Aid.

Arestis, P., De Paula, L. F., and Ferrari, F. (2006). Assessing the Economic Policies of President Lula Da Silva in Brazil: Has Fear Defeated Hope? *Oxford Centre For Brazilian Studies Working Paper* CBS-81-07.

ASPBAE. (2007). *Indonesia Monitoring Research, Indonesia: Summary Report*. Retrieved March, 8 2011 from: http://www.aspbae.org/pdf/indonesia.pdf

Bainton, D. 2009. *Realising Children's Right to Education: Priorities, Strategies, Policies and Trends in International NGOs*. Bristol: Globalisation, Education and Societies. Retrieved June, 10 2011 from: *www.bris.ac.uk/education/research/centres/.../plan-bainton-report.pdf*

Bartholomew, A. (2009). *Mid-Term Evaluation Of The EFA Fast Track Initiative Country Desk Study: Zambia*. Retrieved November 30, 2011 from: http://www.globalpartnership.org/mid-term-evaluation-of-the-efa-fast-track-initiative

Bauzon, P.T. (2007). *Handbook in Legal Bases of Education*. Philippines: National Bookstore.

Behar, A. and A. Prakash. (2004). India: Expanding and Contracting Democratic Space. In *Civil Society and Political Change in Asia: Expanding and Contracting Democratic Space*. Ed. Muthiah Alagappa. California: Stanford University Press.

_____ (2004) *National Common Minimum Programme of the Government of India*. Government of India, New Delhi. Accessed Jan 13, 2010 from http://pmindia.nic.in/cmp.pdf

Benford, R.D., and D. A. Snow. (2000). Framing Processes and Social Movements: An Overview And Assessment. *Annual Review Of Sociology* 26: 611-639.

Bestill, M. M., and E. Corell. 2001. NGO Influence in International Environmental Negotiations: A Framework for Analysis. *Global Environmental Politics 1*(4): 65–85.

Blyth, M. (2002). *Great Transformations: Economic Ideas and Institutional Change in the Twentieth Century*. Cambridge: Cambridge University Press.

Boito Jr., A. (2003). A Hegemonia Neoliberal No Governo Lula. *Revista Crítica Marxista 17*: 9–35.

REFERENCES

Bollmann, M. (2007) A Educação E Os Movimentos De Resistência No Brasil: Uma Reflexão Sobre O Papel Do Fórum Nacional Em Defesa Da Escola Pública. Retrieved October 15, 2008 from: http://www.app.com.br/portalapp/opiniao.php?id1=5

Bonal, X., (2004). Is The World Bank Education Policy Adequate For Fighting Poverty? Some Evidence from Latin America. *International Journal of Educational Development 24*: 649–666.

Borges-Neto, J. M. (2003) Um Governo Contraditório. *Revista Da Sociedade Brasileira de Economia Política, 12*(6): 7–27.

Burstein, P. (1999). Social Movements and Public Policy. In Giugni, M., D. Mcadam and C. Tilly. *How Social Movements Matter.* Minneapolis: University of Minnesota Press. 3-21.

Campanha Nacional Pelo Direto A Educação. (1999*). Introdução, Ideário, Diretrizes, Objetivos.* São Paulo: CBDE.

_____(2001) O Plano Nacional De Educação. *Cadernos Do Observatório.* São Paulo: Ibase.

_____(2007) *Apontamentos Da Campanha Nacional Pelo Direito À Educação Ao 'Documento Referência' Da Conferência Nacional De Educação Básica.* São Paulo: CBDE.

Canieso-Doronila. (1997). An Overview Of Filipino Perspectives On Democracy And Citizenship. In Diokno, M.S.I. (Ed.) *Democracy & Citizenship In Filipino Political Culture,* Quezon City: Third World Study Center, pp. 69–111.

Caoli-Rodriguez, R. (2007). The Philippines Country Case Study. Country Profile Prepared for the Education For All Global Monitoring Report 2008 Education For All By 2015: Will We Make It? UNESCO http://unesdoc.unesco.org/images/0015/001555/155516e.pdf

_____ (2008). Hard-Pressed To Achieve The EFA Goals By 2015 In The Philippines. In *Prospects, 38*: 393–399.

Carino, L. (1999). Beyond the Crossroads: Policy Issues for the Philippine Nonprofit Sector. *International Journal of Voluntary and Nonprofit Organizations, 10*(1): 83–91.

Carreira, D. and Pinto, J. M. De Rezende. (2007). *Custo Aluno-Qualidade Inicial: Rumo A Educação Publica De Qualidade No Brasil.* São Paulo: Editora Global.

CIVICUS. (2007). Understanding LTA [Legitimacy, Transparency And Accountability]. Retrieved April 10, 2010 from http://www.civicus.org/lta/1237

Chapman, J. and Mancini, A. (2009, January 29). The Global Call for Action Against Poverty (GCAP): A Review.

Comissão De Programa De Governo. (2002). Programa De Governo 2002: Coligação Lula Presidente: Um Brasil Para Todos, São Paulo, Comitê Nacional Lula Presidente. Brasilia.

CREATE, The Case Of Ghana 1991-2006, CREATE PATHWAYS TO ACCESS, Research Monograph No. 22, Institute Of Education, University Of London, London.

CSE. (2002). Agenda Básica, La Educación Prioridad Nacional. Retrieved February 1st 2009 from http://www.contratosocialecuador.org.ec/home/index.php

_____(2008). Constitución y Educación. *Boletín Contrato Social,* nº 8. Retrieved February 1st 2009 from http://www.contratosocialecuador.org.ec/home/index.php.

Culey, C., Martin, A., and Lewer, D. (2007). Independent Mid-Term Review of the Global Campaign for Education. London: Firetail.

Dale, R., and S. Robertson. (2007). Beyond Methodological "Isms" In Comparative Education in an Era of Globalisation. In Kazamias and R. Cowan (eds) *Handbook on Comparative Education,* 19-32. Netherlands: Springer.

Darkwa, A., N. Amponsah and E. Gyampoh. (2006). Civil Society in a Changing Ghana, An Assessment Of The Current State Of Civil Society In Ghana, Retrieved July 23 2009 from http://www.civicus.org/media/csi_ghana_country_report.pdf

Della Porta, D. and Diani, M. (2006). *Social Movements: An Introduction.* Oxford: Blackwell Publishers.

Diokno, M.S.I. (Ed.) *Democracy & Citizenship in Filipino Political Culture,* Quezon City: Third World Study Center

Doctor, M. (2007). Lula's Development Council: Neo-Corporatism and Policy Reform In Brazil. *Latin American Perspectives 34*(6): 131–148.

REFERENCES

Economic Commission for Africa. (2002). The PRSP Process In Zambia, *Second Meeting of the African Learning Group on the Poverty Reduction Strategy Papers (PRSP-LG)* 18 - 21 November 2002, Brussels, Belgium.

Eldridge P. (1990). NGOs and The State In Indonesia. In Budiman, A. (ed) *State and Civil Society In Indonesia.* Glen Waverly: Aristoc Press.

FTI (2011). Global Campaign for Education EPDF Grant: Update On The Civil Society Education Fund: May 2010 To March 2011. *Education Program Development Fund/World Bank Annual Progress Report.* Washington DC: FTI. 48-56.

Foster, P. (1965). *Education and Social Change in Ghana.* London: Routledge & Kegan Paul

Gaventa, J. and Mayo, M. (2009). Spanning Citizenship Spaces Through Transnational Coalitions: The Case Of The Global Campaign For Education. *University of Sussex IDS Working Paper.* Vol. 2009, Number 327.

GCE. (2009). *The Next Generation: Why the World's Children Need A Global Fund For Education For All.* Retrieved February 22nd 2009 from http://www.campaignforeducation.org/

_____. (2011a). Draft GCE Strategic Plan 2011-2014. Presented At The 4th General Assembly, Paris, February 22-25, 2011.

_____. (2011b). GCE Board Report 2008-2010. Presented To The 4th GCE General Assembly, Paris, February 22-24, 2011.

_____. (2011c). Regional Civil Society Education Funds Report May 10-December 2010. By Julius Kamera. Johannesburg: GCE.

_____. (2011). Making It Right: The Crisis In Girls' Education. Washington DC And Johannesburg: GCE And RESULTS.

_____. (2009). *Education On The Brink: Will The IMF's New Lease On Life Ease Or Block Progress Towards Education Goals?* Retrieved November 22nd 2009 from: http://www.campaignforeducation.org/en/resource-center/func-startdown/47/

Giugni, M. G. 1998. Was it worth the effort? The outcomes and consequences of social movements. *Annual Review of Sociology 98*: 371–393.

Giugni, M. G., D. Mcadam, and C. Tilly. (1999*). How Social Movements Matter.* Minneapolis: University Of Minnesota Press.

GNECC. (2005). Statement By The Ghana National Education Campaign Coalition, On Ghana's Educational Policy Direction, At The Accra International Press Centre, 18 August 2005

_____. (2008). Pass Education Bill Now, Coalition Calls On Government, Accessed From: http://www.gnecc.org/downloads/esar%20story2.pdf.

_____. (2008b). Ghana National Education Campaign Coalition, Quarterly Narrative Report for Period January – March 2008, Accra.

_____. (2008c). The Face And Phaces Of GNECC in 2008, Annual Report 2008, Accra.

_____. (2009). Education Sector Annual Review 2009 Position Paper.

Gomà, R., P. Ibarra, and S. Martí. (2002). *Creadores de democracia radical. Movimientos sociales y redes de políticas públicas.* Barcelona: Icaria.

Goodwin, J., and J. M. Jasper. (2004). *Rethinking social movements: structure, meaning, and emotion.* Oxford: Rowman & Littlefield.

Government of Ghana, (2003). Education Strategic Plan 2003-2015, Volume 1 Policies, Targets And Strategies, Ministry Of Education, Accra.

_____. (2003b). Growth And Poverty Reduction Strategy (GPRS I) 2003-2005, Accra.

_____. (2005). Growth And Poverty Reduction Strategy (GPRS II) 2006-2009, Accra.

_____. (2007). Ghana Education Reform 2007, Accessed From: www.ghana.gov.gh

Government of India. (2009). The Right of Children to Free and Compulsory Education Act. (C.35), New Delhi: Rajya Sabha.

Guzman, A.B. De. (2003). 'The Dynamics Of Educational Reforms In The Philippine Basic And Higher Education Sector' *Asia Pacific Education Review 4*(1): 39–50.

Guzzini, S. (2005). The Concept of Power: a Constructivist Analysis. *Millennium: Journal of International Studies 33*(3): 495–521.

REFERENCES

Gyimah-Boadi, E. (2008). Ghana's Fourth Republic: Championing The African Democratic Renaissance? *Ghana Center For Democratic Development*, *4*(8): 1–6.

Gyimah-Boadi, E. (2004). New Anti-Corruption Governments: The Challenge Of Delivery – Ghana: A Case Study, Paper Commissioned For The Kenya Meeting On New Governments.

Haas, P. M. (2004). When does power listen to truth? A constructivist approach to the policy process? *Journal of European Public Policy 11*(4): 569-592.

Hart, J. (2009). *Commonwealth Education Fund Final Report*. London: Commonwealth Education Fund.

Hay, C. (2002). *Political Analysis: A Critical Introduction*. New York: Palgrave.

Jalal, F., Sardjunani, N., Musthafa, M., Purawdi, and A., Suharti. (2003). Indonesia's Education for All: National Plan Of Action 2003/2015. National Education Forum Education For All. Retrieved September 17 2010 From: http://planipolis.iiep.unesco.org/upload/indonesia/indonesia_efa_npa.pdf

James, E., King, E. M., Suryadi, A. (1996). Finance, Management, and Costs of Public and Private Schools in Indonesia. *Economics of Education Review*, *15*(4): 387–398.

Jenkins, J.C., and B. Klandermans. (1995). *The politics of social protest: Comparative perspectives on states and social movements*. Minneapolis: Univ Of Minnesota Press.

Kadingdi, H. (2007). Policy Initiatives For Change And Innovation In Basic Education Programmes In Ghana, Accessed From: http://www.educatejournal.org/index.php?journal=educate&page=article&op=viewfile&path%5b%5d=35&path%5b%5d=31.

Keck, M.E. and Sikkink, K. (1998). Transnational Advocacy Networks in the Movement Society. In Meyer, D.S. And S. Tarrow (eds), *The Social Movement Society: Contentious Politics for a New Century*. New York: Rowman & Littlefield.

Keck, M. E., and K. Sikkink. (1998). *Activists Beyond Borders. Advocacy Networks In International Politics*. New York: Cornell University Press.

Korzeniewicz, R. P., and W. C. Smith. 2003. Redes Transnacionales de la Sociedad Civil. *El ALCA y las cumbres de las Américas: ¿una nueva relación público-privado?* Buenos Aires: Biblos. 47–75.

Kristiansen, S. and Pratikno. (2006). Decentralising Education in Indonesia. *International Journal Of Educational Development*, *26*: 513–531.

Lapus, J.A. (2008). The Education System Facing The Challenges Of The 21st Century, Country: The Philippines. Available At: http://www.ibe.unesco.org/national_reports/ice_2008/philippines_nr08.pdf

Luna Tamayo, M. (2009). ¡Mucho Cuidado! EL COMERCIO 5/16/2009. Retrieved October 13th 2009 from: http://Ww1.Elcomercio.Com/Default.Asp

Martin, A., Culey, C., and Evans, S. (2005). *Make Poverty History: 2005 Campaign Evaluation*.

Machila, M. C. M. (2009). State of Youth and Adult Literacy in Zambia, Some Perspectives for Intensifying Joint Actions.

Maitra, Sreya, (2009). Role of Civil Society In Democratisation: A Case Study Of Zambia.

Maney, G. M, P. G Coy, and L. M Woehrle. (2009). Pursuing political persuasion: War and peace frames in the United States after September 11th. *Social Movement Studies 8*(4): 299–322.

McAdam, D. (1996). Conceptual origins, current problems, future directions. In McAdam, D. and McCharthy, J. D. (eds.) *Comparative perspectives on social movements: Political opportunities, mobilizing structures, and cultural framings*. Cambridge: Cambridge University Press. 23–40.

McAdam, D. (2001). Culture And Social Movements. In Crothers, L. and C. Lockhart (eds). *Culture and Politics: A Reader*. NY: Saint Martin's Press. 253–68.

Meyer, D. S., (2004). Protest and Political Opportunities. *Annual Review of Sociology 30*: 125–145.

Meyer, D. S., and D. C. Minkoff. 2004. Conceptualizing Political Opportunity. *Social Forces 82*(4): 1457 -1492.

Milimo J. T., T. Shilito, and K. Brock, (2002). The Poor Of Zambia Speak; Who Would Ever Listen To The Poor? Published By the Zambia Social Investment Fund

Ministerie van Buitenlandse Zaken, (2008). Primary Education In Zambia, IOB Impact Evaluation, Policy And Operations Evaluation Department, No 312.

Ministério Da Educação. (2007). Plano De Desenvolvimento Da Educação: Razões, Princípios E Programas. Brasília: Ministério Da Educação.

Ministry of Education. Government of India. (1968). National Policy of Education, 1968, New Delhi: Ministry Of Education.

_____. (1998). National Policy Of Education, 1986 (As Modified In 1992), New Delhi: Government Of India.

Ministry Of Education, Government of the Republic Of Zambia. (2007), Education Sector National Implementation Framework 2008 – 2010, Implementing The Fifth National Development Plan.

Moriarty, K. (2010). Real World Strategies – Towards Education for All By 2015. A Story of Civil Society Advocacy. A Project Documentation and Assessment Report, Commissioned By The Global Campaign For Education Report.

Mundy, K. Cherry, S. Haggerty, M. Maclure, R. and Sivasubramaniam, M. (2008). Basic Education, Civil Society Participation and the New Aid Architecture: Lessons From Burkina Faso, Kenya, Mali And Tanzania. OISE-UT/CIDA. Available At: http://cide.oise.utoronto.ca/civil_society/

Mundy, K. and M. Haggerty. (2010). The Global Campaign For Education. January 2008- February 2010. A Review. Report Prepared For The Hewlett Foundation's Quality Basic Education In Development Countries Advocacy Appraisal – September 2010

Mundy, K., and L. Murphy. (2001). Transnational Advocacy, Global Civil Society: Emerging Evidence from the Field Of Education. *Comparative Education Review*. *45*(1): 85–126.

Murphy, L., And K. Mundy. (2002). A Review of International Nongovernmental EFA Campaigns, 1998-2002. Background Paper Prepared For EFA Global Monitoring Report 2002.

Muunga, A.M., Mufalo M. and Jule, K. M., (2008). Commonwealth Education Fun, Zambia End Of Project Evaluation Report

Oliver, P. E., and H. Johnston. (2000). What a good idea! Ideologies and frames in social movement research. *Mobilization: An International Quarterly 5*(1): 37–54.

Otis, M. (2005). *Re-Imagining Civil Society in India*. MA Development Studies: Brown University.

Oviedo, A. and Wildemeersch, D., (2008). Intercultural Education And Curricular Diversification: The Case Of The Ecuadorian Intercultural Bilingual Education Model (MOSEIB). *Compare: A Journal of Comparative and International Education 38*(4): 455–470.

Pinto, J., (2002). Financiamento Da Educação No Brasil: Um Balanço Do Governo FHC (1995-2002), *Educação & Sociedade, 80*(23): 108–135.

Peil, M., (1995). Ghanaian Education As Seen From An Accra Suburb. *International Journal Of Educational Development, 15*(3): 289–305.

Ponce Jarrín, J., (2008). *Education Policy and Performance: Evaluating The Impact Of Targeted Education Programs in Ecuador*. Maastricht: Shaker Publishing.

Raya, R. (2007). *'The Missed Education Of The Filipino People' Missing Targets: an Alternative MDG Midterm Report*. Philippines: Social Watch 2007 Report.

Raya, R. and R.G. Mabunga. (2003). *Tracking CSO Participation in The EFA Country Process In Philippines*. Manila: ASPBAE.

Raychaudhuri, T., D. Kumar, M. Desai, and I. Habib. (1983). *The Cambridge Economic History of India, Volume 2 C. 1757 - C. 1970*. New York: Cambridge University Press.

Razon, V. (2008). Programme on Capacity-Building for Education Advocacy: Accelerating Action To Achieve EFA, Evaluation Report ASPBAE & CEF.

Republic of Zambia. (2006). Fifth National Development Plan 2006-2010, Broad Based Wealth And Job Creation Through Citizenry Participation And Technological Advancement

Robertson, S., A. Verger, K. Mundy and F. Menashy. (2012). *Public Private Partnerships in Education: New Actors and Modes of Governance in a Globalizing World*. Edward Elgar: London.

Rodrik, D. (2006). Goodbye Washington Consensus, Hello Washington Confusion? *Journal of Economic Literature 44*(4): 973–987.

Rogers, S. (2004). Philippine Politics and The Rule Of Law. *Journal Of Democracy, 15*(4): 111–125.

Rolleston, C. (2009). Human Capital, Poverty, Educational Access and Exclusion: The Case of Ghana 1991-2006. *CREATE Research Monograph* n° 22.

REFERENCES

Rose, P. (2003). The Education Fast Track Initiative: A Global Campaign Review Of Progress, And Recommendations For Reform. London: Action Aid.

Sabatier, P. A. (2007). *Theories of the Policy Process.* Boulder: Westview Press.

Santos, B. S. (2005). *El Milenio Huérfano. Ensayos para una Nueva Cultura Política.* Madrid: Trotta.

Scholte, J. A. (2007). Civil Society And The Legitimation Of Global Governance. *Journal Of Civil Society* 3(3): 305–326.

Sen, A. (1983). *Poverty and famines: an essay on entitlement and deprivation.* Oxford: Clarendon Press.

Sen, A. (2001). Democracy as a Universal Value. In Diamond, L., and M. F. Plattner. *The global divergence of democracies.* Baltimore: JHU Press. 3-17.

Shiffman, J., and S. Smith. 2007. Generation of political priority for global health initiatives: a framework and case study of maternal mortality. *The Lancet 370*(9595): 1370–1379.

Silva, M. K. and Lima, A.J.F. De. (2007). Dilemmas for Social Factors In Brazil, In Polet, F. (Ed.) *The State Of Resistance: Popular Struggles In The Global South.* London: Zed Books, 23–28.

Slater, D. (1994). Power and Social Movements In The Other Occident: Latin America In An International Context. *Latin American Perspectives 21*(2): 11–37.

Snow, D. A., and R. D. Benford. (2005). Clarifying the relationship between framing and ideology. In H. Johnston and J. A. Noakes (eds.) *Frames of protest: Social movements and the framing perspective.* Oxford: Rowman & Littlefield. 205–212.

Tandon, R. and M. Ranjita. (2003). Introduction: Civil Society And Governance Issues And Problematics. In Rajesh Tandon And Ranjita Mohanty (eds.) *Does Civil Society Matter? Governance In Contemporary India.* California: Sage Publications. 9–23.

Tarrow, S. (1994). *Power In Movement: Social Movements, Collective Action And Politics.* Cambridge: Cambridge University Press.

Tarrow, S. (2001). Transnational Politics: Contention and Institutions in International Politics. *Annual Review of Political Science* 4: 1-20.

Thompson, N.M. and L. Casely-Hayford, (2008). The Financing and Outcomes Of Education In Ghana, Recoup Working Paper 16, Accessible From: http://recoup.educ.cam.ac.uk/publications/wp16.pdf.

Tilak, J. B. G. (2004). Education in The UPA Government Common Minimum Programme (Economic And Political Weekly October 23, 2004).

_____. (2009). Universalizing Elementary Education: A Review Of Progress, Policies, And Problems, In: Preet Rustagi (Ed.), *Concerns, Conflicts And Cohesions: Universalization Of Elementary Education In India.* New York: Oxford University Press.

Tomlinson, K. and Macpherson, I. (2007a). *Driving The Bus: The Journey of National Education Coalitions.* London: Commonwealth Education Fund.

_____. (2007b). *Funding Change: Sustaining Civil Society Advocacy in Education.* London: Commonwealth Education Fund.

UNESCO. (2009). *EFA Global Monitoring Report 2009 – Overcoming inequality: why governance matters.* Paris: UNESCO.

_____. (2011). EFA Global Monitoring Report 2011 - The Hidden Crisis: Armed Conflict And Education. Paris: UNESCO.

UNICEF, (2009). http://www.unicef.org/infobycountry/zambia_1391.html

Verger, A. and Vanderkaaij, S. (2012). The National Politics of Global Policies: Public-Private Partnerships in Indian Education. In Verger, A., Novelli, M. and Altinyelken, H. K. (Eds.) *Global Education Policy And International Development: New Agendas, Issues And Policies.* London: Continuum.

_____. (2009) Join The Second Freedom Struggle To Break The Chains Of Illiteracy. New Delhi: NCE.

World Bank. (2003). EFA In Indonesia: Hard Lessons About Quality. Retrieved August 13, 2010 from: http://siteresources.worldbank.org/education/resources/education-notes/ednotesindonesia.pdf.

Watt, P. (2005). Keeping Education on the International Agenda: The Global Campaign For Education, In Rao, N. and I. Smyth (eds) *Partnerships For Girls Education*. London: Oxfam Great Britain. 22–38.

Wiarda, H.J. (2003). *Civil Society. The American Model and Third World Development*. Colorado and Oxford: Westview Press.

World Education Forum. (2000). *The Dakar Framework for Action*. Paris: UNESCO.

ZANEC. (2007). *Strategic Plan: 2008-2011*.

_____. (2009). Global Action Week, Activity Report Zambia National Education Coalition.

AUTHOR BIOS

Anja Eickelberg holds a MSc in International Development Studies (with distinction) from the University of Amsterdam and a BA in Culture and Literature Studies, Journalism and Sociology from the University of Dortmund, Germany. She is currently a PhD candidate in Public Policy at the Institute of Economy of the Federal University of Rio de Janeiro (UFRJ) where she is focussing on the development and implementation of a more effective and inclusive governance model for megacities. As part of this endeavor, Anja has recently co-founded the "United City Movement" (Movimento Cidade Unida), a group of engaged citizens from the formal and informal city of Rio de Janeiro that seeks to pressure the city government to use the windows of opportunities opened up by upcoming megaevents such as the 2016 summer olympics to foster sustainable social change. Within the broader theme of urban development, Anja's main research interests include quality public education, public sector transparency and accountability, and the role of the academic scholar and new technologies in the public policy process.

Laura Grant graduated from the University of British Columbia with a BA in Anthropology with a focus in archaeology. During that time she worked with various First Nations' groups in identifying places of previous occupation to assist with land claim issues in areas such as the Dundas Island group in British Columbia with the Tlingit and Tsimshian. She also was involved with a community development project with the Splatsin First Nation group in which we lobbied the government for additional resources. It was from these experiences that Laura decided to change her direction of education towards international development. She continued her education at the University of Amsterdam and graduated with an MSc in International Development Studies with a focus in advocacy and education. She spent time in India working with the National Coalition of Education and other civil society organizations, studying the impact that civil society organizations have had on education. She also participated in a nation wide march across Nepal to promote education as a fundamental right to create pressure on the government to make a change in the constitution.

Selma Hilgersom holds a BA Interdisciplinary Social Sciences at Utrecht University with a focus on governance and a MSc on Human Geography at the University of Amsterdam with a focus on international development and civil society advocacy. In the context of this master, Selma did research on the impact of E-Net for Justice, a civil society network organization advocating public education in Indonesia. After completing this study, Selma graduated from a second MSc on Policy and Organization at Utrecht University. Complex organizational structures and governmental policies were main themes during this master. Her main interests lie in international development, civil society organizations, human geography, governance and organizational structures.

Joosje Hoop studied Language and Communication at the University of Amsterdam. Furthermore she was involved in an education development project in Tamale (Ghana) and she experienced many different aspects of the education and development field during her time in Asia. She continued her education at the University of Amsterdam and completed the MSc International Development Studies. As a post-graduate researcher, her experience lies in the Philippines, with a specific interest in civil society advocacy and Education for All. She was also the research assistant of the IS Academie programme between 2009 and 2011. Joosje was invited to present her research results in international conferences in Delhi, India ('Transnational Advocacy Research Project in Asia 2009'), Istanbul, Turkey ('WCCES Congress 2010') and Paris, France ('GCE General Assembly'). More recently, she completed an MSc in Education at the University of Amsterdam and is currently a teacher in a Montessori school.

Karen Mundy is Associate Professor and Canada Research Chair at the Ontario Institute for Studies in Education of the University of Toronto, where she directs the *Comparative, International and Development Education Centre*. Her research has focused on the politics of educational assistance in the developing world, educational reform in Africa, the role of civil society in the reform of educational systems, and on the issue of global education in North American schools. Dr. Mundy has been a consultant for such organizations as UNICEF, UNESCO, CIDA, and the Hewlett Foundation. She is also the founder and current President of the Canadian Global Campaign for Education, a coalition of NGOs, teachers unions and universities committed to advancing education for all.

Mario Novelli is Senior Lecturer in Education and International Development at the University of Sussex, UK. His research focuses on the intersections between globalisation, education and international development, and most recently the relationship between education and conflict. He is particularly interested in the securitisation of aid and the relationship between geopolitics and international development assistance to education in conflict affected states. He has published in journals such as the International Journal of Educational Development; Globalisation, Societies and Education and Educational Review.

Felice van der Plaat studied Human Geography and performed her Master of Science in International Development Studies at the University of Amsterdam. Subsequently she finished her Advanced Master in IDS at the Radboud Universiteit Nijmegen, a course providing a broad understanding of critical development theories and the processes involved in policy development and project implementation. During her undergraduate she did research about the resettlement processes in Tamil Nadu, India that occurred after the tsunami. Furthermore she has research experience in Ghana and Zambia. In 2010 Felice worked for the NGO CARE in The Hague, focusing on organizational learning and planning, monitoring and evaluation. Currently, Felice is working for the United

Nations Environment Programme in Nairobi, Kenya as a Junior Professional Officer dealing with Climate Change Adaptation.

Jonah Sarfaty graduated from the University of Amsterdam with a BA in Cultural Anthropology and an MA in International Development Studies (with honours). As a post-graduate researcher, her main experience and interest lies within the education and development field and more specifically on the Latin American continent. She has spent considerable time doing research in Ecuador and Guatemala. During her time in Central America she participated in *Camino Seguro*, an educative project for elementary school children in Guatemala. She is currently part of the fundraising committee of *Niños de Guatemala*, a non-profit organization focused on contributing to a better future for the people of Guatemala.

Antoni Verger is a 'Ramon y Cajal' senior researcher at the Sociology Department of the *Universitat Autònoma de Barcelona*. His main areas of expertise are global education policy and international development, with a focus on the role of international organizations and transnational civil society networks, and privatization and quasi-markets in education. He has published widely on these topics in international journals such as Comparative Education Review, Globalization Societies and Education, British Journal of Sociology of Education, Journal of Education Policy or the *International Studies in Sociology of Education.* He has conducted research for UNESCO, the GCE, the Spanish Agency of Aid (AECID), the Dutch Ministry of Cooperation and Education International.

CPSIA information can be obtained at www.ICGtesting.com
Printed in the USA
BVOW021448110512

290015BV00002B/7/P